PROFESSOR JEFF MACKIE-MASON
SCHOOL OF INFORMATION
UNIVERSITY OF MICHIGAN
ANN ARBOR, MI 48109-1092

Resource allocation mechanisms derives the general welfare properties of systems in which individuals are motivated by self-interest. Satisfactory outcomes will emerge only if individual incentives are harnessed by means of a communication and payoff process, or mechanism, involving every agent. Professor Campbell employs a formal and abstract model of a mechanism that brings into prominence the criteria by which the performance of an economy is to be judged. The mechanism approach is used to prove some fundamental theorems about the possibility of designing an economic system satisfying the criteria. It also establishes a way of thinking about economic issues that is becoming increasingly useful in special branches of economics, such as industrial organization and public finance.

Resource allocation mechanisms can be viewed as two different, yet connecting, texts: One constitutes an introduction to the theory of mechanism design and the other is a treatment of welfare economics with conventional emphasis on Pareto optimality as well as providing substantial material on incentives, uncertainty, and existence of equilibrium.

Written for graduate students and professional economists, *Resource allocation mechanisms* presents contemporary general equilibrium theory by weaving the central results into a coherent story. Examples abound, and the proofs are rigorous but not intimidating.

Professor Campbell received his Ph.D. from Princeton University and is now Professor of Economics at the University of Toronto. He has published papers in several journals, including *Econometrica* and the *Journal of Economic Theory*.

Resource allocation mechanisms

Resource allocation mechanisms

DONALD E. CAMPBELL
University of Toronto

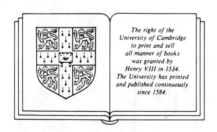

The right of the
University of Cambridge
to print and sell
all manner of books
was granted by
Henry VIII in 1534.
The University has printed
and published continuously
since 1584.

CAMBRIDGE UNIVERSITY PRESS

Cambridge
London   New York   New Rochelle
Melbourne   Sydney

Published by the Press Syndicate of the University of Cambridge
The Pitt Building, Trumpington Street, Cambridge CB2 1RP
32 East 57th Street, New York, NY 10022, USA
10 Stamford Road, Oakleigh, Melbourne 3166, Australia

First published 1987

Printed in the United States of America

Library of Congress Cataloging-in-Publication Data
Campbell, Donald E. (Donald Edward), 1943–
Resource allocation mechanisms.
Bibliography: p.
Includes index.
1. Economics.   2. Resource allocation.
3. Welfare economics.   4. Equilibrium (Economics)
5. Consumption (Economics)   I. Title.
HB171.5.C267   1987   330'.01   85–25556

British Library Cataloguing in Publication Data
Campbell, Donald E.
Resource allocation mechanisms.
1. Equilibrium (Economics)
I. Title
330   HB145

ISBN 0 521 26664 5 hard covers
ISBN 0 521 31990 0 paperback

FOR DIANE

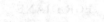

Contents

viii   **Contents**

Preface

This book was inspired by my economic theory lectures to first-year Ph.D. students at the University of Toronto. The *point d' appui* is that any economic system or mechanism is essentially a communication process. Each agent transmits messages to which other agents respond as self-interest dictates. A successful mechanism must harness this self-interest so that each agent, without necessarily understanding the overall process, is induced to cooperate in the determination of a satisfactory (or optimal) menu of goods and services. Adam Smith, of course, is the founder of this approach to the study of economics. This book employs the formal, and abstract, general equilibrium model of resource allocation pioneered by the nineteenth-century economist Léon Walras. Its modern formulation was developed over the last three decades, particularly by Professors K. J. Arrow, G. Debreu, L. Hurwicz, and R. Radner.

Our "mechanism design" approach to economic theory begins with the tacit supposition that the author and the reader have met to design a resource allocation mechanism that will deliver a satisfactory menu of goods and services. Nothing is taken for granted and the designers are not necessarily committed to the existing institutions. As a result, any theorem that does point to a particular system, say, to the private ownership market economy, will have that much more cogency.

The mechanism approach brings into prominence the issue of the criteria by which the performance of an economic system is to be judged, particularly those criteria relating to the interplay between individual incentives and individual messages. It provides a way of thinking about economic affairs that is becoming increasingly useful in special branches of economics, particularly industrial organization and public finance, where strategic equilibrium is an important investigative tool. Even in "institutional" areas such as industrial relations the mechanism design approach can be illuminating: Does there exist an arbitration scheme satisfying certain welfare criteria laid down in advance?

The central actor in our drama is the planner. In the case of a completely decentralized laissez-faire system the planner, after having designed the mechanism, exits to the side of the stage and observes the action without participating. In other cases the planner would continue to play a role, transmitting signals in response to the messages of households and firms, which will in turn respond to the planner's message. In any case, by keeping the planner in mind, we will be forced to recognize important informational constraints that disqualify many schemes as naively utopian.

Each of the chapters in the book can be read independently. The book can even be viewed as two different texts: Chapters 1, 2, 3, 5, and 6 constitute an introduction to the theory of mechanism design that is not readily accessible in other sources. Chapters 3, 4, 5, 6, and 7, along with the material in the appendixes, constitute a conventional treatment of general equilibrium theory and welfare economics with the addition of some material on incentives (Chapter 5) and uncertainty (parts of Chapter 4) not always encountered in texts.

Except for the brief Appendix 3, which proves the existence of a competitive equilibrium and is included for completeness, the entire book can be read by anyone whose background in mathematics includes a good grounding in calculus. Thus, it is accessible to advanced undergraduates as well as to graduate students. Appendixes 1 and 2 have been included to provide an elementary but rigorous treatment of consumer theory without which the many examples in the main body of the text could not be developed.

There are a few notational conventions of which the reader should be aware: R^k is k-dimensional Euclidean space, and R^k_+ is the set of nonnegative vectors in R^k. For any two vectors $p = (p_1, p_2, \ldots, p_k)$ and $q = (q_1, q_2, \ldots, q_k)$ in R^k the inner product $p_1 q_1 + p_2 q_2 + \cdots + p_k q_k$ is denoted pq. If $p_c \geq q_c$ for $c = 1, 2, \ldots, k$, we write $p \geq q; p >> q$ means that $p_c > q_c$ holds for all $c = 1, 2, \ldots, k$.

I have received help along the way from my colleagues Larry Epstein, Mike Peters, and Don Moggridge, and from Tapan Mitra and Hugo Sonnenschein. Their encouragement has been just as important as their constructive criticism. It is a pleasure to acknowledge their help and record my gratitude. I am also very grateful to my students, particularly Pantelis Andreou and Carl Ehrman, for the care with which they read the manuscript.

It is common practice to permit one's typist to bear most of the stress associated with meeting a production deadline, and I did not depart from this useful custom in preparing my own book. Jennifer Johnson deserves the credit in this case for an able and speedy job of typing.

Finally, and with greatest enthusiasm, I thank my children, Samantha and Jordan, and my wife, Diane, for graciously tolerating the book's intrusions into our family life as well as for cheering me on to the finish line. This book is dedicated to Diane, who makes the professional part of my life more pleasurable by making our home life sublime.

D.E.C.

Toronto
March, 1986

CHAPTER 1

Introduction

This book is concerned with the general welfare implications of individual decisions in systems in which some sort of coordination of individual activities is essential to the achievement of a high level of overall welfare. What makes this problematic is the determination of each individual to act in a way that enhances his or her personal well-being. Different configurations of individual decisions produce different outcomes, some of which could be improved upon to the extent of making everyone better off and most of which favor some of the individuals more than others. Even though it will be difficult to claim that a system promotes the general welfare when there will always be some individuals who protest, accurately, that another arrangement would have gone further toward satisfying their material wants, there is no ambiguity in the requirement that a test of welfare be based, somehow, on individual assessments of the outcomes.

We begin, therefore, with a desire to determine which outcomes will emerge and whether these will satisfactorily reflect the tastes and values of the individuals participating in the system. In most economic settings there will be a large number of possible outcomes. It will be assumed at the outset that of all the outcomes that are likely to emerge, only the *equilibrium* outcomes are worthy of attention. In an abstract model of an economy an equilibrium is a state in which all forces are in balance and there is no tendency to change: No agent wishes to revise his decision having observed this state and, because the decisions do not change, the original outcome is maintained. In a working economy, an equilibrium is an outcome that reasserts itself period after period once it is established, however it is initially established. The two notions of equilibrium should coincide; whether they do in fact depends on the real-world phenomenon under study and how it is modeled. Because this book examines abstract models of economic systems, the first notion of equilibrium will be employed. There are still many ways to define an equilibrium, depending on, for example, what is assumed about individual responses to threats, the possibilities for collusion, one person's knowledge of another's situation, and the number of times the agents will be required to play the game. It

1

will be assumed throughout that individuals act independently: There is no collusion. This assumption is still consistent with a variety of definitions of equilibrium, but an equilibrium is essentially a configuration of individual decisions with the property that each individual's decision contributes as much as possible to his or her well-being subject to the limitations inherent in the behavior of others.

Any definition of equilibrium can be resolved into two subtypes: equilibria that give rise to satisfactory outcomes and those that do not. The notion of satisfactory performance that is central to this book and to most of economic theory is *Pareto optimality*. An outcome is Pareto optimal if there is no other feasible outcome that would make everyone simultaneously better off. It must be noted that Pareto optimality is a very weak test of general well-being. An outcome might be Pareto optimal yet stop short of providing the decencies of life to some group of individuals even though these could be obtained at a small sacrifice to others in the community. All that can be inferred from Pareto optimality is that it is not possible to make absolutely everyone better off. Nevertheless, Pareto optimality is ubiquitous as a test of performance of an economic system. There are two reasons for this. First, there are so many possible ways of organizing production in any one industry and so many ways of bringing industries together to provide households with a menu of goods and services that a system that accomplishes this to the extent of providing a Pareto-optimal array of goods and services is truly remarkable. Second, once the economic model is fitted with individual preferences, production recipes, and commodities that have some of the complications of their real-world counterparts, it becomes extremely difficult, and sometimes impossible, to design an economic system that provides even Pareto-optimal outcomes under all circumstances. Even though Pareto optimality is a minimal test of performance, economists have been kept busy for a century trying to design techniques for realizing it in difficult cases.

The rest of this chapter is devoted to six examples of economic systems or mechanisms. They provide an informal introduction to the criteria that will be used throughout the book to evaluate the performance of resource allocation mechanisms. The first three examples elucidate the definition of Pareto optimality in relatively simple models. Each of the six examples attempts to shed light on how and when individual self-interest can be harnessed so that Pareto optimality is achieved at equilibrium. The treatment of equilibrium is informal and intuitive at this stage.

1.1   A trivial case

There are 500 students in a college with a library that can easily accommodate that many individuals. Some individuals prefer to study in their

Table 1.1. *Preferences for meeting times*

Group 1	Group 2	Group 3
10:00 A.M.	10:00 A.M.	2:00 P.M.
Noon	Noon	Noon
2:00 P.M.	2:00 P.M.	10:00 A.M.

rooms and some prefer the library. If each is allowed to choose where he studies *and* individuals are assumed to act in their self-interest, the outcome is Pareto optimal because each will be able to study in his or her preferred location. No other arrangement would make anyone better off, so no other arrangement could make everyone better off. The analysis of the optimality properties of equilibrium is simple in this case because no person's decision has any bearing on anyone else's welfare. This is obviously not typical of economic problems and no further time will be wasted on such cases.

1.2 Majority rule

A university class consisting of an instructor and eleven students is meeting to decide on a weekly time period for their lecture. The instructor does not wish to give her preference more weight than any of the students' and has agreed to settle the matter by majority vote. There will be twelve ballots, including the instructor's. There are three time periods when all twelve individuals are free of other commitments: 10:00 A.M., noon, and 2:00 P.M. Before considering what the outcome will be, we will determine which meeting times are Pareto optimal. Suppose that there are three groups of like-minded individuals. Table 1.1 gives the group rankings of alternatives in order of preference. Every outcome is Pareto optimal in this case. The 10:00 A.M. period is Pareto optimal because no other choice could make the members of group 1 or 2 better off. The 2:00 P.M. period is also Pareto optimal because it is the first choice of the members of group 3. A noon meeting would be Pareto optimal too: Although the 10:00 A.M. meeting time would make eight persons better off, it would be worse from the standpoint of the members of group 3, and therefore there is nothing that would be better for *everyone*. (Each group has four members.)

Although every outcome is Pareto optimal in this example, it is not the case that one of the outcomes cannot be shown to be better than the others in terms of some other generally accepted welfare criterion. From the standpoint of majority rule, for example, the 10:00 A.M. period is best because it is preferred by a majority to every other outcome. This is what will be decided on using the majority rule "mechanism," since no one has an incentive not to cast his ballot for his most preferred meeting time. (Can you prove this?) In this case the outcome of the majority rule process is Pareto optimal.

A simple but cogent demonstration that Pareto optimality by itself is merely a minimal test of satisfactory performance for any system is afforded by an examination of dictatorship. In abstract economic and social systems dictatorship means that one individual controls the outcome. In the present example one individual – perhaps the instructor – is empowered to determine a meeting time without consulting anyone else. In general, the dictator would select the outcome he most prefers. No other outcome would make the dictator better off, so nothing would make everyone better off. Therefore, in formal models dictatorship always guarantees Pareto optimality. But this solution is obviously unsatisfactory in terms of other welfare criteria. Now, we return to majority rule.

Suppose it were true that in every situation there was at least one outcome that no majority would reject in favor of some other feasible outcome. Then some alternative would always emerge as a majority winner and it would be Pareto optimal. (If everyone preferred some alternative x to alternative y, then y would certainly not survive the majority voting process.) Suppose, in other words, that there always exists an equilibrium of the majority rule process. We would then have a mechanism for which an equilibrium always exists and every equilibrium is Pareto optimal. In that case would you be in favor of using majority rule to settle all economic issues, including those presently left to the market system?

The hypothesis of the previous paragraph – a majority winner will emerge in every situation – is false. Suppose that in another classroom or on another occasion the preferences are as set out in Table 1.2. In this case every proposal would be opposed by some majority of voters. In the language of economic theory we say that an equilibrium does not exist for the second configuration of preferences. Even though every equilibrium of the majority decision process is Pareto optimal, this mechanism will fail to achieve optimality whenever an equilibrium does not exist.

1.3   The kingmaker scheme

This is a simple mechanism, devised by Hurwicz and Schmeidler (1978), for which an equilibrium always exists and every equilibrium is Pareto optimal. Suppose there are three individuals and two alternatives. The second assumption is crucial but the first is not. (The reader can no doubt extend the argument to the case of n persons.)

Each person other than individual 1 is required to write down the name

Table 1.2. *Another preference scheme*

Group 1	Group 2	Group 3
10:00 A.M.	Noon	2:00 P.M.
Noon	2:00 P.M.	10:00 A.M.
2:00 P.M.	10:00 A.M.	Noon

of his most-preferred alternative on a ballot. All of the ballots are handed over to individual 1, who determines the outcome by picking one of the nominated alternatives. If 1's most-preferred alternative is among those nominated, he is required to pick it; otherwise 1's second choice will appear on all ballots and that will be the outcome. In effect, person 1 is a kingmaker who picks someone (other than himself) whose preferences will rule.

An equilibrium will always exist. Rather than explain what this means in this context, we will approach the subject indirectly by first demonstrating that the mechanism is *incentive compatible*. A mechanism is incentive compatible if it is always in each individual's interest to behave the way the system's rules instruct him to behave. Any mechanism will require an individual to choose an action that reflects his preferences in a specified way. But an individual's preferences are known only to himself, and a violation of the rule governing the choice of an action cannot be detected. That is why incentive compatibility is such an important requirement; a mechanism cannot be successful if its rules are not followed, but violations of the rules usually cannot be detected.

The last example illustrates nicely. Individual 2 is required to name his most preferred alternative. This is known only to individual 2, but he has no incentive to nominate his second choice, because that strategy would influence the outcome only if it were to force the outcome to change from 2's first choice to his second choice, and this would not be to his advantage. The same argument applies to 3. Individual 1 has no incentive other than to pick his most-preferred outcome, if it has been nominated, and, if it has not, there is no action available to 1 that would render it eligible. Therefore, no one can gain by deviating from the rules. Put another way, if each individual were to submit his preference ranking to a referee who would then complete the game by taking the appropriate actions on behalf of the respective players, no one would have any incentive but to report his true preferences *regardless of the preference rankings reported by the others*. We say that an action by individual i is a dominant strategy for i if it results in the best outcome from i's standpoint, given the actions of the others, *whatever these other decisions may be*. In this example sincere behavior – that is, truthful play, or truthful preference revelation – is a dominant strategy for each agent. This suggests that the mechanism is incentive compatible in the strongest possible sense.

An equilibrium always exists because there is only one strategy that an individual would consider taking and it is independent of the actions of the others. No one will wish to revise his decision upon observing the actions of others because there is only one strategy worth considering.

Every equilibrium is Pareto optimal because 2 and 3 will each nominate their most-preferred alternatives and one of these will be picked by individual 1. Therefore, the outcome will be someone's first choice and hence no other alternative can make everyone better off.

Individual 1 is not a dictator in this context because he will not get his first choice if both 2 and 3 prefer x to y, say, and 1 prefers y to x. Alternative x will be named on both ballots, so the outcome must be x. Nevertheless, if one extended the mechanism to include n individuals and individuals 2 through n were required to submit ballots from which 1 would pick an outcome, the chances would be very high that 1's first choice would be among the alternatives nominated. The system would appear to favor the first individual unduly. This concern will be given formal expression in the next chapter as the *individual rationality* requirement.

1.4   Pollution

Since the passage in England of the Clean Air Act in 1956, London has been free of smog, and the famous pea soup fogs have become rare. The quantity of waste particles in the air has fallen by at least 25 percent. It is probably not far from the truth to say that, even net of the costs of cleanup, the legislation has led to changes that have enhanced the well-being of everyone in the city. For the sake of argument, let us assume that the act did result in a universal increase in well-being. Why, then, did it take an act of Parliament to accomplish something that benefited everyone? If each person had something substantial to gain, why did self-interest not lead to spontaneous individual decisions to take steps to improve the quality of the air?

The answer lies in the structure and interplay of the incentives confronting the residents of London. To bring this out, we can reduce the scope of the problem to one dimension, the choice between hard and soft coal as a fuel for heating one's home. Soft coal is more noxious.

Before the passage of the Clean Air Act households did not choose to purchase hard coal even though everyone is better off in net terms when each household does use hard coal. Whatever decisions others have taken, a single individual will not measurably improve the quality of the air if he consumes hard coal. Since soft coal is cheaper and has virtually the same

Table 1.3. *Payoff matrix*

No. of individuals other than i who choose S	Net value to i of i's choice	
	i chooses S	i chooses H
0	$100 - 80/n$	90
1	$100 - 160/n$	$90 - 80/n$
2	$100 - 240/n$	$90 - 160/n$
3	$100 - 320/n$	$90 - 240/n$
.		
.		
.		
$n - 2$	$20 + 80/n$	$10 + 160/n$
$n - 1$	20	$10 + 80n$

effect on the environment, *given the decisions of others,* each individual finds it in his self-interest to purchase soft coal. In other words, the purchase of soft coal by each household corresponds to an equilibrium and the equilibrium outcome is not Pareto optimal because each household is better off when everyone burns hard coal.

Let us make this precise with the aid of a simple format. We will construct an n-person game that models the preceding discussion. Each individual i ($i = 1, 2, \ldots, n$) decides on an action; he can choose S (burn soft coal) or H (burn hard coal). Table 1.3 gives the net value to i of each action, depending on the number of other individuals who have chosen action S. The net value is determined by considering the cost to i of purchasing the type of coal chosen and the quality of the air; the latter depends on the total number of players choosing S. The values displayed are net of the benefit derived from heating one's home. (Both decisions give rise to the same amount of heat.)

We suppose that n, the number of households, is large, much larger than 100, but not so large that the price of one kind of coal will be affected by the composition of demand. If i chooses S, the net value to i of this decision falls slightly as the number of other households "playing S" increases by 1: The decline in i's net value is $80/n$, a small number. It is due to the increase in the amount of harmful waste products in the air. But, however many individuals have already chosen S, i receives more benefit by playing S than by playing H; the difference of $10 - 80/n$ is due to the lower price of soft coal, which accounts for the 10, and the fact that the number of soft coal users is greater by 1 when i plays S, *given the choices of others,* and this accounts for the term $-80/n$.

Self-interest leads each player to choose S no matter what others have chosen, so the situation in which each individual chooses S is a strong candidate for equilibrium. (There are many notions of equilibrium, some of which will be explored in later chapters, but almost all definitions of equilibrium would be consistent with each player i choosing S in the game under discussion because the choice of S is a dominant strategy). But the outcome, cheaper coal and much smog, is not Pareto optimal. When each person chooses S, the net benefit to each is 20. When each player takes action H, *each* gets a net benefit of 90 and this is considerably larger than 20. The equilibrium that results from the pursuit of self-interest is, in terms of the criterion of benefit to the individual, quite inferior to the outcome that results when each is forced by law to adopt the alternative course of action. In fact, almost any configuration of strategies benefits everyone more than the equilibrium. For example, if $n = 80,000$, as long as the number of individuals taking action S is less than 70,000, everyone will receive a net benefit greater than 20, even those who choose S.

This example shows that the pursuit of self-interest in a market economy can result in suboptimal outcomes in some situations. It does not prove that such difficulties can easily be remedied by the passage of legislation. If the outcome in which each household burns hard coal makes everyone better off than the outcome in which each household burns soft coal, it is only because the preference for clean air by each person is strong enough to outweigh the cost in terms of other goods and services sacrificed when the more expensive fuel is used. Therefore, remedial legislation can be successful only if the government decision-makers obtain all the relevant information on household preferences and resource costs. Whether it is possible to design an economical procedure for eliciting the relevant information in all situations is the theme of this book.

We have seen that the attainment of Pareto optimality cannot be taken for granted (see the last example). But we need not despair of being able to design a mechanism that harnesses self-interest in a way that guarantees Pareto optimality (see the third example). The distinction between the two kinds of equilibria is featured in the final two examples, which bring the market system onto center stage.

1.5   Street lighting

Street lights reduce crime. Consider the placement of lights on a typical city street. Would the residents be served best by having one light in front of each house, one light for the entire street, or some intermediate number? The decision *should* depend on householders' preferences. Preferences will in turn depend on the perceived benefits in terms of crime reduction from the various plans and on the nature of the goods and services – interior lighting, for example – that could be produced instead of a street lamp.

Let us consider the outcome that would be determined by the market system. Assume, therefore, that private firms produce light standards and sell them to private buyers at a price that is expected to maximize profit. Anyone desiring lighting on his street may purchase a lamp, hire a contractor to install it on his front lawn, and pay the monthly electricity charges for its operation. Will this system serve the residents of our street very well? It is highly unlikely.

There is a *free-rider problem*. Any householder will receive the benefit from a lamp installed by his neighbor and will have an incentive to avoid paying for a light on his own property in anticipation of getting the benefit of neighboring lights without paying for them. Of course, each resident has the same incentive, and it is likely that no street lights would be installed. In that case the residents would be in a position to agree that each would be better off if lamps had been installed by the government, with each household paying a share of the total cost. In other words, the market outcome is not Pareto optimal in this case.

Having the government take the initiative for the project does not automatically solve the problem. One has to consider how the government is to discover the extent of household preferences for street lighting and for other goods and services that could be produced with the inputs required to manufacture a street lamp. This is by no means a simple matter. It is one virtue of the market mechanism that for a wide range of goods and services this process of accumulating essential information about household preferences is accomplished simply and neatly. In the case of any commodity for which the benefits are confined to one individual – such a commodity is called a *private good* – a consumer does not derive any benefit unless he pays for the good, and the higher the price, the higher the benefit that must be realized in consumption for the purchaser to justify the purchase decision. However, when the benefits of a commodity can be collectively enjoyed (as in the case of street lights), a very high level of community benefit can be sacrificed when each individual determines that *his* benefit is not great enough to justify *his* paying the purchase price.

Let's try to solve the problem of producing a Pareto-optimal number of street lights by designing a mechanism that imitates the market system's success in the realm of private goods. We will have to face up to the issue of incentives.

Consider a scheme of voluntary contributions based on the degree of benefit received. Specifically, the residents of the street form a club and each household contributes to a fund that is to be used to purchase the lights and pay the monthly electricity bill. To imitate the role of prices in private goods markets, we can impose the rule that a householder's contribution to the fund be proportional to the benefit received. For concreteness, suppose that each household i receives $\alpha_i z$ dollars worth of benefit from z units of lighting and z units of lighting cost $\frac{1}{2}z^2$ dollars. The individual preference parameter α_i is unknown to anyone outside of household i. There are n households on the street.

A Pareto-optimal provision level of street lighting may be found by maximizing the total benefit minus total cost: $\alpha_1 z + \alpha_2 z + \cdots + \alpha_n z - \frac{1}{2}z^2$. Any provision level that would give everyone greater net benefit would result in a larger total net benefit figure. Therefore, any level that maximizes total net benefit is Pareto optimal. Using elementary calculus, we discover that $z^* = \alpha_1 + \alpha_2 + \cdots + \alpha_n$ is a Pareto-optimal outcome. Each individual in the club is required to report α_i, the amount of benefit received per unit of lighting, and is required to pay the fraction $t_i = \alpha_i/(\alpha_1 + \alpha_2 + \cdots + \alpha_n)$ of the total cost of whatever amount of street lighting is decided on. A household is not only asked to report its benefit parameter but is also required to propose a value for z. An equilibrium is declared when each household demands the same value of z. Household i will want the level of z that maximizes $\alpha_i z - t_i(\frac{1}{2}z^2)$. Equating the first derivative to zero allows us to solve for z^i, the amount of street lighting that i is required to "demand." The solution is $z^i = \alpha_1 + \alpha_2 + \cdots + \alpha_n = z^*$.

We see that our mechanism provides a Pareto-optimal equilibrium *as long as the benefit parameters are reported faithfully.* But there is no incentive for the individual to do so. If household 1 misrepresents the benefit it receives from street lighting and reports a benefit parameter of zero, then it will not be required to pay part of the cost of providing lights. However, it will be able to enjoy the benefit of the amount $\hat{z}$ of lighting installed. Now $\hat{z}$ will be smaller than z^* because $\hat{z} = \alpha_2 + \alpha_3 + \cdots + \alpha_n$ when 1 falsely reports a benefit parameter of zero. But the net benefit to 1 from misrepresentation will be $\alpha_1 \hat{z} = \alpha_1(\alpha_2 + \alpha_3 \cdots + \alpha_n)$, and this will be larger than the net benefit from truthfully reporting α_1 as long as $\alpha_2 + \alpha_3 + \cdots + \alpha_n > \alpha_1 > 0$. We now verify this. When each α_i is truthfully reported, z^* units of output are produced and i pays $\frac{1}{2}t_i(z^*)^2$ dollars into the club's fund. The computation of 1's net benefit, $\alpha_1 z^* - \frac{1}{2}t_1(z^*)^2$, is straightforward:

$$\alpha_1 z^* - \left(\frac{\alpha_1}{\alpha_1 + \alpha_2 + \cdots + \alpha_n}\right)\frac{1}{2}(z^*)^2$$

$$= \alpha_1^2 + \alpha_1\hat{z} - \left(\frac{\alpha_1}{\alpha_1 + \hat{z}}\right)\frac{1}{2}(\alpha_1 + \hat{z})^2$$

$$= \alpha_1^2 + \alpha_1\hat{z} - \frac{\alpha_1}{2}(\alpha_1 + \hat{z})$$

$$= \frac{\alpha_1^2}{2} + \frac{\alpha_1\hat{z}}{2}$$

The increase in net benefit as a result of reporting a benefit parameter of zero is $\alpha_1 \hat{z} - (\frac{1}{2}\alpha_1^2 + \frac{1}{2}\alpha_1\hat{z}) = \frac{1}{2}\alpha_1(\hat{z} - \alpha_1)$, which is positive if $\hat{z} > \alpha_1 > 0$.

The mechanism we have defined yields Pareto-optimal outcomes when everyone plays by the rules, but there is a strong incentive for individuals to violate the rules and report false benefit parameters. It is not even necessary for a household to possess detailed information about other households' benefit parameters in order to be able to misrepresent preference to its own advantage. If it derives positive benefit from the "public good," then reporting a zero benefit parameter will yield more net benefit than truthful revelation as long as the household does not receive more gross benefit per unit than all other households in total.

In the language of the rest of the book, the mechanism under consideration is not *incentive compatible* because the equilibria that provide Pareto-optimal outcomes are not *competitive equilibria:* Playing strictly by the rules does not maximize net benefit, given the actions of others. If, as we assume throughout, each individual attempts to maximize his net benefit, then a system that requires the individual to pursue a different course is not consistent with individual incentives.

1.6 Land use

Suppose that a particular block of land in the heart of a city contains some dilapidated buildings that are to be torn down. The neighboring sites contain office buildings. The block in question will be available for any conceivable building or commercial outlet. How should the community decide to use this land, which has just "become available?"

Let's consider two possibilities: allowing the community to vote on the issue and using the private ownership market system to determine the outcome. To simplify further, suppose there are only two projects under consideration:

A. Use of the land for the location of carpet warehouses, automobile showrooms, and other activities that require a great deal of land for the storage of bulky commodities
B. Use of the land for restaurants, movie theaters, and stores supplying goods having a high value but little bulk, such as jewelry or clothing

Consider first what might happen if the community settled the issue by means of a simple majority vote. It is not inconceivable that 60 percent of the community favors A over B. Those preferring A feel that even though carpets and automobiles are purchased infrequently, there is some small advantage to having these outlets near their place of work for the rare occasions when they are needed. Option A would be taken if majority rule were employed to settle the conflict.

However, it is unlikely that the outcome would be Pareto optimal. Preferences are taken into account in the voting process in only a very crude way, at least in this instance. Each person has only one vote to cast no matter how profoundly he is affected by the issue. There is no possibility of the outcome reflecting *intensity of preference* if only two options are presented. Suppose, for example, that the 60 percent who favor A have only a very slight preference for A over B owing to the infrequency of purchase of automobiles and carpets. Suppose further that the 40 percent who favor B have a great deal at stake. Their working day would be rendered much more pleasant by the availability of restaurants for the lunch hour and movies after work. (You can think instead of a gymnasium that would extend life expectancy if it helps you appreciate the example.) If those who favor A have a preference that is so slight that they are almost indifferent while those who favor B prefer that alternative by a very wide margin, then Pareto optimality would seem to require the adoption of B. (Suppose that stores were run for profit, as they are in a market system, and rents were higher in the center of the city, where restaurants and movie theaters tend to be, and lower in the suburbs, where automobile showrooms and carpet warehouses tend to be. Then carpets would be cheaper than if they were sold in the center of the city and the 60 percent favoring A would actually prefer this to A: Their preference of A over B is so weak that the possibility of cheaper carpets more than compensates for the slightly less favorable location. The 40 percent who prefer B to A will also prefer this third alternative, even though restaurant prices are higher than in other areas, owing to the higher rents, since they greatly prefer having restaurants handy to their offices than having carpet warehouses nearby. If we can make everyone better off, the original voting outcome is not Pareto optimal.)

We can try to repair the defect that results when the vote of the individual with a very weak preference has the same weight as that of someone with a very strong preference by allowing each individual to cast up to 1000 votes, depending on his strength of preference. The rule to be followed would be that an individual who strongly prefers A to B casts a proportionately large number of votes for A and an individual who mildly prefers A to B and is almost indifferent casts relatively few votes for A. *If* everyone follows this rule, the outcome would be optimal. Under the present hypothesis 60 percent of the community would vote for A, but each vote would be low so the total would not be large, where all those favoring B would cast a high vote for it. Then B would be adopted, since it would receive far more votes than A.

This extended voting scheme works well if each voter follows the rules, but there would be no incentive for those favoring A to do so. In fact, each voter would cast 1000 votes for the alternative he favored in order to increase its chance of being adopted; one might as well try to obtain what one prefers if there is no additional cost in doing so, even if the strength of preference is weak. Then the outcome is identical to the one-person, one-vote scheme, and Pareto optimality would in fact be violated.

We have already indicated how the issue would be settled in a market system. Entrepreneurs wishing to use the land as a site for selling a particular product or service would bid for it and the amount of rent charged would reflect the desirability of the land to the highest bidder.

The entrepreneur who stayed in the bidding longest – the one who eventually signs the contract and pays the market-determined rent – cannot continue using the land unless he or she can avoid losses. That is one of the rules of the game in a market system. This rule serves a crucial purpose. Since the land can be used for a wide range of purposes, optimality requires that it be used in the way that yields the greatest benefit to the community. If the general benefit from one particular use truly is high, consumers generally will be prepared to pay a lot for whatever good or service results. (This does not imply that the price of the commodity will be high; the price might be low, yet a very large number of consumers purchase the output of a small unit of land.) An entrepreneur will stay in the bidding for the land only if he or she expects to be able to pay the rent by taking in enough revenue from customers. The customers will pay only if the entrepreneur provides a good or service that yields a benefit proportional to the amount paid. In effect, customers are voting for goods and services, and in a market system they can increase or decrease the number of votes cast for a particular good. Since the votes are cast in the form of dollars given up, which represent other goods and services sacrificed, there is no incentive for a consumer to overstate the benefit he receives for any commodity. We have Pareto optimality: The outcome reflects individual preferences, not just crudely, but precisely, since it reflects the intensity of individual preference. We also have incentive compatibility, since there is no incentive for a consumer to misrepresent his preferences. If the benefit to be derived from a commodity is very slight, it would be foolish to pretend that it is high by casting a large number of dollar votes – paying a high price for the good – since one will have to give up these dollars to get the good and they could be used instead to purchase something yielding substantial benefit.

The various entrepreneurs bidding for parts of this block of land are in effect representing various groups of consumers. The entrepreneur seeking a location for a retail carpet output is representing consumers who will at

some time in the near future want to buy a carpet. The would-be restaura-
teur is representing office workers who would like to have a handy restaurant at lunch hour, and so on. The group of consumers with the keenest
preference will in the end "win out," since they will – almost by definition
– be prepared to pay the most for their desired commodity, thus enabling
the entrepreneur representing them to stay in the bidding process longest
because he will anticipate the largest flow of revenues compared to all
other entrepreneurs. As a result, it is not necessary for any one of these
consumer groups to form a pressure group, political party, or club to have
their preferences effectively represented. We can claim that the market
outcome is *informationally efficient* in this case: It would seem to mini-
mize the costs of achieving an optimal outcome.

(It is not even necessary for the entrepreneur to be able to guess accurately the amount of potential demand for the firm's output. Entrepreneurs
who have seriously overestimated the value to the public of the service
they provide will be informed of the fact. The messenger bearing the bad
news will appear in the form of a loss figure at the end of the firm's income
statement. And the rules of the market game require a firm that continually
operates at a loss to discontinue its activities.)

1.7   Summary

The fifth example (Section 1.5) is an instance of the failure of the market
system to deliver a Pareto-optimal outcome. On the other hand, the sixth
example highlights a setting in which the market system generates a
Pareto-optimal equilibrium without an inordinate amount of information
processing. How can the two examples be reconciled? The commodity
featured in the fifth example is one that provides substantial spillover benefits, and the market system runs into difficulties in such cases because it
relies on an incentive structure to elicit information about individual – or
private – benefit derived from consumption. If the benefit from consumption is not confined to the individual taking the action, the information
provided by the market system will be incomplete and the incentives will
be inappropriate.

Simple examples (such as the first four) help illustrate a point or two
concerning the way in which self-interest may be harnessed in order to
identify a satisfactory outcome, but they do not make it clear why resource
allocation mechanisms are worthy of serious study. What makes the success of any mechanism problematic is the dispersion of knowledge phenomenon: Whether or not an economywide outcome or plan (specifying
the consumption of each household and the production activities of each
firm) is Pareto optimal depends on what other plans are feasible and

whether any of these are generally preferred to the given outcome. This means that a test of Pareto optimality depends on detailed knowledge of almost every aspect of each individual's preferences and each firm's production recipes. This knowledge is initially dispersed throughout the economy; no individual knows much more than his or her tastes and no plant manager knows much more than his or her production techniques. A successful resource allocation mechanism must somehow draw out this information, as a ballot reveals something about a voter's preferences. It must take into consideration the fact that economic behavior is usually motivated by self-interest, and it must somehow coordinate the activities of individuals and firms by forcing each to adjust to the observable implications of others' actions in a way that guides the system as a whole to an equilibrium that satisfactorily reflects the preferences of the participants. All of this is made formal and precise in the next chapter.

1.8 Background

Adam Smith was the first influential economist to recognize the need to explain why a decentralized economy that depends on the individual pursuit of self-interest would not result in chaos. He also began the task of explaining why this was so. For the most part, he used a simple performance criterion: maximum national output and wealth measured in terms of market prices. This is a crude measure of welfare, but one that was appropriate for a society attempting to shed the arbitrary restraints of mercantilism. The Italian economist Vilfredo Pareto suggested the subtle and powerful criterion that now bears his name. His optimality criterion was proposed in 1909, although it was not until later that he made it clear that an infinite number of allocations qualify as Pareto optimal (Pareto, 1927). The genius of the Pareto criterion lies in the fact that it rules out every conceivable type of waste. Because the criterion identifies an infinite number of outcomes as Pareto optimal in an economy and it does not address ethical considerations of *distributional* justice, subsequent authors asked whether Pareto optimality could be strengthened, most notably Bergson (1938). In 1951 Arrow proved that there exists no welfare criterion satisfying the Pareto criterion in addition to a few other mild conditions (Arrow, 1963). Since then economists have been less impatient to refine the Pareto criterion, although the attempt continues.

One reason for the profession's willingness to employ Pareto optimality as *the* welfare standard, in spite of its indecisiveness, is the fact that there are so many situations in which the Pareto criterion is violated. The conditions under which the price system fails to yield Pareto-optimal outcomes were identified by Young (1913). The understanding of why things went wrong was developed by Knight (1924), Pigou (1932), and Scitov-sky (1954), among others. The development of the literature on the public goods problem is sketched in the background notes for Chapters 3 and 5.

The refinement of the notion of a noncooperative equilibrium began with Cournot (1897), who employed what is now known as Nash equilibrium. (In certain contexts it is called a Cournot–Nash equilibrium.) The characteristic feature of a Nash equilibrium is that each agent, or player, chooses a strategy on the assumption that the previously announced strategies of the other agents will not change as a result of his own choice. The landmark contributions are by von Neumann and Morgenstern (1944) and Nash (1950). Recently some inadequacies in the Nash definition of equilibrium have been exposed and refinements proposed, beginning with Selten (1975).

EXERCISES

1.1 A feasible outcome is *strongly* Pareto optimal if there is no other feasible outcome that would make at least one person strictly better off and no one worse off. For the simple allocation problem of Section 1.1 show that every outcome but one is Pareto optimal, although there is only one strongly Pareto-optimal outcome. This suggests that mere Pareto optimality provides an inadequate test of efficiency *in this context*. Would Pareto optimality be less demanding than strong Pareto optimality in a conventional economic setting?

1.2 Let X be a finite set of alternatives. Suppose that no one is indifferent between any two distinct members of X. Suppose that each individual has *transitive* preferences: If x is strictly preferred to y and y is strictly preferred to z, then x is strictly preferred to z. Prove that there is a unique Pareto-optimal alternative if and only if everyone has the same first choice. Construct an example that violates transitivity of individual preference for which there exists no Pareto-optimal alternative.

1.3 Prove that the Pareto-optimal amount of the public good, z^*, in Section 1.5 is unique if each household is required to have some money left over after making its contribution to the financing of the public good. Show that there are an infinite number of Pareto-optimal *allocations*.

1.4 Consider the problem of dividing a cake among n persons. Let $x = (x_1, x_2, \ldots, x_n)$ be a typical outcome, with x_i denoting the fraction of the cake awarded to individual i. Prove that x is Pareto optimal if and only if $x \geq 0$ and $\sum_{i=1}^{n} x_i = 1$. Be explicit about the assumptions on individual preferences necessary to validate this claim.

1.5 Two individuals wish to share a cake. Suppose that person 1 cuts the cake into two pieces, however he likes, and person 2 is allowed to choose whichever of these pieces he wants for himself. What is the equilibrium of this allocation scheme?

CHAPTER 2

Performance criteria

A successful resource allocation mechanism is one that provides house-holds with the goods and services they would choose for themselves *if* they knew all of the production recipes for transforming inputs into out-puts and also the size of the economy's stock of primary inputs. The no-tion of a group of consumers deciding among themselves the best menu of commodities is an ambiguous one. Let us suppose, briefly, that it is sufficient for the mechanism to cater to the preferences of just one con-sumer. We might call this consumer a dictator. Let us see what difficulties the dictator would have in designing a resource allocation mechanism to suit his preferences. Then we will see what additional difficulties arise when an economy is required to cater to individual wants generally.

The limitations implied by production recipes, or techniques, and by the stock of primary inputs will constrain the dictator's choice. But no individual can be expected to know all of the recipes and all of the details concerning input availability. Each important fact relevant to production is known by someone, but no one individual, even if he is a dictator, is privy to even a substantial fraction of the relevant information. In other words, *knowledge is dispersed*. The key to the successful operation of a resource allocation mechanism is its ability to organize and exploit essential infor-mation by means of a communication process. This communication pro-cess, which is central to the operation of a mechanism, consists in the transmission of messages by economic agents and the reaction of agents to the messages transmitted by others. The transmission of a message can be more or less costly. For example, a firm's message might be a complete description of its production technology, and if such a message were trans-mitted to the dictator by each firm, the former would have enough infor-mation to calculate the set of feasible consumption menus. Reaction to messages could in this case consist of the computation by the dictator of the feasible set and a choice made by him, reflecting his tastes, from that set. Both steps would be very costly; a substantial amount of time and other resources would be used up both in the transmission of messages and in the reaction to them. It would not be unwise for the dictator to attempt to design an alternative mechanism for achieving the same goal of arriving at the most preferred consumption menu subject to the constraint implied by production technology and resources.

If the economy is to serve more than one individual, the dispersion of knowledge phenomenon presents even more of a challenge to the designer of a resource allocation mechanism. When the preferences of each individual or household are to be reflected to some degree in the outcome, the mechanism must be able to elicit information about preferences as well as production information. A successful mechanism will be more intricate when more than one consumer plays a role. The analysis of such a system is much more complicated because two new issues must be addressed.

First, the notion of catering to individual wants must be defined. Second, a mechanism that provides outcomes that somehow reflect individual preferences must be sensitive to individual behavior. If different actions on the part of one household lead to different outcomes, the course of action that the mechanism's rules require the household to take may lead to an outcome that is less favorable to it than another outcome resulting from some other action. In other words, a mechanism that generates outcomes that are satisfactory from the standpoint of society as a whole, provided that its rules are followed, will be unsatisfactory in practice if agents have an incentive to violate the rules of the game. These concerns take precise form in the shape of five performance criteria spelled out below (in Sections 2.2–2.6). Together these criteria are very demanding, but if one of them is omitted, the task of designing a mechanism that satisfies the others is in most cases a trivial one.

In examining the performance of a resource allocation process, attention will be confined to equilibrium outcomes. There are several definitions of equilibrium that have some claim to plausibility. One reason for this is that an individual agent may be assumed either to act on his own or to explicitly coordinate his strategy with other agents for their joint benefit. In the latter case various assumptions can be made about the costs of coalition formation and the nature of admissible coalitions. This book is concerned exclusively with noncooperative decision making; this is not an assumption intended to reflect the real world but a partial delineation of the scope of our treatment of economic systems. In plain words, it will be assumed throughout that no agent joins forces with other agents for the purpose of coordinating activities in order to influence the outcome of the economic process. Although most firms in a private ownership market economy are owned collectively by a large group of individuals, we will think of the firm itself as a single agent and thus it is implicit that the firm is formed exogenously. This is one of many reasons why a study of the formation of the producing units is beyond the scope of this book.

Under the assumption of noncooperative decision making, many definitions of equilibrium are still available, depending on what is assumed about the response of one agent to another's threats and about the knowledge possessed by one agent concerning another's characteristics and likely response to a change in the former's strategy. For example, a state that is in equilibrium *if* each agent takes the system's parameters to be given independently of his own behavior – whether or not they are in fact – may not be in equilibrium if at least one agent can conjecture how the parameters, and hence his consuming opportunities, would change as a result of a change in his behavior.

The abstract version of a mechanism sketched in the next section is centered on the idea of equilibrium, but the definition of equilibrium is not made explicit. Chapter 6, Section 2.6, and Sections 4.7–4.9 deal directly with the problem of determining a meaningful equilibrium concept.

2.1   Abstract economies

There are n consumers, or households, and m firms; $I = \{i_1, i_2, \ldots, i_n\}$ denotes the set of households and $J = \{j_1, j_2, \ldots, j_m\}$ denotes the set of firms. The set of agents is $A = I \cup J$. Some mechanisms require the planner to play an explicit role in the communication process, responding to the messages announced by households and firms with a signal of her own. In that case we will add a zero to the set A, which will then denote the set of all agents, including the planner; the planner is agent zero. In other words, $A = \{0, i_1, \ldots, i_n, j_1, \ldots, j_m\}$ if the planner plays an explicit role and $A = \{i_1, \ldots, i_n, j_1, \ldots, j_m\}$ otherwise. When we deal with households and firms separately, we will simplify by letting $\{1, 2, \ldots, n\}$ denote the set of households and $\{1, 2, \ldots, m\}$ denote the set of firms. The terms I and J, respectively, will still denote these sets; i and j, respectively, will denote arbitrary members of those sets.

There are k private goods and l public goods. Each household i consumes a bundle $(x_i, h) \geq 0$ consisting of a k-vector x_i of private goods and an l-vector h of public goods. Each unit of any public good produced is consumed simultaneously by all households. The *consumption set* X_i is the set of all bundles (x_i, h) that i is capable of consuming. Household i's preference over commodity bundles is represented by a real-valued function u_i, called a *utility function*, on X_i: $u_i(x_i, h) > u_i(x_i', h')$ signifies that i strictly prefers bundle (x_i, h) to bundle (x_i', h'). In fact, the utility function representation is just a convenience: It suffices for most of the results in this book, and for most of the important results in economic theory, to keep track of the order of preference between pairs of bundles. Finally, each household i has an *endowment* w_i, a k-vector in X_i: w_{ic} is the amount of commodity c, for example, an amount of some type of labor, that i holds. The endowments comprise the primary inputs on which all production and consumption activity is founded.

Each firm j produces an input–output vector (y_j, z_j), where y_j is a k-vector specifying j's production and employment of private goods and z_j is an l-vector of public goods produced by firm j. If the cth component y_{jc} of y_j is negative, then $-y_{jc}$ units of commodity c are required as input in order to carry out the plan (y_j, z_j). If y_{jc} is positive, then the plan (y_j, z_j) generates y_{jc} units of good c as output, which will then be available for consumption by the household sector or for use as input by another firm. The plan (y_j, z_j) generates the nonnegative vector z_j of public goods; z_j is nonnegative because public goods are never used as inputs. The set Y_j, a *technology set*, is the set of plans that are feasible for j: If $(y_j, z_j) \in Y_j$, then it is technologically possible for j to carry out the plan (y_j, z_j), provided that $-y_{jc}$ units of c can be obtained for any commodity c such that $y_{jc} < 0$.

Let e represent one specification of agent characteristics and let $F(e)$ denote the set of allocations that are feasible for *environment e*. An allocation $f = (x, y, z)$ belongs to $F(e)$ if and only if conditions 2.1 (*individual feasibility*) and 2.2 (*global feasibility*) both hold:

$$(x_i, h) \in X_i \qquad \text{for } i \in I$$

$$h = \sum_{j \in J} z_j \quad \text{and} \quad (y_j, z_j) \in Y_j \qquad \text{for } j \in J \tag{2.1}$$

$$\sum_{i \in I} x_i \le \sum_{i \in I} w_i + \sum_{j \in J} y_j \tag{2.2}$$

If condition 2.2 holds as a strict equality, we say that the allocation has the *material balance* property.

Let E denote the family of environments over which a mechanism is required to operate successfully. For example, E might have the property that for each e in E and each firm j, $z_j = 0$ if (y_j, z_j) is in Y_j. In that case only private goods need be considered; Y_j might rule out increasing returns to scale and u_i might be required to be continuous and exhibit diminishing marginal rates of substitution.

A resource allocation mechanism operates by having the individual agents (and the planner in some cases) transmit *messages* until an *equilibrium* configuration of messages is reached, at which point the rules of the game defining the mechanism determine an allocation or *outcome*.

The presence of an auctioneer or planner in the model is not necessarily intended as a reflection of the real world. In a model of the market system one often wishes to capture the idea that individual agents behave as if their messages or actions had no effect on prices, even though, with a finite number of firms and individuals, any individual agent's demands or supplies will have a positive – even if practically insignificant – effect on prices. If this effect is indeed tiny, it will not pay the individual to take it into account when making decisions. In terms of the professional argot, the individual will then be a *price-taker:* He optimizes given the current prices, implicitly assuming that prices will not change as a result of his optimizing behavior. If each agent is a price-taker – and this assumption is the idealization of the notion of competition in a market economy – then it is difficult to assemble a formal model of the market mechanism without a deus ex machina to announce prices and to adjust prices when supply does not exceed demand.

An abstract model of a market system with an auctioneer can be validated by showing that a more realistic model has the same equilibria – approximately – and that price-taking behavior is rational *at equilibrium* for an individual agent. This is problematic. If, for example, there are only one or two firms producing a particular good for which close substitutes are not available, we cannot justify price-taking behavior, even at equilibrium, as an idealization of reality. A monopolist will not choose the input–output combination that maximizes profit at current prices if a lower level of activity would lead to a substantial increase in the price of that firm's output and yield more profit at the new price. This book does not examine at length the conditions under which price-taking behavior is rational for firms, although Chapter 5 is devoted to the general phenomenon of rational behavior by households in relation to the rules of the game.

On the other hand, it must be made clear that evidence of price setting by a firm in the real world is not sufficient to vitiate a formal model that assumes price-taking behavior *at equilibrium*. If there is a large number of firms producing a particular good and at the given price configuration the total demand exceeds total supply, then an arbitrary firm can raise its own price somewhat without fearing that its customers will desert to a rival firm, since most other firms will be unable to fill all outstanding orders.

An *allocation* $f = (x, y, z)$ is a triple specifying the private goods consumption x_i of each household $i \in I$ and the production plan (y_j, z_j) of each firm $j \in J$. The consumption h of public goods by each household is implicit: $h = z_1 + z_2 + \cdots + z_m$. Whenever it is convenient, u_i will be exhibited as a function of the entire allocation – as $u_i(f)$ – although in most cases u_i will depend only on x_i and h.

Let F denote the universal set of allocations. Specifically, $F = (R_+^k)^n \times (R^k)^m \times (R_+^l)^m$, where R^t is t-dimensional Euclidean space and

R^t_+ is its nonnegative orthant. An *environment e* is a specification of the characteristics of the individual agents: e_a is the characteristic of agent $a \in I \cup J$. If a is a household, then e_a specifies a consumption set X_a, an endowment vector w_a, and a utility function u_a. If a is a firm, then e_a specifies a technology set Y_a. It will not be necessary to explicitly demonstrate the dependence of X_a, w_a, and so forth, on e_a. In some cases the characteristic e_a will have other features in addition to those just listed. For example, the Walrasian mechanism, which is defined below, requires e_i to specify the shares of firms owned by household i. In formulating the Walrasian mechanism to represent the market system, we do not attempt to capture the price setting of firms out of equilibrium; we leave this to an auctioneer, since we are concerned only with equilibrium. We are not even explicit about how the auctioneer adjusts prices; we say only that the auctioneer will adjust some prices unless demand equals supply in every market.

There are many ways of modeling the market system, even if the role of price setting is placed in the hands of an auctioneer. This is especially true if uncertainty is recognized. In addition, there are systems other than the market system that are worthy of serious attention, especially if public goods are acknowledged. Therefore, we require a definition of a resource allocation mechanism that is exceedingly general.

Formally, a *mechanism* $\mathcal{M}$ on the family of environments E is a triple $\mathcal{M}$ $= (M, \mu, g)$ consisting of a message set M, an equilibrium correspondence μ, and an outcome function g:

1. The *message set M* is the product of the individual agent message sets M_a $(a \in A)$; that is, each message configuration $m \in M$ specifies the message m_a transmitted by each agent a. Here M_a is the set of messages that a may transmit, although the particular message selected by a at any instant will be constrained by e_a and the messages of other agents. The individual messages may be more or less complex. Depending on the mechanism, m_i for household i could be a k-vector of amounts demanded of each private good, a demand function for each good, or a complete description of i's characteristic e_i, to name just a few possibilities. The complexity of the members m of M is a matter of some concern. Some message sets M will require the transmission of messages that are so complex that the signaling process will be very costly.

2. The equilibrium correspondence μ identifies for each environment e in E a set $\mu(e) \subset M$ of messages. If $m \in \mu(e)$, then m is in equilibrium for the environment e. Since e varies as preferences, endowments, and technologies vary, so will the notion of a satisfactory outcome. If the mechanism is to be successful, the equilibrium must change when the set of acceptable outcomes changes, as it will when e varies. Therefore, the

equilibria will depend on e and this is exhibited by the correspondence μ, which embodies most of what is of interest in a mechanism: It incorporates the rules by which each agent is required to react to the messages (such as prices) transmitted by other agents. If $m^* \in \mu(e)$, then the rules require agent a to transmit m_a^* if each $b \neq a$ announces m_b^* and the environment is e.

3. The outcome function g translates an equilibrium outcome m^* in $\mu(e)$ into a feasible allocation $g(m^*)$ in $F(e)$.

As an example of a mechanism, we define the *Walrasian mechanism* (WM) on a family E of environments that excludes public goods. Since $z_j = 0$ for each $(y_j, z_j) \in Y_j$, we will ignore the public goods component of any production plan or consumption bundle. The Walrasian mechanism, $\mathcal{M}^1$, has the following properties:

1. The planner's message set M_0 is the set of price vectors $p = (p_1, p_2, \ldots, p_k)$ such that $p \geq 0$ and $p_1 + p_2 + \cdots + p_k = 1$. For household $i \in I$, M_i is the set of demand vectors $x_i \geq 0$ $(M_i = R_+^k)$. For firm $j \in J$, M_j is the set of input–output plans y_j $(M_j = R^k)$.

2. Household i's message, or demand, is constrained by its wealth, which consists of the value of its endowment,

$$pw_i = p_1 w_{i1} + p_2 w_{i2} + \cdots + p_k w_{ik}$$

and its share of profits. Let α_{ij} denote the share of firm j owned by i. Of course, $\alpha_{ij} \geq 0$ for all i, j and $\alpha_{1j} + \alpha_{2j} + \cdots + \alpha_{nj} = 1$ for all j. Now,

$$py_j = p_1 y_{j1} + p_2 y_{j2} + \cdots + p_k y_{jk}$$

is the profit of firm j, since $p_c y_{jc} = -p_c |y_{jc}|$ if commodity c is an input and $p_c y_{jc} = +p_c |y_{jc}|$ if c is an output. Then $\alpha_{ij} py_j$ is i's share of j's profit and $\Sigma_{j \in J} \alpha_{ij} py_j$ denotes i's total profit earnings. Therefore, i's demand x_i must satisfy the *budget constraint* $px_i \leq pw_i + \Sigma_{j \in J} \alpha_{ij} py_j$. This constraint obviously depends on the messages of the firms and the planner.

The set of equilibrium message configurations, $\mu(e)$, is the set of $m = (p, x, y)$ satisfying the following:

(i) x_i belongs to X_i, x_i satisfies the budget constraint, given p, $y_1, \ldots, y_m$, *and* x_i yields the highest utility, $u_i(x_i)$, of all those commodity vectors in X_i satisfying the budget constraint.

(ii) y_j belongs to Y_j and $py_j \geq py_j'$ for any $y_j' \in Y_j$: y_j maximizes profit over Y_j *given* the price vector p.

(iii) $\Sigma_{i \in I} x_{ic} = \Sigma_{i \in I} w_{ic} + \Sigma_{j \in J} y_{jc}$ for each commodity c for which $p_c > 0$ and

$$\sum_{i \in I} x_{ic} \leq \sum_{i \in I} w_{ic} + \sum_{j \in J} y_{jc} \qquad \text{if } p_c = 0$$

[Note that conditions 2.1 and 2.2 are satisfied at equilibrium and (p, x, y) $\in \mu(e)$ if (i), (ii), and (iii) hold simultaneously.]

3. $g(p, x, y) = (x, y)$ for all $m = (p, x, y)$

The central condition is the demand-equals-supply requirement (iii). If a commodity has a price of zero at equilibrium, it can be in excess supply, but demand must equal supply at equilibrium for any good with a positive price. Equality of demand and supply must be achieved while the households and firms are maximizing utility and profit, respectively. In general terms, a configuration m of messages is in equilibrium if each agent a in A announces m_a and no agent, including the planner, wishes to revise his message after observing the messages transmitted by the other agents. In particular, if demand does not equal supply for some good with a positive price, the auctioneer (or planner) will change her message p. If the price vector p changes, the rules embodied in μ require households and firms to change their messages, as a result of the new optimizing exercises, and demands and supplies will then change.

Evidently, it is possible to define *individual* equilibrium correspondences μ_0, μ_i $(i \in I)$ and μ_j $(j \in J)$ that depend only on the respective agent's characteristic and in such a way that $(p, x, y) = m \in \mu(e)$ if and only if $m_a \in \mu_a(e_a)$ for each agent a. (In the case of the auctioneer e_0 can be any constant.) Equivalently, $\mu(e) = \cap \mu_a(e_a)$, where intersection is taken over A.

$$\mu_0 = \left\{ (p, x, y): p \in M_0 \text{ and for any } q \in M_0 \ p\left(\sum_{i \in I}(x_i - w_i)\right.\right.$$

$$\left.\left. - \sum_{j \in J} y_j \right) \geq q\left(\sum_{i \in I}(x_i - w_i) - \sum_{j \in J} y_j\right)\right\}$$

$$\mu_i(e_i) = \left\{ (p, x, y): x_i \in X_i, \ px_i \leq pw_i + \sum_{j \in J}\alpha_{ij}py_j \text{ and if } u_i(x_i')\right.$$

$$\left. > u_i(x_i) \text{ then } px_i' > pw_i + \sum_{j \in J}\alpha_{ij}py_j\right\}$$

$$\mu_j(e_j) = \{(p, x, y): y_j \in Y_j \text{ and } py_j' > py_j \text{ implies } y_j' \notin Y_j\}$$

It is easy to show that $\mu(e) = \cap \mu_a(e_a)$. All we need to do is show that (iii) holds if (p, x, y) belongs to $\cap \mu_a(e_a)$. We have individual feasibility 2.1 by definition of μ_i and μ_j. If $(p, x, y) \in \mu_i(e_i)$, then x_i satisfies the budget constraint. Summing this inequality over all households yields

$$\sum_{i \in I}px_i \leq \sum_{i \in I}pw_i + \sum_{j \in J}py_j$$

since $\Sigma_{i \in I}\alpha_{ij} = 1$. Now,

$$p\left(\sum_{i\in I}x_i - \sum_{i\in I}w_i - \sum_{j\in J}y_j\right) \leq 0$$

and $(p, x, y) \in \mu_0(e_0)$ implies condition 2.2, global feasibility: If $\Sigma x_{ic} > \Sigma w_{ic} + \Sigma y_{jc}$ for some commodity c, set $q_c = 1$ and $q_b = 0$ for $b \neq c$. Then $q(\Sigma x_i - \Sigma w_i - \Sigma y_j) > 0 \geq p(\Sigma x_i - \Sigma w_i - \Sigma y_j)$, contradicting $(p, x, y) \in \mu_0(e_0)$. Finally, if preferences are such that all income is spent on consumption, we will have, for each i, $px_i = pw_i + \Sigma_{j\in J}\alpha_{ij}py_j$ and hence $p\Sigma x_i = p\Sigma w_i + p\Sigma y_j$. This, along with global feasibility and $p \geq 0$, implies that $p_c = 0$ if $\Sigma x_{ic} < \Sigma w_{ic} + \Sigma y_{jc}$.

Before turning to the specific performance criteria, we consider whether it is necessary for the planner to know $\Sigma_{i\in I}w_i$. The definition of μ_0 depends on this knowledge, but this dependence can be avoided formally in precisely the way in which it is avoided in practice. Suppose that instead of signaling x_i, the vector of gross demands, household i announces its *excess demand* (or net demand) $d_i = x_i - w_i$. If $d_{ic} > 0$, then i has a net demand for c and consumes its endowment w_{ic} plus an additional d_{ic} units that are purchased. In that case i's total consumption is $w_{ic} + d_{ic} = x_{ic}$. If $d_{ic} < 0$, then i supplies $-d_{ic}$ units of c to the community and its consumption is again $w_{ic} + d_{ic} = x_{ic}$. The excess demands are observable and the constraint $\Sigma_{i\in I}x_i \leq \Sigma_{i\in I}w_i + \Sigma_{j\in J}y_j$ is equivalent to $\Sigma_{i\in I}d_i \leq \Sigma_{j\in J}y_j$. The last inequality is defined in terms of the agent messages d_i and y_j, and thus each correspondence $\mu_a(e_a)$ for all a, including $a = 0$, depends only on e_a, the agent's own characteristic, and on the messages of other agents. Nevertheless, we will always think of household i's message (in WM) as the gross demand vector x_i in order to simplify the exposition and the proofs of theorems.

Now we begin our discussion of the performance criteria.

2.2 Privacy preservation

If we permit the message transmitted by one agent to reflect the characteristics of other agents, we can assume away almost all of the difficulties of resource allocation with which economists are occupied: Simply require some agent, say, the first, to report a Pareto-optimal allocation. Accordingly, define the mechanism $\mathcal{M}^2$.

> There is no planner, so M_0 need not be defined. Set $M_1 = F$ and $M_a = \{0\}$ for all $a \neq 1$, since agents other than 1 play no essential role in the message transmission process. For each e, $\mu(e) = \{(f^*, 0, 0, \ldots, 0)\}$, where f^* is some appropriate Pareto-optimal allocation in $F(e)$. Of course, $g(f^*, 0, 0, \ldots) = f^*$.

This mechanism is successful in the sense that each equilibrium is Pareto optimal. It can be modified so that f^* is whichever allocation in $F(e)$ that is considered ideal. But it cannot be taken seriously, since it fails to come to terms with the dispersion of knowledge phenomenon. Mechanism $\mathcal{M}^2$ assumes that individual 1 knows every detail of e without the need for individual agents to communicate data pertaining to their characteristics to agent 1. A simple way to rule out this highly unrealistic kind of mechanism is to insist that μ be a coordinate correspondence.

The family of environments is E. Let E_a be the set of e_a such that $e_a = e'_a$ for some $e' \in E$; E_a is the family of characteristics of agent a that are represented in E. The correspondence $\mu: E \to M$ is a *coordinate correspondence* if for each agent a there exists a correspondence $\mu_a: E_a \to M$ such that $\mu(e) = \cap \mu_a(e_a)$ for all e in E, where intersection is taken over all agents a. (The planner's E_0 can be any singleton set, say, $E_0 = \{1\}$.) If μ is a coordinate correspondence, we say that the mechanism is *privacy preserving*.

The Walrasian mechanism is privacy preserving for the reasons given at the end of Section 2.1.

Now let us see why $\mathcal{M}^2$ is not privacy preserving. Assume two households, two private goods, no production, and no public goods. Then each e in E defines a pure exchange economy. Fix $u_1 = u_2$ for all e in E: $u_i(x_i) = x_{i1} \cdot x_{i2}$. Only the endowments w_i vary and $w_i \in \{(1, 0), (0, 1)\}$ for each e in E. For definiteness, let f^* be the Walrasian equilibrium for e. If $w_1 = w_2 = (1, 0)$ or $w_1 = w_2 = (0, 1)$, there is no basis for trade and $f^* = w$. If $w_1 \neq w_2$, then $x^* = ((\frac{1}{2}, \frac{1}{2}), (\frac{1}{2}, \frac{1}{2}))$ is the Walrasian equilibrium allocation. [To verify, set $p^* = (\frac{1}{2}, \frac{1}{2})$. Then $x_i^* = (\frac{1}{2}, \frac{1}{2})$ maximizes u_i subject to the budget constraint $\frac{1}{2}x_{i1} + \frac{1}{2}x_{i2} \leq \frac{1}{2}$.]

If $\mathcal{M}^2$ *is* privacy preserving, then $\mu(e) = \mu_1(e_1) \cap \mu_2(e_2)$ for all e. We can set $e = w$, since endowments are the only variables within E.

$$\mu_1(1, 0) \cap \mu_2(0, 1) = \mu((1, 0), (0, 1)) = \{(x^*, 0)\}$$
$$\mu_1(0, 1) \cap \mu_2(1, 0) = \mu((0, 1), (1, 0)) = \{(x^*, 0)\}$$

Therefore, $(x^*, 0) \in \mu_1(1, 0) \cap \mu_1(0, 1)$ and $(x^*, 0) \in \mu_2(1, 0) \cap \mu_2(0, 1)$. Therefore, $(x^*, 0) \in \mu_1(1, 0) \cap \mu_2(1, 0) = \mu((1, 0), (1, 0)) = \{((1, 0), (1, 0), 0)\}$, a contradiction. Hence $\mathcal{M}^2$ is not privacy preserving.

2.3   Individual rationality

This condition is a general welfare requirement even more elementary than Pareto optimality. It is imposed to ensure that every household benefits from participating in the economic system. The need for such a condition can easily be demonstrated by ignoring production (set $Y_j = \{0\}$ for every firm j) and by restricting E so that each household i's utility depends only on the commodity bundle assigned to i and increases when the consumption of any good increases, ceteris paribus. Now define $\mathcal{M}^3$. For each i, M_i is the set of nonnegative k-vectors; it is interpreted as the set of conceivable endowment vectors. Set $\mu_i(e_i) = \{m = (m_1, m_2, \ldots, m_n) \in M : m_i = w_i\}$. Then $\mu(e) = \cap \mu_i(e_i) = \{w\}$. Each household reports its endowment: The vector of endowments is the equilibrium message configuration. Finally, $g(w) = (\Sigma_i w_i, 0, \ldots, 0)$: Individual 1 consumes everything.

The equilibria of $\mathcal{M}^3$ will be Pareto optimal because individual i's utility can be increased only by reducing 1's consumption. Nevertheless, the equilibria are highly unsatisfactory for many reasons. Above all, every individual except the first will be much worse off for having participated in the economy. To eliminate this possibility, the following *individual rationality* condition is imposed:

> For every household $i \in I$ and every economy $e \in E$ such that u_i is independent of the private goods consumption of each household $a \neq i$, $u_i(g(m)) \geq u_i(f)$ for all $m \in \mu(e)$, where f denotes the allocation that assigns w_i to i and has zeros everywhere else.

If public goods are excluded from consideration, this reduces to $u_i(x_i) \geq u_i(w_i)$, where x_i is i's consumption at equilibrium: At equilibrium, i must be at least as well as when he consumes his endowment; otherwise, i would not wish to participate in the system.

If i's utility is adversely affected by the consumption of others, it would be unreasonable to insist that the system permit i to reach as high a level of utility as he had initially when only the endowments were available for consumption. For in that case i would be able to veto almost any allocation by claiming that the consumption of others left his own level of utility unacceptably low. On the other hand, for the subfamily of E within which individual utility depends exclusively on own consumption and on the provision of public goods, it is quite reasonable to require the mechanism to be utility enhancing for everyone. (It might even be desirable to strengthen the hypothesis of individual rationality so that it is in force only when each household receives benefit from public goods.)

The Walrasian mechanism has the individual rationality property as long as each firm is assured of a nonnegative profit at equilibrium by having the option of reducing costs to zero by reducing output to zero. In that case i will have enough purchasing power to buy its endowment w_i, and therefore whatever i chooses to consume must give at least as much utility as w_i if the private goods consumption of others is not an argument of i's utility function.

2.4   Pareto optimality

A feasible allocation f is *Pareto optimal* if and only if there exists no feasible allocation f' such that $u_i(f') > u_i(f)$ for every household i. If each utility function u_i depends only on x_i, the vector of private goods assigned to i by $f = (x, \ldots)$, then f is Pareto optimal if and only if it is feasible and there exists no feasible allocation $f' = (x', \ldots)$ such that $u_i(x_i') > u_i(x_i)$ for all $i \in I$.

An allocation that assigns all goods and services produced to individual 1 is Pareto optimal if 1 always prefers more to less and there is no other feasible menu that 1 would rather consume. This makes it very clear that Pareto optimality is merely a minimal test of satisfactory economic performance. Nevertheless, there are so many real-world situations in which a system falls short of Pareto optimality that it is by far the most widely used standard by which economists judge economic performance.

We will say that a feasible allocation f is *strongly Pareto optimal* if there is no feasible allocation f' such that $u_i(f') \geq u_i(f)$ for each household i and $u_i(f') > u_i(f)$ for at least one $i \in I$. In most instances the two definitions are equivalent. If an agent's utility is not adversely affected by the consumption of others and $u_1(x_1') > u_1(x_1)$ while $u_i(x_i') = u_i(x_i)$ for $i = 2,$ $\ldots, n$, then individual 1 can give a tiny amount of some good to every other consumer while remaining better off than he was with x_1, yet raising everyone else's utility slightly above $u_i(x_i')$. This results in a new allocation f'' with the same production plans but with $u_i(x_i'') > u_i(x_i)$ for *all* i.

Let us design a simple mechanism that does not generate Pareto-optimal outcomes. Suppose there are two households, one firm, and three (private) goods. Commodity 1 is not desired by consumers but can be used to produce the other two goods according to the recipe

$$Y_3 = \{(\delta, \beta, \gamma): \delta \leq 0, \beta \geq 0, \gamma \geq 0, \text{ and } \delta + \beta + \gamma \leq 0\}$$

(Agent 3 is the firm.) Set $u_1(\beta, \gamma) = 2\beta + \gamma$ and $u_2(\beta, \gamma) = \beta + 2\gamma$. Only individual endowments change as e varies within E. To define $\mathcal{M}^4$, set $M_1 = M_2 = \{\delta: \delta \text{ is a nonnegative real number}\}$. Set $\mu_i(e_i) = \{w': w_i' = w_i\}$ for $i = 1, 2$ and $\mu_3(e_3) = \{1\}$, since e_3 specifies the constant technology set Y_3. For any $m = (\delta_1, \delta_2) \in M$ let $g(m) = (x_1, x_2, y)$, where $y = (-\delta_1 - \delta_2, \frac{1}{2}(\delta_1 + \delta_2), \frac{1}{2}(\delta_1 + \delta_2))$ and $x_1 = (0, \frac{1}{4}(\delta_1 + \delta_2), \frac{1}{4}(\delta_1 + \delta_2)) = x_2$.

The households report their endowments. There is no need for the firm to transmit a message, since its technology never changes and can be assumed to be known from the start. The total endowment is used to produce equal amounts of commodities 2 and 3. The mechanism is individually rational, since no utility is derived from the endowment, which merely consists of the input good. The equilibrium allocations are not Pareto optimal, however, since

$$u_1(\tfrac{1}{2}(\delta_1 + \delta_2), 0) > u_1(\tfrac{1}{4}(\delta_1 + \delta_2), \tfrac{1}{4}(\delta_1 + \delta_2))$$

and

$$u_2(0, \tfrac{1}{2}(\delta_1 + \delta_2)) > u_2(\tfrac{1}{4}(\delta_1 + \delta_2), \tfrac{1}{4}(\delta_1 + \delta_2))$$

if either δ_1 or δ_2 is positive.

The next chapter explores the conditions under which equilibria of the Walrasian mechanism are Pareto optimal and every Pareto-optimal allocation is a Walrasian equilibrium allocation for some redistribution of endowments and firm shares.

2.5 Informational viability

A direct way of realizing a Pareto-optimal allocation without violating the first two criteria is to appoint a central planner who canvasses individuals and firms to ascertain their respective utility functions, endowments, and technologies; the feasible set $F(e)$ can be determined from the latter two components of e, and a complete specification of individual preferences permits the planner to identify an individually rational and Pareto-optimal member of $F(e)$.

To this end, define the mechanism $\mathcal{M}^5$. Set $M_0 = F$ and $M_a = E_a$ for all $a \neq 0$. Let $g: E \to F(e)$ be a function that selects a Pareto-optimal and individually rational member of $F(e)$ for each $e \in E$. Set $\mu_0 = \{m = (f, e): f = g(e)\}$, and $\mu_a(e_a) = \{m' = (f', e'): e'_a = e_a\}$ for all $a \neq 0$.

This mechanism places an enormous computational burden on the central authority. Even a large firm finds the calculation of every detail of a profit-maximizing set of activities beyond the capability of the fastest electronic computer, and an economy is vastly more complex than even a giant firm. In addition, the process of transmitting and receiving information about the characteristic e_a is a very costly one in a real sense; time and other resources are consumed while individual agents communicate the information required for the central planner to identify e_a. An individual consumer, for example, will find it very difficult to characterize his preferences.

This is not to say that central planning is not informationally viable but merely that $\mathcal{M}^5$ is not. One natural way of imposing informational viability is to insist that each agent's message set be a subset of some finite-dimensional Euclidean space. In that way each message is a list of numbers, and unless E is so narrow in scope that individual characteristics have a parameterization of fixed and finite length, mechanisms such as $\mathcal{M}^5$ will be inadmissible. Accordingly, a mechanism will be termed *informationally viable* if each agent's message set is a subset of some finite-dimensional Euclidean space.

Obviously, the Walrasian mechanism is informationally viable. On this account it is quite remarkable that it generates Pareto-optimal equilibria for a wide class of environments, although the proof of this could hardly be simpler, as we will see in the next chapter.

2.6   Incentive compatibility

Consider once again the mechanism $\mathcal{M}^3$. It will probably have occurred to the reader that a sensible individual will not announce his true endowment vector w_i if whatever is declared is confiscated and given to individual 1. Even if Pareto optimality were the only test of satisfactoriness and one Pareto-optimal allocation were just as good as another, $\mathcal{M}^3$ could not be called a success, even in the pure exchange context. *If* each agent followed the rules embodied in μ, $\mathcal{M}^3$ would provide a Pareto-optimal allocation, but each agent other than the first has a strong incentive not to do so. The best message for i to transmit is $m_i = 0$. This would allow i to consume w_i without having to yield any of it to agent 1. In general, if no agent has anything to gain from departing from the rules of behavior embodied in the equilibrium correspondence, we will say that the mechanism is *incentive compatible*. Since an agent's perception of how his behavior can influence the equilibrium can be more or less acute, there are many degrees of incentive compatibility.

In order to define incentive compatibility precisely, it is necessary to make a distinction between a *notional equilibrium* and an *observed equilibrium*, or, as we will call it, a *stationary point*. Let e denote the actual environment. Any message configuration m in $\mu(e)$ is called a notional equilibrium for e. If each agent a announced m_a and there were no subsequent revision of messages, the planner would observe the equilibrium m. Since e_a itself cannot be directly observed, the planner cannot ascertain whether m really belongs to $\mu_a(e_a)$ [although there may be many e'_a that are inconsistent with m in the sense that $m \notin \mu_a(e'_a)$]. Therefore, if m is observed in period t and no agent revises his message in the next period $t + 1$, we will call m a stationary point. It cannot be taken for granted that m is a notional equilibrium for e.

The equilibrium correspondence μ_a defines the expected behavior of agent a. The agent's actual behavior will be described by means of a *response function* $s_a : M \to M_a$. If the message configuration m^t is observed in period t, then agent a will announce the message $m_a^{t+1} = s_a(m^t)$ in the next period. The degree of sophistication employed by a in formulating strategies for announcing messages will be characterized by a correspondence S_a on E mapping E into the family of response functions, or strategies. Then $S_a(e)$ is the set of strategies that a would willingly employ when the environment is e.

It may strike the reader as odd that, having been circumspect in emphasizing that knowledge is dispersed and that μ must be a coordinate correspondence, we now suppose that agent a can employ a strategy that depends on components of e other than e_a. However, a successful mechanism must elicit information about individual characteristics. This information is transmitted as messages are announced and then revised, leading to the chronicle $m^1, m^2, \ldots, m^t, m^{t+1}, \ldots$. Whatever information is revealed about e by this sequence can in principle be exploited by some household or firm as well as by the mechanism.

If each agent a employs the strategy $s_a \in S_a(e)$, a message configuration m is a stationary point if and only if $s_a(m) = m_a$ for each a.

Agent a is said to behave *sincerely* if S_a depends only on e_a and every $s \in S_a(e_a)$ is consistent with μ_a in the sense that $m_a = s_a(m)$ if and only if $m \in \mu_a(e_a)$. If every agent is sincere, then m is a stationary point if and only if it belongs to $\mu(e)$. Let $S_a^0(e_a)$ denote the set of response functions for which a can be said to behave sincerely.

Agent a behaves *competitively* if S_a is independent of e_b for $b \neq a$ and for every s in $S_a(e_a)$ and every m in M, $s_a(m)$ is a *best response* to m. In the case of a household, a best response to m is a message $m_a' \in M_a$ that maximizes $u_a(g(m'))$ subject to $m_b' = m_b$ for $b \neq a$. Let $S_a^1(e_a)$ denote the set of competitive response functions. If agent a is a firm, it is difficult to determine what *best response* might mean. In the case of the Walrasian mechanism a best response would presumably be one that maximized the firm's profit. This is because profit has a direct bearing on the utility of the firm's shareholders. Since this book is mainly concerned with household behavior, we will not define *best response* for a firm in the general case.

Consumer i behaves competitively when he announces $m_i^{t+1} = s_i(m^t)$ in period $t + 1$, even though $m^t \in \mu_i(e_i)$ and $m_i^{t+1} \neq m_i^t$, because m_i^{t+1} results in a higher level of utility for i than m_i^t, *given the messages of others*. In other words, sincere behavior is not always compatible with individual incentives.

A *very* sophisticated individual would recognize that although m_i^{t+1} yields a higher level of utility given the messages of others, these messages will be revised, even if others behave sincerely, because m^{t+1} is not likely to be a stationary point even if $m^t \in \mu(e)$ and $m_a^{t+1} =$

m_a^t for $a \neq i$. The stationary point that is eventually realized might even afford i less utility than m^t. To prevent this, a sophisticated individual can anticipate the responses of other agents to a change in his message. To see how this can be done advantageously, suppose that every agent a other than i is known to behave sincerely in all situations. Then i knows that whatever stationary point is realized it will belong to $\mu_a(e_a)$ for each $a \neq i$. If there is some $e_i^* \in E_i$ such that $u_i(g(m^*)) > u_i(g(m))$ for all $m^* \in \mu(e^*)$, where $e_a^* = e_a \; \forall a \neq i$, and $m \in \mu(e)$, then i will be better off by behaving as though his characteristic were e_i^* when it actually is e_i. To ensure that m^* will be realized, i can employ a sincere strategy from $S_i^0(e_i^*)$. In general, we say that the response function s_i is *manipulative* – and that i *manipulates* at e – if $s_i \notin S_i^0(e_i)$ and there is some $e_i^* \in E_i$ such that $s_i \in S_i^0(e_i^*)$. Let $S_i^2(e) = \cup S_i^0(e^*)$, where union is taken over all those e_i^* such that $u_i(g(m^*)) > u_i(g(m))$ for some $m^* \in \mu_i(e_i^*) \cap \{\mu_a(e_a): a \neq i\}$ and some $m \in \mu(e)$. If there are no such e_i^*, then we set $S_i^2(e) = S_i^0(e_i)$, since i has nothing to gain from departing from sincere behavior. The correspondence S_i^2 represents the most extreme type of sophisticated behavior that will be considered in this book.

The next two examples highlight the distinction between sincere behavior and competitive behavior on the one hand and competitive behavior and manipulative behavior on the other hand.

Both examples involve two households, two commodities, no production, and constant endowments $w_1 = (1, 0)$ and $w_2 = (0, 1)$. Only individual preferences vary and each utility function u_i in E_i is defined by a single parameter δ_i:

$$u_i(x_i) = (x_{i1})^{\delta_i}(x_{i2})$$

Restrict δ_i to the interval $[\frac{1}{4}, 1] = \{\delta_i: \frac{1}{4} \leq \delta_i \leq 1\}$ and set $E_i = [\frac{1}{4}, 1]$, $i = 1, 2$, for convenience.

Define a new mechanism $\mathcal{M}^6$. Set $M_i = E_i$: Each household reports its utility parameter. Then

$$\mu_i(\delta_i) = \{(\lambda_1, \lambda_2): \lambda_i = \delta_i\}$$

and

$$g(\lambda_1, \lambda_2) = ((\tfrac{1}{2}, \lambda_2/(\lambda_1 + \lambda_2)), (\tfrac{1}{2}, \lambda_1/(\lambda_1 + \lambda_2)))$$

Verify that $x = g(\delta_1, \delta_2)$ is Pareto optimal for the economy $e = (\delta_1, \delta_2)$.

Suppose $\delta_1 = \delta_2 = \frac{1}{2}$. Then $g(\overline{m}) = ((\frac{1}{2}, \frac{1}{2}), (\frac{1}{2}, \frac{1}{2})) = \overline{x}$ if each person behaves sincerely and $\overline{m}$ is a stationary point. But, given that person 2 has announced $\overline{m}_2 = \frac{1}{2}$, person 1 can maximize $u_1(x_1) = (x_1)^{1/2}(x_2)$, the true utility function, by announcing $m_1 = \frac{1}{4}$. To see this, maximize $u_1(x_1)$ subject to $x = g(m_1, \frac{1}{2})$ and $m_1 \in [\frac{1}{4}, 1]$. In that case $x_1 = (\frac{1}{2}, \frac{1}{2}/(m_1 + \frac{1}{2}))$

and x_{12} will be largest when m_1 is smallest. Individual 2 has the same incentive to depart from sincere behavior. Indeed, whatever the value of δ_i, person i will achieve the highest level of utility, given the other's message, by announcing $m_i = \frac{1}{4}$. We can expect both to announce $m_i = \frac{1}{4}$ in every case, and this will lead to $g(\frac{1}{4}, \frac{1}{4}) = \bar{x}$, which will be Pareto optimal if and only if $\delta_1 = \delta_2$, since the marginal rates of substitution, $\delta_i x_{i2}/x_{i1}$, will be equal at $\bar{x}$ if and only if $\delta_1 = \delta_2$. So $\mathcal{M}^6$ generates Pareto-optimal outcomes if each agent follows the rules – plays sincerely – but each agent has a strong incentive to behave competitively and as a result the outcome is not Pareto optimal.

The Walrasian mechanism $\mathcal{M}^1$ is an example of a system in which sincere behavior and competitive behavior are identical; the rules of the Walrasian game require an agent to play his best response to the messages of others. The mechanism $\mathcal{M}^6$ is one for which competitive behavior and manipulative behavior are identical, because a message amounts to a description of the agent's characteristic and, by announcing $m_i = \frac{1}{4}$ on all occasions, i is behaving as he would be required to if his utility function really were $u_i(x_i) = (x_{i1})^{1/4}(x_{i2})$. To find an example of a mechanism for which competitive behavior and manipulative behavior are quite different, we need only consider the Walrasian mechanism for the family E just defined.

Suppose $e = (\frac{1}{2}, \frac{1}{2})$. Then, using WM, $g(\bar{m}) = \bar{x} = ((\frac{1}{3}, \frac{1}{3}), (\frac{2}{3}, \frac{2}{3}))$ for $\bar{m} = (\bar{p}, \bar{x}) \in \mu(e)$ and $\bar{p} = (\frac{1}{3}, \frac{2}{3})$: $\bar{x}_i$ maximizes $u_i(x_i) = (x_{i1})^{1/2} x_{i2}$ subject to $\bar{p} x_i \leq \bar{p} w_i$. But if agent 1 applies the Walrasian rules to $e_1^* = 1$, pretending that his utility function is $u_1^*(x_1) = x_{11} x_{12}$, the equilibrium is $m^* = (p^*, x^*)$ for $p^* = (\frac{2}{3}, \frac{1}{3})$ and $x^* = ((\frac{1}{2}, \frac{1}{3}), (\frac{1}{2}, \frac{2}{3}))$, as long as 2 behaves sincerely. (To define the manipulative response function of 1 simply maximize u_1^* subject to 1's budget constraint.) Since $u_1(x_1^*) = \sqrt{\frac{1}{2}}/3 > \sqrt{\frac{1}{3}}/3 = u_1(\bar{x}_1)$, individual 1 has an incentive to manipulate.

It is not difficult to motivate household 1's behavior in straightforward terms. Household 1 is the sole supplier of good 1, and by rationalizing his behavior by u_1^*, he is overstating his demand for that commodity – compare marginal rates of substitution – and this will result in a higher price of good 1 at equilibrium, allowing 1 to consume more of both goods than when he plays sincerely and good 1 has a lower price.

Whether an agent can advantageously manipulate depends on how much it is necessary for him to know about the characteristics and behavior of others and how costly it is to obtain this information. At one extreme, $\mathcal{M}^6$ can be manipulated without any additional knowledge by an agent other than the system's rules: Announcing $m_i = \frac{1}{4}$ is a dominant strategy in the sense that it gives rise to more utility than any other message available to i given any announcement by the other agent. The mechanism of Section 1.5 can be manipulated with the acquisition of just a slight amount of information by household i; i need only conjecture that the total benefit received by all other agents from the consumption of a unit of the public good exceeds i's benefit. The Walrasian mechanism requires a household to know something of how a change in his demand will affect the equilibrium price, and this presumes some knowledge of the utility functions, or at least the demands, of other households. Even if this knowledge is very hard to come by, it is premature to assume that agents will not formulate more sophisticated strategies than are embodied in the competitive response functions.

Therefore, we will carry two definitions of incentive compatibility. First, a mechanism is *compatible with competitive behavior* if $S_a^0 = S_a^1$ for every agent a. This means that the equilibria identified by μ are competitive equilibria; the mechanism assumes and depends on competitive behavior. Second, a mechanism is *compatible with manipulative behavior* if for every agent a and all $e \in E$, $S_a^2(e) = S_a^0(e_a)$; no agent can gain by misrepresenting his characteristic, and he might as well play sincerely.

Suppose that a mechanism is not compatible with competitive behavior. If $m \in \mu_i(e_i)$ but $u_i(g(m')) > u_i(g(m))$ for some $m' \notin \mu_i(e_i)$ such that $m_a' = m_a$ for all $a \neq i$, then $S_i^2 \neq S_i^0$ if $m' \in \mu_i(e_i^*)$ for some e_i^*. If $m_i = s_i(m)$ for $s_i \in S_i^1(e_i)$ but $m \notin \mu_i(e_i)$ while $m' \in \mu_i(e_i)$ for some m' such that $m_a' = m_a$ for all $a \neq i$, then $u_i(g(m)) > u_i(g(m'))$ and again $S_i^2 \neq S_i^0$ if $m \in \mu_i(e_i^*)$ for some e_i^*. This establishes, somewhat informally, that a mechanism that is compatible with manipulative behavior is also compatible with competitive behavior. Therefore, compatibility with manipulative behavior is more demanding than compatibility with competitive behavior. It would seem to make sense to carry only the one, stronger, incentive compatibility requirement. However, as demonstrated in Chapter 5, there does not exist a mechanism that is compatible with manipulative behavior unless (1) E is severely, and unrealistically, limited in scope; (2) the mechanism is dictatorial (recall $\mathcal{M}^3$); or (3) the mechanism is not required to generate Pareto-optimal equilibria. (Points 1 and 3 are addressed in Exercises 2.6 and 2.7 at the end of this chapter.) For this reason, there is no point in formally defining strategies that are more sophisticated than manipulation. For the same reason, it would be rash to discard the weaker version of incentive compatibility, compatibility with competitive behavior.

2.7   Summary

We seek an *informationally decentralized* resource allocation mechanism that satisfies Pareto optimality and individual rationality in a wide variety of situations. To be completely successful, the mechanism must be compatible with individual incentives and operate by means of a relatively efficient exchange of information among agents. The privacy preservation property formalizes the idea of informational decentralization.

2.8 Background

The study of the welfare properties of resource allocation mechanisms was begun in earnest by Adam Smith. But the mechanism design approach is relatively new. "This new approach refuses to accept the institutional status quo of a particular time and place as the only legitimate object of interest and yet recognizes constraints that disqualify naive utopias" (Hurwicz, 1973:1). Oscar Lange and F. M. Taylor are among the innovators; in separate papers collected in Lippincott (1938), they attempted to overcome skepticism that a socialist economy could meet the computational challenge of locating an optimal allocation of resources by showing how agents could be required to respond to prices just as in a private ownership market economy. Lerner (1944), von Hayek (1935), and Marschak (1955) contributed to the debate, and their contributions were to affect the way economists study resource allocation. Taking his cue from Hayek, Hurwicz (1960) showed how two mechanisms could be compared with respect to the information-processing demands made by each. Another important strand of the mechanism design literature is concerned with the convergence properties of particular planning processes. Of course, game theory (von Neumann and Morgenstern, 1944) has had an enormous impact on the study of resource allocation mechanisms as it has on all of economics, indeed on the social sciences in general. Hurwicz (1973) outlines the history of the mechanism approach.

The Walrasian model of the market system was first sketched by the nineteenth-century French economist Léon Walras [Walras (1874–7)]. He not only defined a general market equilibrium but also sought to represent the adjustment process by which equilibrium is reached. Walras invented the device of an auctioneer crying out prices *au hasard* at the outset and then adjusting them in response to demands and supplies until an equilibrium is reached. The artifice of an auctioneer is extremely useful and it has only been recently that economists have constructed models in which the auctioneer's services can be dispensed with (Hurwicz, 1979a; Walker, 1984). Arrow (1959) explained how to reconcile the practical fact that each firm sets the price of its own output with the theoretical assumption that firms take prices as given *at equilibrium*. Results on the stability of the adjustment process are summarized in Arrow and Hahn (1971) and Hahn (1982).

The privacy preservation and individual rationality conditions formalized in this chapter made their first appearance in Hurwicz (1960). Pareto optimality is discussed in the background notes to Chapter 1. The development of incentive compatibility is sketched in the background notes for Chapter 5.

The informational viability requirement made its formal debut in Hurwicz (1960). This paper inspired proofs that the Walrasian mechanism is actually *informationally efficient* in the sense that no mechanism can guarantee Pareto-optimal equilibria over the classical family of environments by means of a message space of smaller dimension than the Walrasian message space. This investigation was begun by Mount and Reiter (1974) and completed by Hurwicz (1977), Walker (1977), and Osana (1978).

In a recent paper Jordan (1982b) showed that the Walrasian mechanism – or a copy of it – is the only mechanism that is informationally efficient if Pareto optimality and individual rationality are imposed. This means that the Walrasian mechanism emerges as the solution to a well-defined problem. This is a strong vindication of the mechanism design approach. A similar claim can be made for Hurwicz (1979a, b), Hammond (1979), and Sonnenschein (1974).

EXERCISES

2.1 A commodity is *desirable* if any increase in its consumption, ceteris paribus, increases utility. Let $f = (x, y, z)$ be a feasible allocation such that every household has a positive amount of a particular private good that everyone finds desirable. Suppose that each individual's utility function is continuous and independent of the private goods consumption of everyone else. Prove that f is Pareto optimal if and only if it is strongly Pareto optimal.

2.2 Consider a two-person, two-commodity exchange economy with endowments $w_1 = (10, 0)$ and $w_2 = (0, 10)$. Each person's consumption set is the nonnegative quadrant. Let (a, b) represent an allocation, with 1 consuming $a = (a_1, a_2)$ and 2 consuming $b = (b_1, b_2)$. A particular economy e^t ($t = 1, 2, \ldots, 9$) is specified below by defining the utility functions u_1 and u_2. Determine the set of Pareto-optimal allocations for each economy, being careful about cases where someone is assigned zero units of some good or some good is not used up.

e^1: $u_1(a) = a_1 + a_2$ and $u_2(b) = b_1 + b_2$

e^2: $u_1(a) = 2a_1 + a_2$ and $u_2(b) = b_1 + 2b_2$

e^3: $u_1(a) = a_1 a_2$ and $u_2(b) = b_1 b_2$

e^4: $u_1(a) = a_1^2 a_2$ and $u_2(b) = b_1 b_2$

e^5: $u_1(a) = \min\{a_1, a_2\}$ and $u_2(b) = \min\{b_1, b_2\}$

e^6: $u_1(a) = \min\{2a_1, a_2\}$ and $u_2(b) = \min\{b_1, 2b_2\}$

e^7: $u_1(a, b) = a_1 + a_2 - b_2$ and $u_2(b) = b_1 + b_2$
(individual 1 is adversely affected by 2's consumption of commodity 2)
e^8: $u_1(a, b) = a_1 + a_2 + b_2$ and $u_2(b) = b_1 + b_2$
e^9: $u_1(a) = \max\{a_1, a_2\}$ and $u_2(b) = \max\{b_1, b_2\}$

2.3 Are there any Pareto-optimal allocations that are not strongly Pareto optimal in any of the economies of Exercise 2.2?

2.4 Consider a two-commodity economy with one household and m firms. The consumption set is the nonnegative quadrant; $u(x) = x_1 x_2$ and $w = (\omega, 0)$. Firm j's technology set is characterized by the positive real number β_j:

$$Y_j = \{y_j: y_{j1} \leq 0 \leq y_{j2} \leq -\beta_j y_{j1}\}$$

Characterize the set of Pareto-optimal allocations.

2.5 Consider a two-commodity economy with one household identical to the household of Exercise 2.4 and one firm with technology set $Y = \{y: y_1 \leq 0 \leq y_2$ and $y_2 \leq \sqrt{-y_1}\}$. Characterize the set of Pareto-optimal allocations.

2.6 There are two households, two private goods, no public goods, and no production. Endowments are fixed at $w_1 = (0, 1)$ and $w_2 = (1, 0)$. Let E be the set of pairs (δ_1, δ_2) of nonnegative real numbers. Each (δ_1, δ_2) defines an economy in which the utility functions are $u_1(a) = \delta_1 a_1 + a_2$ and $u_2(b) = \delta_2 b_1 + b_2$. Cast into formal language the mechanism in which each household i reports a nonnegative real number λ_i and the outcome is w unless $\lambda_1 > \lambda_2$, in which case the outcome is $((1, 0), (0,1))$. The mechanism is obviously informationally efficient; no mechanism could have a smaller message space. Prove that the mechanism is also privacy preserving, individually rational, and Pareto optimal. Prove that the mechanism is incentive compatible in the strongest possible sense: For each i, reporting the true utility parameter δ_i is a dominant strategy.

2.7 Design an individually rational, informationally viable, and privacy preserving mechanism that is incentive compatible in the strongest possible sense even when there is more than one household and E includes all conceivable environments. (Pareto optimality will necessarily be violated.)

2.8 Design a mechanism that has the same equilibria as the Walrasian mechanism in the pure exchange context but that has the planner announcing an allocation x and each household i responding by reporting its vector of marginal rates of substitution at x_i. Can you extend the coverage of the mechanism to include cases where marginal rates of substitution are not defined?

2.9 Consider an n-person pure exchange economy with strictly private goods and such that each utility function depends exclusively on the consumption of the individual in question. Prove that if the endowments are identical, then at any Walrasian competitive equilibrium no consumer would want to exchange commodity vectors with anyone else, regardless of how the individual preferences are specified.

2.10 Let E be the family of environments defined by Exercise 2.4 as $(\beta_1, \beta_2, \ldots, \beta_m)$ varies over the nonnegative orthant of R^m. Set $\omega = 1 : w = (1,0)$.

Describe formally a mechanism that requires each firm to report β_j and awards half a unit of good 1 to one of the firms reporting the largest β_j and zero units to every other firm. Which of the five properties discussed in Chapter 2 are satisfied by this mechanism? Now set $m = 2$ and replace the technology set of firm 2 with

$$Y_2 = \{y_j: y_{j1} \le 0 \le y_{j2} \le 1 - \beta_2(1 + y_{j1}) - (1 - \beta_2)(1 + y_{j1})^2\}$$

Let E^* be the family of environments with u, w, and Y_1 as defined in Exercise 2.4 and Y_2 as just defined. Prove that the mechanism defined in this question does not satisfy Pareto optimality on E^*.

2.11 Prove that if (p, f) is a Walrasian competitive equilibrium, then so is $(\lambda p, f)$ for any positive real number λ.

CHAPTER 3

The Arrow–Debreu world

A utility function that is sensitive only to the private goods consumption of the agent in question will be termed *self-regarding*. A firm's technology set is self-regarding if it does not depend on the activities of other agents. We will show that a Walrasian competitive equilibrium allocation is Pareto optimal as long as household utilities and firm technologies are self-regarding *and* each commodity that affects someone's utility is traded in some market. Section 3.9 demonstrates that self-regarding preferences and technologies are not really required for Pareto optimality, but the assumption of competitive behavior loses its plausibility without it.

E^{AD} will denote the largest family of environments for which all utility functions and technology sets are self-regarding. Section 3.4 proves that a Walrasian competitive equilibrium allocation is Pareto optimal if the environment belongs to E^{AD}. There are many members of E^{AD} for which an equilibrium does not exist, however; this issue is taken up in Chapter 6, which shows that there is a very wide class E^* of environments overlapping E^{AD} for which equilibria exist. Therefore, the result of Section 3.4 is not vacuous. Section 3.6 will show that for every economy e in $E^* \cap E^{AD}$ and any Pareto-optimal allocation f of e there is an economy e' in $E^* \cap E^{AD}$ that is the same as e except with respect to endowments and profit shares and such that f is a Walrasian competitive equilibrium allocation for e'. In other words, e' is obtained from e by redistributing wealth.

3.1   What is a commodity?

In the Arrow–Debreu world all decisions are made at one time prior to the delivery of goods, whether these deliveries will take place in the present or in the future. Since it matters to a consumer whether he obtains a particular good now or later, we will have to treat units of a particular good delivered at different times as different commodities. Suppose that there are k_1 commodities when commodities are identified according to their physical characteristics only and that there are k_2 time periods under consideration. Then $k = k_1 \times k_2$ is the total number of commodities.

A commodity bundle x_i assigned to household i is a k-vector $x_i = (x_{i1}, x_{i2}, \ldots, x_{ik})$. If x_{i1} is a quantity of apples for present consumption, then x_{ic} for $c = k_1 + 1$ is the quantity of apples to be delivered and consumed one period later, and x_{ic} for $c = 2k_1 + 1$ is the quantity of apples to be delivered and consumed two periods later, and so on.

Just as there are as many different "types" of apples as there are time periods, there will be the same number of prices for apples. If p is a system of prices (a k-vector), then p_1 is the price *paid now* for apples delivered now, p_c for $c = k_1 + 1$ is the price *paid now* for apples delivered one period from now, and p_c for $c = 2k_1 + 1$ is the price *paid now* for apples delivered two periods from now. We would expect to find that p_1 is larger than p_{k_1+1}: It costs less (now) to buy apples for future delivery.

There is no money in the Arrow–Debreu world. The prices serve to define the rate at which a consumer can trade one good for another. At price system p a household i can make any vector x_i of demands on the social stockpile of goods that satisfies its budget constraint. Money in the real-world market system ensures that an individual does not violate the budget constraint. (Money has other functions as well.) For supplying w_i to the economy, the individual receives $p \cdot w_i$ dollar notes, and for every unit of commodity c the individual purchases, he must hand over p_c dollars to the shopkeeper. (What incentive does the shopkeeper have to enforce this rule?) We abstract from this aspect of market exchange and assume that individuals satisfy their budget constraints without the discipline of money. The theoretical treatment of money in a market economy is very difficult, and we will circumvent the difficulties by banishing this commodity from the model. (The planner can enforce the budget constraint without money by requiring goods to be exchanged directly for goods of equal value. However, a barter system involves high costs of search – for a compatible trading partner – and incentive difficulties would be exchanged for informational inefficiencies if this scheme were adopted.)

3.2   Private ownership

The firms are owned by individual households. Let α_{ij} be the share of firm j owned by household i. Then $0 \leq \alpha_{ij} \leq 1$ and $\Sigma_{i \in I} \alpha_{ij} = 1$ for each firm $j \in J$. (I is the set of households and J is the set of firms.)

An individual's wealth has two components: the market value $p \cdot w_i$ of his endowment w_i and the profits received from the firms in which he owns a share. Individual i's profit income is $\Sigma_{j \in J} \alpha_{ij} \Pi_j$ where Π_j is the profit earned by firm j and $\alpha_{ij} \Pi_j$ is his share of that profit.

The individual is able to purchase a commodity bundle x_i at prices p if and only if $p \cdot x_i \leq p \cdot w_i + \Sigma_{j \in J} \alpha_{ij} \Pi_j$.

3.3 Walrasian competitive equilibrium

The Walrasian mechanism was defined formally in Section 2.1. It is intended as an idealization of a private ownership market economy in which individual agents are price takers and their messages are solutions to individual maximization problems. In the case of a household i the message is a vector x_i of demands, but we can also think in terms of the net demand vector $x_i - w_i$; if $x_{ic} - w_{ic}$ is positive, then i is a net demander of commodity c, and if $x_{ic} - w_{ic}$ is negative, individual i supplies $w_{ic} - x_{ic}$ units of c to the rest of the economy. If we treat i's message as a net demand $x_i - w_i$, then the demand equal supply condition is $\Sigma_{i \in I}(x_i - w_i) = \Sigma_{j \in J}y_j$, which is equivalent to $\Sigma_{i \in I}x_i = \Sigma_{i \in I}w_i + \Sigma_{j \in J}y_j$, where y_j is the input–output vector of firm j. In fact, we allow $\Sigma_{i \in I}(x_{ic} - w_{ic}) < \Sigma_{j \in J}y_{jc}$ at equilibrium, but only if the price of c is zero.

The essential properties of a Walrasian competitive equilibrium are reviewed at this point. Recall that X_i, i's consumption set, is the set of commodity bundles that i can conceivably consume. Household i's endowment, w_i, is a k-vector in X_i and i's preferences are represented by a real-valued utility function u_i on X_i. The technology set of firm j, Y_j, is the set of input–output plans that can be carried out by j assuming it can obtain the required inputs. If $y_j \in Y_j$ and y_{jc} is negative, then the plan y_j requires $-y_{jc}$ units of commodity c to be used as input. Therefore, the profit from y_j is py_j under price regime p.

A list (p^*, x^*, y^*) of messages is a Walrasian competitive equilibrium if conditions (3.1) – (3.4) hold.

x_i^* solves household i's optimization problem:
max $u_i(x_i)$ subject to $x_i \in X_i$ and

$$p^*x_i \leq p^*w_i + \sum_{j \in J}\alpha_{ij}p^*y_j^* \qquad (3.1)$$

y_j^* solves firm j's optimization problem:
max p^*y_j subject to $y_j \in Y_j$ \qquad (3.2)

$$\sum_{i \in I}x_i^* \leq \sum_{i \in I}w_i + \sum_{j \in J}y_j^* \quad \text{and} \quad p^* \geq 0 \qquad (3.3)$$

The last equilibrium condition,

$$p^*\sum_{i \in I}x_i^* = p^*\sum_{i \in I}w_i + p^*\sum_{j \in J}y_j^* \qquad (3.4)$$

which is part of the planner's adjustment rule, will not be needed for any of the proofs. In words, x_i^* maximizes i's utility subject to i's budget constraint given prices p^* and firm profits [condition (3.1)], y_j^* maximizes

j's profit given p^* and subject to the technological constraint Y_j [condition (3.2)], and demand equals supply for each commodity c unless $p_c^* = 0$ and supply exceeds demand [conditions (3.3) and (3.4)].

The equilibrium (p^*, x^*, y^*) is a *competitive* equilibrium since each agent is required by the rules of the mechanism to announce a best response to the messages transmitted by others. The messages determine the household's budget constraint and the profitability of alternative production plans available to the firm.

3.4   The first welfare theorem

Pareto optimality was formally defined in Chapter 2. When each household's utility depends only on its own consumption of private goods, we can say that a feasible allocation (x, y) is Pareto optimal for economy e if there is no feasible allocation (x', y') such that $u_i(x_i') > u_i(x_i)$ for each household i. [An allocation (x, y) is feasible if $x_i \in X_i$, $y_j \in Y_j$, $\forall i \in I$, $\forall j \in J$, and $\Sigma_{i \in I}(x_i - w_i) \leq \Sigma_{j \in J} y_j$.] Public goods are not considered until Section 3.7 and they will be ignored until then.

Theorem 3.1. *For any Arrow–Debreu economy e in E^{AD} a Walrasian competitive equilibrium is Pareto optimal.*

Proof: Suppose that (p^*, x^*, y^*) is a Walrasian competitive equilibrium for e. Suppose that it is not Pareto optimal and there is a feasible allocation (x, y) such that $u_i(x_i) > u_i(x_i^*)$ for each household i. Since x_i gives each i more utility than x_i^*, which was in fact chosen, the bundle x_i must violate i's budget constraint at prices p^*. Then (3.1) implies (3.5):

$$p^* x_i > p^* w_i + \sum_{j \in J} \alpha_{ij} p^* y_j^* \tag{3.5}$$

Summing (3.5) over all $i \in I$ yields (3.6):

$$p^* \sum_{i \in I} x_i > p^* \sum_{i \in I} w_i + \sum_{i \in I} \sum_{j \in J} \alpha_{ij} p^* y_j^* \tag{3.6}$$

Since $\Sigma_{i \in I} \Sigma_{j \in J} \alpha_{ij} p^* y_j^* = \Sigma_{j \in J} p^* y_j^* \Sigma_{i \in I} \alpha_{ij}$ and $\Sigma_{i \in I} \alpha_{ij} = 1$, inequality (3.6) is equivalent to (3.7).

$$p^* \sum_{i \in I} (x_i - w_i) > p^* \sum_{j \in J} y_j^* . \tag{3.7}$$

If allocation (x, y) is feasible, then $y_j \in Y_j$ ($\forall j \in J$), and therefore condition (3.2) implies $p^* y_j^* \geq p^* y_j$ ($\forall j \in J$). This, along with (3.7), implies (3.8):

$$p^*\sum_{i\in I}(x_i - w_i) > p^*\sum_{j\in J}y_j \tag{3.8}$$

But $p^* \geq 0$ so (3.8) is inconsistent with $\Sigma_{i\in I}(x_i - w_i) \leq \Sigma_{j\in J}y_j$, contradicting the claim that (x, y) is feasible. Therefore, (x^*, y^*) is Pareto optimal.   Q.E.D.

Notice that the proof does not depend on the existence of a utility function to represent an individual's preference scheme. If x_i is strictly preferred to x_i^* by i, then x_i must have been too expensive when x_i^* was chosen. For the proof of Theorem 3.1 it suffices to assume that an individual's preference scheme is independent of the consumption of others.

3.5   Other properties

It has just been established that Walrasian equilibria are Pareto optimal in the Arrow–Debreu world of *complete markets*. Markets are complete in the sense that all plans and decisions concerning the future are made in the present and contracts are struck in order to ensure that desired exchanges will actually take place according to plan. This completeness assumption is examined in detail in the next section and the next chapter.

As explained at the end of Section 2.1, the Walrasian mechanism is privacy preserving. Also, the mechanism is compatible with competitive behavior. If strategic maneuvering by individuals is limited to the selection of messages that maximize individual utility given the messages announced by other agents, then households will be following prescribed behavior, as is the case with firms striving to maximize profits *given* the prices announced by the auctioneer. Whether competitive behavior is itself plausible is the subject of Chapter 5.

The Walrasian mechanism is individually rational for e if $0 \in Y_j$ for all j since this assumption implies that profits are not negative at equilibrium. This in turn means that $p^*x_i \leq p^*w_i + \Sigma_{j\in J}\alpha_{ij}p^*y_j^*$ holds for $x_i = w_i$ if (p^*, x^*, y^*) is a Walrasian equilibrium. Therefore, anything chosen by i must provide at least as much utility as w_i since the endowment is affordable at equilibrium.

The Walrasian mechanism is obviously informationally viable. It is even informationally efficient in the sense that there exists no other mechanism that generates Pareto-optimal equilibria and that has individual messages in a Euclidean space of dimension less than k, the length of the message list announced by an agent for the Walrasian mechanism. (If E is severely restricted, or discontinuities are tolerated in a mechanism, then this informational efficiency assertion is false.)

## 3.6	The second fundamental theorem

Let us examine Walrasian equilibrium in a simple economy. There are two goods and two consumers but no production. Let E be defined so that w_1 always equals $(1, 0)$ and w_2 always equals $(0, 1)$. Only the preferences are unknown at the outset; the utility functions of 1 and 2 are defined by means of parameters δ and β (with $0 < \delta < 1$ and $0 < \beta < 1$): $u_1(x_1) = x_{11}^{\delta} x_{12}$ and $u_2(x_2) = x_{21}^{\beta} x_{22}$. At equilibrium $p_1/p_2 = \beta(1 + \delta)/(1 + \beta)$ and $x_1 = (\delta/(1 + \delta), \beta/(1 + \beta)) = (1, 1) - x_2$. If δ and β are large, then 1 will have almost everything.

Obviously, most people would reject some of the Pareto-optimal allocations as undesirable on other grounds but would also insist that Pareto optimality is at least a minimum performance standard. The purpose of this section is to show that every Pareto-optimal allocation $\hat{x}$ is a Walrasian competitive equilibrium with respect to some reassignment of endowments. Consider the example just presented. Let $\hat{w}_1 = (1, \varepsilon)$ and $\hat{w}_2 = (0, 1 - \varepsilon)$ represent a transfer from person 2 to person 1, where $0 < \varepsilon < 1$. An equilibrium with respect to $\hat{w}$ results in a price ratio $p_1^*/p_2^* = [\beta(1 + \delta) + \varepsilon(\delta - \beta)]/(1 + \beta)$. The corresponding equilibrium allocation x^* assigns

$$x_1^* = \left(\frac{\delta(\beta + \varepsilon)}{\beta(1 + \delta) + \varepsilon(\delta - \beta)}, \frac{\beta + \varepsilon}{1 + \beta} \right)$$

to household 1 and

$$x_2^* = \left(\frac{\beta(1 - \varepsilon)}{\beta(1 + \delta) + \varepsilon(\delta - \beta)}, \frac{1 - \varepsilon}{1 + \beta} \right)$$

to household 2. Pareto optimality requires equality of marginal rates of substitution in this case, and therefore $\hat{x}_{12} = \beta\hat{x}_{11}/[\delta - \hat{x}_{11}(\delta - \beta)]$. (Prove that this must hold, in this example, even if some x_{ic} is zero.) Note that x^* satisfies this equality. Allocations x^* and $\hat{x}$ are identical if

$$\varepsilon = \frac{(\delta + \beta)\hat{x}_{11} - \delta\beta}{\delta - \hat{x}_{11}(\delta - \beta)} \tag{3.9}$$

As asserted, an appropriate transfer of endowments, given by (3.9) for this example, results in a Walrasian competitive equilibrium at the given Pareto-optimal allocation $\hat{x}$. The argument of Maskin and Roberts (1980) will be used to prove this in general.

In order to prove the result, called the second fundamental theorem of welfare economics, we will need an additional assumption on preferences. A utility function u_i is *strongly monotonic* if an increase in the consumption of any good increases utility, ceteris paribus. The second welfare theorem can be proved without this assumption; it is employed here in order to simplify the proof. Recall that E^* is the family of environments e for which a Walrasian competitive equilibrium exists. Let E^0 be that subset of $E^* \cap E^{AD}$ for which each individual utility function has the strong monotonicity property. Recall that allocation $(\hat{x}, \hat{y})$ is *strongly* Pareto optimal if there is no feasible allocation (x, y) such that $u_i(x_i) \geq u_i(\hat{x}_i)$ for all $i \in I$ and $u_i(x_i) > u_i(\hat{x}_i)$ for some $i \in I$ (assuming that preferences are self-regarding). Now we turn to formalities.

> *Strong monotonicity:* u_i is strongly monotonic if $x_i \geq x_i'$ and $x_i \neq x_i'$ implies $u_i(x_i) > u_i(x_i')$.

Theorem 3.2. *Suppose that $(\hat{x}, \hat{y})$ is Pareto optimal for environment $e \in E^0$. Then there is a price system $\hat{p}$ such that $(\hat{p}, \hat{x}, \hat{y})$ is a Walrasian competitive equilibrium for some environment $\hat{e}$ that is identical to e except for a redistribution of endowments and profit shares.*

Proof: Allocation $(\hat{x}, \hat{y})$ is actually *strongly* Pareto optimal for e since preferences are strongly monotonic, self-regarding, and continuous. (E^* requires continuity.) This was established informally in Section 2.4. (See also Exercise 2.1.) Therefore, there exists no feasible allocation (x, y) such that $u_i(x_i) \geq u_i(\hat{x}_i)$ for all i and $u_i(x_i) > u_i(\hat{x}_i)$ for at least one i.

Define a mechanism that is identical to the Walrasian mechanism except that for any price vector p announced by the planner household i's expenditure is limited by $p\hat{x}_i$. That is, i's budget constraint is $px_i \leq p\hat{x}_i$ instead of $px_i \leq pw_i + \Sigma_{j \in J}\alpha_{ij}py_j$. As demonstrated in Chapter 6, there is a wide class of mechanisms, including the Walrasian mechanism and the modified one just defined, for which an equilibrium exists for all $e \in E^0$. Let (p^*, x^*, y^*) be an equilibrium for the mechanism with the modified budget constraints. Then, by definition, $u_i(x_i^*)$ maximizes u_i subject to $px_i \leq p^*\hat{x}_i$, y_j^* maximizes p^*y_j for $y_j \in Y_j$, and $\Sigma_{i \in I}(x_i^* - w_i) \leq \Sigma_{j \in J}y_j^*$. We will prove (3.10)–(3.12).

$$u_i(x_i^*) = u_i(\hat{x}_i) \quad \text{for each household } i \tag{3.10}$$
$$p^*x_i^* = p^*\hat{x}_i \quad \text{for each household } i \tag{3.11}$$
$$p^*y_j^* = p^*\hat{y}_j \quad \text{for each firm } j \tag{3.12}$$

Since $\hat{x}_i$ satisfies i's budget constraint, $p^*x_i \leq p^*\hat{x}_i$, and x_i^* maximizes u_i subject to that constraint, we must have $u_i(x_i^*) \geq u_i(\hat{x}_i)$ for all $i \in I$. We cannot have $u_i(x_i^*) > u_i(\hat{x}_i)$ for any i since $(\hat{x}, \hat{y})$ is strongly Pareto optimal for e and (x^*, y^*) is feasible for e. Therefore, equation (3.10) holds.

If $p^*x_i^* < p^*\hat{x}_i$, then, by strong monotonicity,

$$u_i(x_i) > u_i(x_i^*) \text{ for } x_i = x_i^* + (\varepsilon, \varepsilon, \ldots, \varepsilon)$$

and

$$\varepsilon = (p^*\hat{x}_i - p^*x_i^*) \Big/ \sum_{c=1}^{k} p_c^* > 0$$

But $p^*x_i = p^*\hat{x}_i$, contradicting the fact that x_i^* maximizes u_i subject to $p^*x_i \le p^*\hat{x}_i$. Therefore, equation (3.11) must hold.

Since y_j^* maximizes j's profit given p^*, we have $p^*y_j^* \ge p^*\hat{y}_j$ ($\forall j \in J$). If $p^*y_j^* > p^*\hat{y}_j$ for some j, then

$$p^*\sum_{j\in J} y_j^* > p^*\sum_{j\in J} \hat{y}_j = p^*\sum_{i\in I}(\hat{x}_i - w_i) = p^*\sum_{i\in I}(x_i^* - w_i) \quad (3.13)$$

The last of these equalities is a consequence of equation (3.11). The equality $p^*\Sigma_{j\in J}\hat{y}_j = p^*\Sigma_{i\in I}(\hat{x}_i - w_i)$ follows from strong monotonicity and Pareto optimality: $\Sigma_{j\in J}\hat{y}_j \ge \Sigma_{i\in I}(\hat{x}_i - w_i)$ since $(\hat{x}, \hat{y})$ is feasible. If $\Sigma_{j\in J}\hat{y}_{jc} > \Sigma_{i\in I}(\hat{x}_{ic} - w_{ic})$ for some commodity c, then the excess supply of good c could be divided among all the households, increasing the utility of each and contradicting Pareto optimality.

Since $\Sigma_{i\in I}x_i^* \le \Sigma_{i\in I}w_i + \Sigma_{j\in J}y_j^*$, statement (3.13) implies that $\Sigma_{i\in I}x_{ic}^* < \Sigma_{i\in I}w_{ic} + \Sigma_{j\in J}y_{jc}^*$ holds for some commodity c. Therefore, we can construct a new feasible allocation (x', y') by giving a share of the undistributed surplus of commodity c to each individual, leaving unchanged all other features of the original allocation (x^*, y^*). By strong monotonicity, $u_i(x_i') > u_i(x_i^*)$ for all i in I. By equation (3.10), $u_i(x_i') > u_i(\hat{x}_i)$ for all i in I, contradicting Pareto optimality of $(\hat{x}, \hat{y})$. Therefore, $p^*\Sigma_{j\in J}y_j^* = p^*\Sigma_{j\in J}\hat{y}_j$ and, for each j, $p^*y_j^* \ge p^*\hat{y}_j$. Equation (3.12) follows.

Now equations (3.10) and (3.12) imply that $(p^*, \hat{x}, \hat{y})$ is a Walrasian competitive equilibrium for any economy $\hat{e}$ such that

$$p^*\hat{x}_i = p^*\hat{w}_i + \sum_{j\in J}\hat{\alpha}_{ij}p^*\hat{y}_j \quad (\forall i \in I)$$

where $\hat{w}_i$ and $\hat{\alpha}_{ij}$ are the endowments and profit shares specified by environment $\hat{e}$, which is otherwise identical to e. (Check that demand equals supply for each good.) Set

$$\lambda_i = p^*\hat{x}_i \Big/ p^*\sum_{a\in I}\hat{x}_a$$

$$\hat{w}_i = \lambda_i \sum_{a\in I} w_a$$

and

$$\hat{\alpha}_{ij} = \lambda_i \quad (\forall i \in I, \forall j \in J).$$

Since $\lambda_i \geq 0$ and $\Sigma_{i \in I} \lambda_i = 1$, environment $\hat{e}$ is obtained from e by redistributing endowments and profit shares. Since

$$p^* \sum_{i \in I} \hat{x}_i = p^* \sum_{i \in I} w_i + p^* \sum_{j \in J} \hat{y}_j$$

we have

$$p^* \hat{x}_i = p^* \hat{w}_i + \sum_{j \in J} \hat{\alpha}_{ij} p^* \hat{y}_j \text{ for all } i \in I$$

as desired.   Q.E.D.

A Walrasian competitive equilibrium exists for each $e \in E^0$ and every equilibrium is Pareto optimal. The Walrasian mechanism is *unbiased* over E^0 in the sense that every Pareto-optimal allocation is a Walrasian competitive equilibrium allocation for some distribution of wealth. All of this means that the Walrasian mechanism is *Pareto satisfactory* on E^0.

3.7   Public goods

This section considers whether optimality can be achieved with public goods included in the model. Theorem 3.1 will be extended by modifying the Walrasian mechanism to allow taxes to be imposed on individuals so that the government can finance the public goods it purchases from the private sector and provides to consumers at no user cost. (Consumers pay indirectly through taxes, of course.)

Let q_i, a nonnegative l-vector, represent the taxes imposed on household i per unit of each of the l public goods provided. If the vector h of public goods is made available to consumers, then household i will pay a tax of $q_i h = q_{i1} h_1 + q_{i2} h_2 + \cdots + q_{il} h_l$, where q_{ic} is the tax paid by i per unit of public good c supplied and h_c is the total amount of public good c made available for consumption.

Firms produce public goods for profit, and these goods are sold to the government. The price paid by the government for public good c is $q_{0c} = \Sigma_{i \in I} q_{ic}$, which is the sum of the unit taxes on good c paid by households. Then $q_0 = (q_{01}, \ldots, q_{0l})$ is an l-vector of public goods prices charged by the private sector for the production of public goods. As part of the specification of the mechanism we have $q_0 = \Sigma_{i \in I} q_i$.

It may be the case that $q_i = q_0/n$ for all i (proportional taxation) or that q_i is a vector (somehow arrived at) of l marginal rates of substitution for public goods (in which case the mechanism is closely related to the *Lindahl mechanism*, defined below). The theorem to follow holds in any case as long as $q_0 = \Sigma_{i \in I} q_i$ and q_i is nonnegative for all i. There is really an entire family of mechanisms, one for each rule by which the public goods price vectors $q_0, q_1, \ldots, q_n$ are determined. They will be referred to as *linear tax mechanisms* (LTM).

Firm j is required to select a feasible input–output plan (y_j, z_j) that maximizes profit, $py_j + q_0 z_j$, given the announced price vectors p and q_0. The vector $y_j \in R^k$ specifies inputs and outputs of private goods, with $y_{jc} < 0$ if commodity c is required as input, and $z_j \geq 0$ is an l-vector of public goods produced by the plan.

The household's role in selecting a message is an extension of its role in the Walrasian mechanism. Household i's message $m_i = (x_i, v_i)$ is a pair of vectors: x_i is a k-vector of private goods demands and v_i is an l-vector of proposed changes in the mix of public goods. If $v_{ic} < 0$, then i requests a reduction of $-v_{ic}$ units in the supply of public good c. The condition $\Sigma_{i \in I} v_i = \Sigma_{j \in J} z_j$ will be added to the standard demand-equals-supply requirement. If $m = (p, q, x, v, y, z)$ is an equilibrium configuration of messages, then the allocation $g(m) = (x, y, z)$ is the outcome; the consumption of public goods, $h = \Sigma_{i \in I} v_i = \Sigma_{j \in J} z_j$, is implicit.

Each LTM requires individual utility maximization subject to a budget constraint. Given the message configuration $m = (p, q, x, v, y, z)$, household i's income is $I_i(m) = pw_i + \Sigma_{j \in J} \alpha_{ij} (py_j + q_0 z_j)$, where α_{ij} is i's share of firm j's profit. If i demands (x_i, v_i), its expenditure will be $px_i + q_i v_i + q_i \Sigma_{a \neq i} v_a = px_i + q_i h$ (for $h = \Sigma_{a \in I} v_a$): i's share of the cost of public goods "demanded" by others is $q_i \Sigma_{a \neq i} v_a$; if $v_i \neq 0$, then i is requesting a change in the vector of public goods, from $\Sigma_{a \neq i} v_a$ to $v_i + \Sigma_{a \neq i} v_a$, and i's net income available for expenditure on private goods will decrease by $q_i v_i$. We do not require $v_i \geq 0$, but i's choice must satisfy $v_i + \Sigma_{a \neq i} v_a \geq 0$, given v_a for $a \neq i$. To summarize, i is required to choose (x_i, v_i) so as to maximize utility, $u_i(x_i, v_i + \Sigma_{a \neq i} v_a)$, subject to the budget constraint $px_i + q_i v_i + q_i \Sigma_{a \neq i} v_a \leq I_i(m)$, given the messages of other agents.

A configuration $m = (p, q, x, v, y, z)$ is in equilibrium if for any $i \in I$ (x_i, v_i) solves i's utility maximization problem given m_a $(a \neq i)$, for any $j \in J$ (y_j, z_j) solves j's profit maximization problem given m_a $(a \neq j)$, $\Sigma_{i \in I}(x_i - w_i) \leq \Sigma_{j \in J} y_j$ with $p_c = 0$ for private good c if $\Sigma_{i \in I}(x_{ic} - w_{ic}) < \Sigma_{j \in J}(y_{jc})$, and, finally, $\Sigma_{i \in I} v_i = \Sigma_{j \in J} z_j$. Set $h = \Sigma_{j \in J} z_j$ for convenience. By definition, an equilibrium of the LTM is a competitive equilibrium.

Theorem 3.3 establishes that any equilibrium of an LTM is Pareto optimal. The proof is an adaptation of the proof of Theorem 3.1.

Theorem 3.3. *Suppose that technology set Y_j is self-regarding for each firm j and that each household i's preferences depend only on the public* *goods provided and on i's own consumption of private goods. Then any equilibrium of an LTM is Pareto optimal.*

Proof: Let $m^* = (p^*, q^*, x^*, v^*, y^*, z^*)$ be an equilibrium. Suppose that (x, y, z) is a feasible allocation and $u_i(x_i, h) > u_i(x_i^*, h^*)$ for all i, with $h = \Sigma_{j \in J} z_j$ and $h^* = \Sigma_{i \in I} v_i^* = \Sigma_{j \in J} z_j^*$. Set $v_i = h - h^* + v_i^*$. Then $h \geq 0$ by feasibility, and therefore $v_i + \Sigma_{a \neq i} v_a^* = h \geq 0$. Since m^* is an equilibrium, budget-constrained utility maximization implies

$$p^* x_i + q_i^* h > p^* w_i + \sum_{j \in J} \alpha_{ij} (p^* y_j^* + q_0^* z_j^*)$$

$$p^* \sum_{i \in I} x_i + q_0^* h > p^* \sum_{i \in I} w_i + p^* \sum_{j \in J} y_j^* + q_0^* \sum_{j \in J} z_j^*$$

if we sum over all i in I, set $q_0^* = \Sigma_{i \in I} q_i^*$, and recall that $\Sigma_{i \in I} \alpha_{ij} = 1$. Since $p^* y_j^* + q_0^* z_j^* \geq p^* y_j + q_0^* z_j$ for all $j \in J$, the last inequality implies

$$p^* \sum_{i \in I} x_i + q_0^* h > p^* \sum_{i \in I} w_i + p^* \sum_{j \in J} y_j + q_0^* \sum_{j \in J} z_j$$

Since $q_0^* \geq 0$ and $h = \Sigma_{j \in J} z_j$ by definition, we have

$$p^* \sum_{i \in I} x_i > p^* \sum_{i \in I} w_i + p^* \sum_{j \in J} y_j$$

But this inequality is inconsistent with the feasibility requirement $\Sigma_{i \in I}(x_i - w_i) \leq \Sigma_{j \in J} y_j$ since $p^* \geq 0$. The contradiction establishes that (x^*, y^*, z^*) is Pareto optimal.   Q.E.D.

One type of LTM is the proportional tax mechanism (PTM), which requires the planner to set $q_i = q_0/n$ for each i: Each i pays the average cost $q_0 h/n$ of the public goods h provided. This is a very simple mechanism; we have just shown that its (competitive) equilibria are Pareto optimal. However, PTM equilibria rarely exist.

Consider as an illustration the following simple model.

Set $k = 1$ (one private good) and $l = 1$ (one public good) and assume one firm with a fixed technology set $Y = \{(y, z): y \leq 0 \text{ and } y + z \leq 0\}$. The private good cannot be produced, but it can be used as an input to produce the public good with a maximum of one unit of the public good for each unit of the private good employed. At equilibrium $p = 1 = q_0$ must hold. (Normalize and set $p = 1$: if $q_0 < 1$, production cannot take place without a loss, and if $q_0 > 1$, there will be an infinite supply of the public good and an infinite demand for input.) All prices are constant because the PTM requires $q_i = 1/n$. Let E be further streamlined so that

$u_i(x_i, h) = x_i + \delta_i h - \frac{1}{2}\beta h^2$ with the positive utility parameter δ_i and the endowment of the private good being the only variable. Since δ_i is the marginal utility of the public good at a zero level of consumption, we will assume that $\Sigma_{i \in I}\delta_i > 1$; the marginal benefit exceeds the marginal cost at $h = 0$, and the public good makes a contribution to welfare.

Every LTM is individually rational: By setting $v_i = -\Sigma_{a \neq i}v_a$, individual i can block the production of public goods, thereby ensuring that he pays no taxes and as a result has enough income to purchase his endowment. If we assume that the maximum utility that i can obtain without any private goods consumption is less than w_i, and this is equivalent to assuming that $\delta_i^2/2\beta < w_i$, then i will have a positive amount of the private good at equilibrium since his utility cannot be less than $u_i(w_i, 0) = w_i$. Therefore, E can be further restricted so that $x_i > 0$ at equilibrium for all $i \in I$. This inequality and Pareto optimality imply that the (public good) marginal utilities sum to unity at equilibrium. If the sum is less than 1, then a small reduction in the supply of the public good can increase everyone's utility if the private good so liberated is distributed in proportion to individual marginal utility. If the sum of the marginal utilities exceeds 1, then a small increase in the public good can be financed in a way that increases everyone's utility (since everyone has a positive amount of the private good at equilibrium). If we equate the sum of the marginal utilities to 1 and then solve for h, we get

$$h^0 = \left(\sum_{i \in I}\delta_i - 1\right)\bigg/ n\beta \tag{3.14}$$

For any economy in E an equilibrium of an LTM is individually rational and Pareto optimal. Therefore, equation (3.14) will hold at equilibrium. If (x^*, y^*, z^*) is a PTM equilibrium, then, $x_i = x_i^*$ and $d_i = 0$ maximize $x_i + \delta_i(h^0 + d_i) - \beta(h^0 + d_i)^2/2$ subject to $x_i + (h^0 + d_i)/n \leq w_i$. (Note that profit is zero at equilibrium.) The first-order condition for this maximization problem is $\delta_i - \beta(h^0 + d_i) - 1/n = 0$. If $d_i = 0$, we have $\delta_i = 1/n + \beta h^0$, which, when summed over all $i \in I$, yields equation (3.14). However, $\delta_i = 1/n + \beta h^0$ implies $\delta_i = \delta_a$ for all households i and a. In other words, an equilibrium exists only if the utility functions are identical.

In general, the first-order condition yields $d_i = (n\delta_i - 1)/n\beta - h^0$. Suppose that the δ_i's are not identical. At h^0 the marginal utility of the public good to i is $\delta_i - \beta h^0$. There must be at least one individual for whom this is larger than $1/n$ since $\Sigma\delta_i - n\beta h^0 = 1$ and the *average* marginal utility is $1/n$. If $\delta_i - \beta h^0 > 1/n$, the marginal benefit to i of a little more of the public good exceeds i's share of the additional cost and i will demand a little more. That is, h^0 is not consistent with equilibrium if each q_i is fixed at $1/n$ and the δ_i's are distinct. (There will also be an individual for whom the marginal utility of the public good is less than $1/n$ at h^0, and this person will demand a little less of the public good.) Therefore, the PTM succeeds only when preferences are identical. In general, equilibria are always Pareto optimal, but competitive equilibria rarely exist.

If one substitutes q_i^* for $1/n$ in the utility maximization exercise and then derives the first-order condition, one gets $\delta_i - \beta(h^0 + d_i) - q_i^* = 0$: setting $d_i = 0$ yields $q_i^* = \delta_i - \beta h^0 \geq 0$. We have $\Sigma_{i \in I} q_i^* = 1 = q_0^*$. Then if the LTM allows variable personal public goods charges, equilibrium is not unattainable. Before exploring this possibility, we consider an important relative of the LTMs, the *Lindahl mechanism*.

The Lindahl mechanism is the same as an LTM except that the planner announces, along with p, the vector h of public goods to be provided and each household responds with a vector q_i of marginal rates of substitution (or Lagrangians) for public goods. Given p^*, h^*, and profit income, household i announces a pair of vectors (x_i^*, q_i^*) such that $x_i = x_i^*$ and $h = h^*$ maximizes $u_i(x_i, h)$ subject to the constraint $p_i^* x_i + q_i^* h \leq p^* w_i + \Sigma_{j \in J} \alpha_{ij}(p^* y_j^* + q_0^* z_j^*)$. Each firm is required to maximize profit, demand must equal supply for each private good as usual, and $h^* = \Sigma_{j \in J} z_j^*$. If each of these conditions holds over all households and firms at the message configuration $m^* = (p^*, h^*, x^*, q^*, y^*, z^*)$, then m^* is a Lindahl equilibrium if $q_0^* = \Sigma_{i \in I} q_i^*$ also holds. We suppose that the planner announces the vector $\Sigma_{i \in I} q_i^*$ of public goods prices paid to firms after households announce their Lagrangian vectors q_i^*. It should be obvious that if m^* is a Lindahl equilibrium, then $(p^*, q^*, x^*, v^*, y^*, z^*)$ is an LTM equilibrium for $v_i^* = h^*/n$ ($\forall i \in I$). Therefore, any Lindahl equilibrium is Pareto optimal by Theorem 3.3. In addition, existence of a Lindahl equilibrium is guaranteed under the standard conditions on preferences and technologies (Chapter 6).

Equilibria of both the proportional tax mechanism (PTM) and the Lindahl mechanism are Pareto optimal. PTM equilibria are competitive but they rarely exist. Lindahl equilibria exist, but they are not compatible with competitive behavior. Therefore, neither mechanism comes close to solving the resource allocation problem.

It is easy to see why Lindahl equilibria are not competitive equilibria. Given the private goods price vector p^* and the public goods vector h^* announced by the planner, household i's best response is to announce $q_i = 0$ allowing all of i's income to be devoted to the purchase of private goods without interfering with the consumption of the vector h^* of public goods. With respect to the provision of public goods the household becomes a *free rider*, consuming the public goods financed by others but avoiding any charges for these goods. This competitive behavior by i constitutes a violation of the rules of the Lindahl mechanism: Although $q_i = 0$ is a best response for i, h^* will not be part of the solution to i's utility maximization problem since $q_i = 0$ implies, in most cases, that u_i can be increased without limit by increasing h without affecting the amount of income available for expenditure on private goods. To further illustrate why the free-rider problem is central to the study of public sector economics, let us consider what would happen if the provision of public goods were left to the private ownership market economy.

If public goods are sold as if they were private goods, individuals will also succumb to the temptation to be free riders. Specifically, any individual can purchase public goods directly from firms just as private goods are purchased in the market system. Consider again the simple model with $u_i = x_i + \delta_i h - (\beta/2)h^2$. Pareto optimality implies $h^0 = (\Sigma \delta_i - 1)/n\beta$ [equation (3.14)]. If i purchases v_i units of the public good, then $h = \Sigma v_i$. Now, $q_0 = 1 = p$ at equilibrium. Household i chooses (x_i, v_i) to maximize $u_i(x_i, v_i + \Sigma_{a \neq i} v_a)$ subject to $x_i + v_i \leq w_i$. (Profit is zero at equilibrium.) Utility maximization implies $x_i + v_i = w_i$, or $x_i = w_i - v_i$. Then $u_i = w_i - v_i + \delta_i h - (\beta/2)h^2$. Marginal utility with respect to v_i is $-1 + \delta_i - (\beta/2)h$, which is no greater than $\delta_i - 1$. If $\delta_i < 1$, then i optimizes by setting $v_i = 0$. Each household does this, and we have $h = \Sigma v_i = 0$, which obviously does not equal h^0, assuming that $\Sigma \delta_i > 1$. In words, each household attempts to be a free rider by devoting all its income to the purchase of private goods while it receives the full benefit of the public goods purchased by others. If no one provides public goods, however, the outcome will be far from Pareto optimal in most cases.

This leaves us with one possibility of all those discussed so far. If we employ an LTM with variable personal public goods prices, q_i, we can have Pareto-optimal competitive equilibria, and the equilibria will exist in most cases. If q_i depends on v_i in an obvious way, then competitive behavior will not be plausible: Individual i will select a value of v_i that will result in a low value of q_i, allowing most of his income to be applied to expenditure on private goods rather than choosing a value of v_i that maximizes utility *given* prices. Groves and Ledyard (1977) were the first to show how i's taxes could be made to depend on all of the v_a in a way that is subtle enough to make the assumption of competitive behavior somewhat realistic.

3.8   The Groves–Ledyard mechanism

The Groves–Ledyard mechanism employs a planner whose message set M_0 is the set of nonnegative price vectors (p, q), where p is a k-vector of private goods prices and q is an l-vector of public goods prices. The message set M_i of household i is the set of vectors (x_i, v_i) such that x_i is a nonnegative k-vector of private goods demands and v_i is an l-vector, not necessarily nonnegative, of changes proposed by i to the vector of public goods proposed in the aggregate by others. The message set M_j of firm j is the set of plans (y_j, z_j) such that y_j is an input–output vector of private goods and z_j is a nonnegative vector of public goods produced by j.

If $m = (p, q, x, v, y, z)$ is an equilibrium of the Groves–Ledyard mechanism, then the vector $h = \Sigma_{i \in I} v_i$ of public goods is provided to all without user charge. The planner purchases the public goods from private firms at a total cost of qh. No firm j has available a production plan that yields more profit than $py_j + qz_j$. And x_i maximizes i's utility subject to the budget constraint $pw_i + \Sigma_{j \in J} \alpha_{ij}(py_j + qz_j) - t_i(q, v)$. Of course, $t_i(q, v)$ is the tax paid by household i; it depends on the public goods prices and on the proposals v_a of other households $a \neq i$ as well as on i's proposal v_i. Specifically, t_i depends on

(i) $\lambda_i qh$, i's share of the cost of public goods ($\lambda_i \geq 0$ and $\Sigma_{i \in I} \lambda_i = 1$);
(ii) $A_i = \Sigma_{a \neq i} v_a / (n - 1)$, the average of all other proposals; and
(iii) $B_i^2 = \Sigma_{a \neq i} (v_a - A_i)^2 / (n - 2)$, a deviation term.

Equation (3.15) defines t_i exactly:

$$t_i(q, v) = \lambda_i qh + \frac{\gamma}{2} \left[\frac{n - 1}{n}(v_i - A_i)^2 - B_i^2 \right] \tag{3.15}$$

The parameter γ can be any positive constant; we really have a family of mechanisms depending on the specification of γ and the λ_i's.

We make the following claims with respect to the Groves–Ledyard mechanism: First, $\Sigma_{i \in I} t_i(q, v) = qh$ for all q and v ($h = \Sigma_{i \in I} v_i$). Second, a competitive equilibrium is Pareto optimal. Third, the mechanism is *not* individually rational. Fourth, every Pareto-optimal allocation is a competitive equilibrium of the mechanism for some distribution of endowments and profit shares. Finally, a competitive equilibrium exists under standard conditions. Existence of equilibrium is dealt with in Chapter 6. The first claim is proved at the end of this section. Instead of proving the other assertions, we will illustrate them with two examples. Both involve three households, one firm, one private good, and one public good. Set $\gamma = 1$ and $\lambda_1 = \lambda_2 = \lambda_3 = \frac{1}{3}$. Set $u_i(x_i, h) = x_i + \delta_i h - \frac{1}{2}h^2$ to define individual utility. The set $Y = \{(y, z): y \leq 0 \text{ and } y + z \leq 0\}$ specifies the firm's technology. At equilibrium $p = q$ and we can set both prices equal to unity. Individual i will maximize $w_i - t_i(q, v) + \delta_i(v_1 + v_2 + v_3) - \frac{1}{2}(v_1 + v_2 + v_3)^2$ with respect to v_i. Taking the derivative and setting it equal to zero yields $-\frac{1}{3} - \frac{2}{3}(v_i - A_i) + \delta_i - h = 0$. Summing over all individuals allows us to solve for h: $-1 - \frac{2}{3}h + \frac{2}{3}h + \Sigma\delta_i - 3h = 0$. Simplifying, $h = \frac{1}{3}(\Sigma\delta_i - 1)$, which agrees with equation (3.14): The equilibrium is Pareto optimal. (Note that $\Sigma_{i \in I} A_i = h$ in general.) The individual first-order condition may now be solved for v_i by setting $A_i = \frac{1}{2}(h - v_i)$ and this will yield $v_i = \delta_i - \frac{1}{3} - \frac{2}{3}h = \delta_i - h - \frac{1}{3} + \frac{1}{3}h$. Therefore, i's message is the benefit from public goods at the margin, $\delta_i - h$, less the average cost of the public good at the margin ($\frac{1}{3}$) *plus* the average amount of the public good. In transmitting a message to the planner, household i takes into consideration the proposals of others on average because t_i penalizes i for submitting a proposal v_i that is much different from the average A_i of the other proposals since $(v_i - A_i)^2$ enters as a term in t_i. It is this feature that prevents i from being exclusively concerned with the trade-off between tax avoidance resulting from a reduced demand for the public good and the associated loss in benefit from a lower level of provision of the public good, and that accounts for the success of the mechanism.

The second example uses a linear utility function and a quadratic production function. Set $u_i(x_i, h) = x_i + \delta_i h$ and $Y = \{(y, z): y \leq 0$ and $y + \frac{1}{2}z^2 \leq 0\}$. As before, $\gamma = 1$ and $\lambda_1 = \lambda_2 = \lambda_3 = \frac{1}{3}$. Profit maximization implies $q = z$ if we normalize and set $p = 1$. Again, obtain the first-order condition by setting the derivative with respect to v_i of $u_i = [w_i + i$'s share of profit $- t_i(q, h) + \delta_i h]$ equal to zero: $-\frac{1}{3}q - \frac{2}{3}(v_i - A_i) + \delta_i = 0$. Sum over all i and set $q = h$ to solve for h: $-h - \frac{2}{3}h + \frac{2}{3}h + \Sigma\delta_i = 0$, or $h = \delta_1 + \delta_2 + \delta_3$. It is easy to verify that the equilibrium allocation is Pareto optimal. Once again we can solve for v_i, obtaining $v_i = \delta_i$. Now we can use this example to show why individual rationality is not guaranteed by the Groves–Ledyard mechanism.

Suppose that $\delta_1 = 0$ and $\delta_2 = \delta_3 = 1$. Then $h = 2$ at equilibrium. Even though household 1 gets no benefit from public goods, it will have a substantial tax bill because the success of the Groves–Ledyard mechanism relies on the absence of a strategy that one can use to avoid paying taxes while enjoying the benefits of public goods financed by others. In this case the tax burdens at equilibrium are given by $t_1 = 20/12$, $t_2 = t_3 = 14/12$. Now $u_1(w_1, 0) = w_1$, but at equilibrium we will have $u_1(w_1 - t_1, h) = w_1 - (20/12) < w_1$.

We have demonstrated the first welfare theorem by example; a competitive equilibrium identifies a Pareto-optimal allocation. Consider next the second welfare theorem. In our two examples an allocation that allows each individual a positive amount of the private good is Pareto optimal if and only if the sum over all individuals of the marginal utilities of the public good equals the marginal cost of production and any amount of the private good not used in production is delivered to households. (This is true of any two-commodity economy in which each i's utility is $x_i + b_i(h)$, where x_i is i's consumption of the private good and $b_i(h)$ is i's public good benefit function. If the sum of marginal utilities exceeds the marginal cost, there is a way of financing a small increase in the supply of the public good that would make everyone better off, as long as $x_i > 0$ for each i. If the sum of the marginal utilities falls short of the marginal cost, a reduction in the supply of the public good will release enough of the private good to make everyone better off if it is appropriately distributed.)

If, as is the case with the two examples, total marginal benefit net of marginal cost declines as h increases, there will be only one level of h consistent with equality of total marginal benefit and marginal cost. Therefore, specifying a Pareto-optimal allocation is equivalent to specifying the distribution of whatever amount of the private good is left over after *the* Pareto-optimal level h^* of the public good has been produced. In both examples the value of v_i at equilibrium is independent of income. Therefore, if (x^*, h^*) is a Pareto-optimal allocation with $x_i^* > 0$, $i = 1$, $2, \ldots, n$, we can choose w_i and i's profit share so that $w_i + i$'s share of profit is equal to $x_i^* + t_i(q^*, v^*)$. This can easily be done because q^* and v^*, and hence profit, are independent of the distribution of wealth in these examples. We will be assured that h^* units of the public good will be supplied at equilibrium and that i's consumption of the private good will equal x_i^*.

To conclude this section, we prove that the total amount of tax collected equals the cost of the public goods ordered by the government from the private sector whether the system is in equilibrium or not.

Lemma

$$\sum_{i \in I} t_i(q, v) = qh$$

Proof: We will show that

$$\sum_{i \in I} \left[\frac{n-1}{n} (v_i - A_i)^2 - B_i^2 \right] = 0$$

Set $h = \sum_{i \in I} v_i$.

$$\sum_{i \in I} \left[\frac{n-1}{n} \left(v_i - \frac{\sum\limits_{a \neq i} v_a}{n-1} \right)^2 - \frac{1}{n-2} \sum_{a \neq i} \left(v_a - \frac{\sum\limits_{b \neq i} v_b}{n-1} \right)^2 \right]$$

$$= \sum_{i \in I} \left[\frac{n-1}{n} \left(v_i - \frac{h - v_i}{n-1} \right)^2 - \frac{1}{n-2} \sum_{a \neq i} \left(v_a - \frac{h - v_i}{n-1} \right)^2 \right]$$

$$= \sum_{i \in I} \left\{ \frac{n-1}{n} \left(\frac{n}{n-1} v_i - \frac{h}{n-1} \right)^2 - \frac{1}{n-2} \right.$$

$$\left. \times \sum_{a \neq i} \left[v_a^2 - \frac{2}{n-1} v_a(h - v_i) + \frac{h^2 - 2v_i h + v_i^2}{(n-1)^2} \right] \right\}$$

$$= \sum_{i \in I} \left\{ \frac{n}{n-1} v_i^2 - \frac{2v_i h}{n-1} + \frac{h^2}{n(n-1)} - \frac{1}{n-2} \right.$$

$$\left. \times \left[\sum_{a \neq i} v_a^2 - \frac{2}{n-1}(h - v_i) \sum_{a \neq i} v_a + \frac{h^2 - 2v_i h + v_i^2}{n-1} \right] \right\}$$

$$= \frac{n}{n-1} \sum_{i \in I} v_i^2 - \frac{2h^2}{n-1} + \frac{h^2}{n-1} - \frac{n-1}{n-2} \sum_{i \in I} v_i^2$$

$$+ \frac{2}{(n-1)(n-2)}$$

$$\times \sum_{i \in I} \left[(h - v_i)(h - v_i) \right] - \frac{nh^2 - 2h^2 + \sum_{i \in I} v_i^2}{(n-1)(n-2)}$$

$$= [(n-1)(n-2)]^{-1} \{ h^2 [-(n-2) + 2(n-2) - (n-2)]$$

$$+ \sum_{i \in I} v_i^2 \left[n(n-2) - (n-1)(n-1) + 2 - 1 \right] \}$$

$$= [(n-1)(n-2)]^{-1} \left[h^2 \cdot 0 + \sum_{i \in I} v_i^2 \cdot 0 \right] = 0 \qquad \text{Q.E.D.}$$

3.9   Consumption externalities in general

The public goods resource allocation problem is based on a particular kind of interdependence among consumers. Any amount of some public good obtained by any household will be consumed in equal measure by all other households. This can be generalized by writing individual i's utility as a function of $x = (x_1, x_2, \ldots, x_n)$, which specifies the private goods consumption of each household $a = 1, 2, \ldots, n$. If $u_i(x) = u_i(x')$ whenever $x_i = x_i'$, the utility function is self-regarding: i's utility depends only on i's own consumption. This is the classical case. The public goods problem is also consistent with the generalization $u_i(x)$. Let $K = \{1, 2, \ldots, k + l\}$ be the set of commodities and let L be an l-element subset of K. If for each i, $u_i(x) = u_i(x')$ holds whenever $x_{ic} = x_{ic}'$ for all $c \in K - L$ and $\sum_{a \in I} x_{ac} = \sum_{a \in I} x_{ac}'$ for all $c \in L$, then the members of L can be viewed as public goods and each individual's utility is independent of the private goods consumption ($K - L$ contains the private goods) of others. Therefore, representing u_i as a function of x gives us a very general model. It certainly allows one person's consumption of private goods to have a direct effect, positive or negative, on the utility of someone else.

Consider a simple exchange economy with $k = 2 = n$, $w_1 = w_2 = (1, 1)$, $u_1(x) = x_{11} + x_{12} - x_{21}$, and $u_2(x) = x_{21} + x_{22} - x_{12}$. This means that 2's consumption of good 1 lowers 1's utility and 1's consumption of good 2 lowers 2's utility. It is obvious that (p^*, x^*) is a *competitive* equilibrium of the Walrasian mechanism for $p^* = (1, 1) = x_1^* = x_2^*$: If i consumes x_i^*, then a ($\neq i$) cannot increase his utility above $u_a(x^*) = 1$ without violating the budget constraint $x_{a1} + x_{a2} \leq 2$. But x^* is Pareto inferior to the allocation $x = ((2,0), (0, 2))$ since $u_i(x) = 2 - 0 = 2 > 1 = u_i(x^*)$ for $i = 1, 2$.

This establishes that a competitive Walrasian equilibrium is not necessarily Pareto optimal outside of the Arrow–Debreu framework E^{AD}. The same conclusion obtains if we set $u_i(x) = x_{i1} + x_{i2} + x_{aa}$ for $a \neq i$. It does not matter whether one individual's consumption affects another positively or negatively; Pareto optimality is no longer logically entailed in the conditions of Walrasian competitive equilibrium.

The effect of one person's actions on another's utility is called an externality if there is no signaling and incentive scheme by which the former is forced to take this interdependence into account in his or her decision making. It is a connection between the actions of one individual (choice of a commodity bundle) and the utility of another individual that is external to the mechanism. There are many cases of interrelationships between i's actions and a's utility that are *not* instances of externality because the prices that the former confronts reflect the utility the latter derives. If, for example, a and others like him have an urgent need for a commodity c, they will have a high demand for this good, forcing its price to be relatively high given the cost conditions. This causes another individual i to economize on his consumption of c, *as if i* were aware of the high level of benefit others derived from the good *and* acted in their interest by reducing his consumption of it.

Why does the market mechanism fail to achieve Pareto optimality when externalities are present? There are not enough markets. One can rephrase the first fundamental welfare theorem in this way: If a competitive market exists for each commodity that enters individual utility functions, then the Walrasian competitive equilibrium is Pareto optimal. If markets are *incomplete*, if there are commodities for which no market exists, then an equilibrium will not likely be Pareto optimal. (This important result is discussed at length in the next chapter in connection with uncertainty.) A simple example will illustrate how this observation leads to new insight into the problem of market failure in the presence of externalities.

Suppose that it is possible to inoculate an individual against the common cold at a cost of $400. Suppose that each individual would pay a maximum of $200 for the inoculation, which would guarantee that the individual inoculated would never again catch a cold. This commodity would not be viable in the usual private market context. This outcome is *not* Pareto optimal if one supposes that the entire population could be prevented from catching cold as the result of a government scheme that provided free inoculations to the youngest quarter of the population and taxed every individual $100 to pay for the program. Each individual would receive a net benefit of $200 − $100 = $100 if cold viruses are not viable when a quarter of the population is ineligible as carriers and communicators. (The virus population becomes extinct.) The difficulty with the market solution is that each individual receiving an inoculation gets a negative net *personal* benefit of $200 − $400 = − $200 but confers a benefit on others with whom he comes in contact; if he does not catch cold, he does not pass the virus along to his friends. *If* he were permitted to charge for this benefit and *if* his acquaintances could be relied on to report truthfully the value to them of a reduced probability of catching cold and *if* the high transactions cost of an individual collecting hundreds of small payments from acquaintances were to be ignored, the *notional* market equilibrium would be Pareto optimal. (When we leave the Arrow–Debreu world, notional and competitive Walrasian equilibrium can be quite different.) The restoration of Pareto optimality is a consequence of the creation of new markets for the commodities – for example, the service that i provides to a when the former purchases an inoculation – that are otherwise not valued and hence not taken into account in individual decision making. Obviously, a decentralized resource allocation scheme cannot induce Pareto optimality if signals of important effects on individual welfare are not transmitted to the relevant individuals or if the transmission takes place but there is no incentive for agents to react.

To make this claim of Pareto optimality with complete markets quite rigorous, we formalize and generalize the argument of the previous paragraph. We define the PWM, or *pseudo-Walrasian mechanism*, exactly as the Walrasian mechanism except that we treat i's consumption of good 1 as it affects a as a different commodity from i's consumption of good 1 as it affects b and these different commodities can have different prices. There will then be $k \times n$ prices for each individual and therefore $n \times k \times n$ prices in total, and from these will emerge the values that guide producers' decisions. The planner's message is a price system p: p specifies a k-vector p^0 of commodity prices at which firms trade and that are received by households from the sale of their endowments, *and* for each household $i \in I$ a k-vector p_a^i of prices at which i can order goods for consumption by household a ($a = 1, 2, \ldots, n$). All payments for goods are received by their suppliers – firms, or households in the case of en- dowments – and therefore p must satisfy $p^0 = \Sigma_{i \in I} p_a^i$ for each $a \in I$. This might seem an odd way of impessing on i the benefit that his consumption confers on a, but since a will also pay for i's consumption, the competitive forces acting on firms will cause the prices of the goods that i buys for his direct consumption, the p_{ic}^i for $c = 1, 2, \ldots, k$, to be lower than if there were no market in which a could "demand" that i increase his consump- tion of some commodity.

Each household i announces a nonnegative $k \times n$ vector $x^i = (x_1^i, x_2^i, \ldots, x_n^i)$, where x_a^i is the commodity vector that i would like a to con- sume given that i must pay $p_a^i x_a^i$ for this demand on a. The planner an- nounces the price regime p and adjusts prices until demand equals supply for each good and $x^i = x^a$ for all households i and a. Each firm j simply announces a feasible input–output vector y_j that maximizes profit given p^0. $(p, x^1, x^2, \ldots, x^n y)$ is a competitive equilibrium of the PWM if:

(i) $x^1 = x^2 = \cdots = x^n$ and $\Sigma_{i \in I}(x_i^i - w_i) = \Sigma_{j \in J} y_j$;
(ii) for each household i, x^i maximizes u_i given the budget constraint $\Sigma_{a \in I} p_a^i x_a^i \le p^0 w_i + \Sigma_{j \in J} \alpha_{ij} p^0 y_j$; and
(iii) for each firm j, y_j is feasible and $p^0 y_j \ge p^0 y_j'$ for all feasible plans y_j'.

Theorem 3.4. *An equilibrium $(\hat{p}, \hat{x}, \hat{y})$ of the PWM is Pareto optimal.*

Proof: $\hat{x} = (\hat{x}^1, \hat{x}^2, \ldots, \hat{x}^n)$ and at equilibrium $\hat{x}^1 = \hat{x}^2 = \cdots = \hat{x}^n$. Suppose that (x, y) is a feasible allocation and $u_i(x) > u_i(\hat{x}^1)$ for all $i \in I$. Since x is preferred by i and $\hat{x}^i$ was chosen, the former was not affordable at equilibrium. Therefore,

$$\sum_{a \in I} \hat{p}_a^i x_a > \hat{p}^0 w_i + \sum_{j \in J} \alpha_{ij} \hat{p}^0 \hat{y}_j.$$

Summing over all $i \in I$ and recognizing that $\hat{p}^0 \hat{y}_j \ge \hat{p}^0 y_j$ for all $j \in J$ yields

$$\sum_{i \in I} \sum_{a \in I} \hat{p}_a^i x_a > \hat{p}^0 \sum_{i \in I} w_i + \hat{p}^0 \sum_{j \in J} y_j$$

But

$$\sum_{i \in I} \sum_{a \in I} \hat{p}_a^i x_a = \sum_{a \in I} x_a \sum_{i \in I} \hat{p}_a^i$$

and

$$\sum_{i \in I} \hat{p}_a^i = \hat{p}^0.$$

Therefore we have

$$\hat{p}^0 \sum_{a \in I} x_a > \hat{p}^0 \sum_{a \in I} w_a + \hat{p}^0 \sum_{j \in J} y_j.$$

This is inconsistent with $\sum_{a \in I}(x_a - w_a) \le \sum_{j \in J} y_j$; therefore, (x, y) is not feasible and this contradiction establishes Pareto optimality of the equilibrium.   Q.E.D.

Although the PWM provides Pareto-optimal equilibria even though one person's consumption affects another's utility, this mechanism cannot be taken seriously. Its purpose is to illustrate the difficulty of designing a successful resource allocation mechanism in the presence of externalities. First, the PWM is not incentive compatible, not even with competitive behavior. Household i is required, in effect, to propose an allocation x^i given the price regime for i and the proposals of others. But the proposal of another household a includes the commodity vector x_a^a directly consumed by a and the benefit that this provides to i can be enjoyed whether or not i contributes to the financing of a's consumption. By maximizing u_i, given the actions of others, agent i will violate the rules of the PWM. The PWM does require competitive behavior with respect to prices, but even this is implausible. Household i is the only agent on the demand side of the market affecting the price p_{ac}^i, the price paid by i for consumption of commodity c by household a. In other words, the markets are *thin*. Agent i would be very much aware of the effect of his decisions on p_{ac}^i and would have no incentive to take this price as given.

3.10   Summary

The private ownership market system, as idealized by the Walrasian mechanism, performs remarkably well under a wide range of conditions. The most important of these is that every commodity that affects someone's utility is traded in some market where buyers and sellers behave competitively. This assumption is quite plausible if all goods are private goods. (The discussion of Chapter 5 will add more weight to this assertion.)

If consumption interdependence is limited to pure public goods, it is possible to design a mechanism that harnesses competitive behavior in a way that achieves optimality much as the Walrasian mechanism does in the private goods realm. (Whether competitive behavior remains plausible will also be discussed in Chapter 5.)

If uncertainty is added to the model, the opportunities for mutually advantageous trade among individuals are extended since the random events will affect individual wealth in different ways. One person could offer to give another some of his entitlement to goods and services should one event be realized in return for an agreement by the other to reciprocate in case of some other event taking place. Since additional kinds of welfare-improving trades are possible, new kinds of markets will have to be created if Pareto optimality is to be achieved at equilibrium. In other words, the completeness-of-markets condition will take on a new significance.

3.11   Background

Walras (1874–7) began the task of formulating a model of the competitive market process with enough clarity and rigor to enable one to ask precise questions about the performance of the market system. The relation between Pareto optimality and market equilibrium, summarized as the two fundamental theorems of welfare economics, was developed by Pareto (1927), Lerner (1934), Hotelling (1938), and Lange (1942), among others. Arrow (1951) brought theoretical welfare economics into step with modern convex analysis and showed how some extreme assumptions – smooth indifference curves and positive consumption of every good by every household – could be dispensed with. Debreu (1954) provided further refinements.

Two crucial aspects of the market process are not addressed in this book: the role of money, and the birth, growth, and death of firms. This shortcoming reflects the extreme difficulties involved in incorporating these two features of the real world into an abstract general equilibrium model. Section 3.1 refers briefly to the fact that without money individual incentives will lead to the violation of the budget constraint unless each individual is closely monitored or individuals are restricted to transactions in which goods exchange for goods of equal value (bilateral balance). In either case significant costs are imposed on the operation of the system. As explained in Ostroy (1973), when goods are exchanged for money and money for goods, the budget constraint can be enforced in an informationally efficient way since the large number of transactions required by bilateral balance is substantially reduced. What is really required, however, is a model in which money is created by private market forces. Hahn (1965) was first among modern general equilibrium theorists to stress the need for at least a model in which money has a positive price at equilibrium even though it has no intrinsic value.

At every point we assume that the number and nature of firms are determined outside of the model. Novshek (1980, 1985) and Novshek and

Sonnenschein (1978) have made considerable progress toward making firm creation endogenous.

The idea of creating new markets in order to overcome the market failures that result from externalities can be traced to Meade (1952). Arrow (1970) gave it a rigorous foundation in the Walrasian model. Starrett (1972) showed how the convexity assumption on which classical welfare economics rests would be violated in the process of extending markets to accommodate externalities.

Wicksell (1896) was the first economist to recognize the free-rider problem in the context of public goods. He argued that although Adam Smith had demonstrated how individual self-interest could be successfully harnessed in allocating private goods, this could not be accomplished in the public goods realm, and reliance would ultimately have to be placed on some scheme of consultation and cooperation. Lindahl (1919) began the search for a competitive adjustment process for achieving Pareto optimality with public goods. He provided a characterization of optimality in that setting and suggested a procedure, in the spirit of benefit taxation, for achieving optimality by requiring an individual to pay a share of the cost in proportion to the benefit he receives at the margin. This scheme is now presented in a general equilibrium setting as the Lindahl mechanism. Lindahl's suggestion did not confront the free-rider problem and is more in the spirit of an algorithm for locating a Pareto-optimal allocation assuming that individual preferences are known. Drèze and de la Vallée Poussin (1971) and Malinvaud (1971) independently discovered a satisfactory planning algorithm that is compatible with a limited, myopic type of strategic behavior.

Samuelson (1954, 1955) made the seminal contribution to the modern theory of public goods. For the first time it was made clear that there can be an infinite number of Pareto-optimal levels of the public good output. Two decades later Groves and Loeb (1975), drawing their inspiration from Groves (1973), identified the family of mechanisms that would force self-interested individuals to reveal their preferences for public goods. Clarke (1971) independently discovered a member of this class. The key idea was already available in an overlooked paper by Vickrey (1961). These mechanisms have the dominant strategy property – truthful preference revelation is optimal for an agent regardless of the strategies of others – but they cannot be grafted onto a private goods allocation mechanism in a way that guarantees Pareto optimality overall. (See Walker, 1978.)

Groves and Ledyard (1977) defined a mechanism that guarantees Pareto optimality under competitive behavior. Their device requires an auctioneer and does not satisfy individual rationality. Hurwicz (1979a) and Walker (1981) have designed auctioneerless mechanisms that yield Lindahl allocations, which are always individually rational, at Nash equilibrium points. Maskin (1977) and Williams (1984) establish conditions under which an arbitrary definition of optimality can be implemented at Nash equilibrium points.

Chapter 5 demonstrates that there does not exist a *dominant strategy* mechanism for allocating public goods without violating Pareto optimality. Several procedures are available for achieving Pareto optimality at *Nash equilibrium* points. Can we say that the free-rider problem has been solved? Meunch and Walker (1981) are skeptical: They show that a mechanism will either fail to yield Pareto-optimal outcomes or, as in the case of mechanisms that rely on Nash equilibria, will be extremely unstable.

EXERCISES

3.1 Characterize the Walrasian competitive equilibria for each of the economies e^1–e^6 of Exercise 2.2.

3.2 Verify that each of Walrasian competitive equilibrium allocations for e^t is Pareto optimal, $t = 1, 2, \ldots, 6$ (e^t is defined in Exercise 2.2).

3.3 Show that each Pareto-optimal allocation in e^t is a Walrasian competitive equilibrium allocation for some distribution of wealth ($t = 1, 2, \ldots, 6$; e^t is defined in Exercise 2.2).

3.4 Compute the Walrasian competitive equilibria of the economy of Exercise 2.4.

3.5 Find the Pareto-optimal allocations and the Walrasian competitive equilibria for the following one-household, one-firm, two-commodity economy:

$$u(x) = (x_1 + 3)x_2, \qquad w = (\omega, 0)$$
$$Y = \{y: y_1 \leq 0 \leq y_2 \leq \beta^{-1}(-y_1)^\beta\}$$
$$(\omega > 0 \text{ and } 0 < \beta < 1).$$

3.6 This question concerns a one-household, two-firm economy with three goods A, B, and T. Commodity T is not produced and is not desired by the household whose endowment consists of one unit of T. The utility function is $u(a, b) = a + b$, where a and b are the amounts consumed of A and B. Firm 1 produces A according to the production function $a(t_1) = \varepsilon t_1$ (t_j denotes the amount of T employed by firm j). Firm 2 produces B according to the production function $b(t_2) = t_2^\beta$. Both ε and β are nonnegative real numbers. The entire allocation is specified by t_1, assuming $t_2 = 1 - t_1$ and that everything produced is consumed. Determine the Pareto-optimal value, or values, of t_1 for various assumptions about the relative size of ε and β. (*Hint:* There are nine cases corresponding to $\beta < 1$, $\beta = 1$, $\beta > 1$, $\varepsilon < \beta$, $\varepsilon = \beta$, and $\varepsilon > \beta$.)

3.7 Determine the Walrasian competitive equilibria for each of the cases considered in Exercise 3.6.

3.8 For the two-person, two-commodity exchange economy defined by

$$u_i(x_i) = x_{i1}^{\lambda i} x_{i2}^{1-\lambda i}, \qquad w_i = (1, 1), \qquad i = 1, 2$$

determine the set of Pareto-optimal allocations and the Walrasian competitive equilibria. (Assume $0 < \lambda_i < 1$.) For any given Pareto-optimal allocation x characterize the set of endowment points for which x is an equilibrium allocation.

3.9 Consider an economy with one private good, one public good, one firm, and n households. Household i's endowment consists of w_i units of the private good. The firm can produce z units of the public good by employing $f(z)$ units of the private good as input. Household i's utility function is $u_i(x_i, z) = x_i + b_i(z)$, where x_i is its consumption of the private good, z is the amount of the public good produced, and b_i is a real-valued function. Assume that $b_i'(z) > 0$, $b_i''(z) < 0$, $f'(z) > 0$, and $f''(z) > 0$ for all i and z. Say that an allocation is *admissible* if every household is assigned a positive amount of the private good and all of the private good not used in production is consumed. Prove that an admissible allocation is Pareto optimal if and only if

$$b_1'(z) + b_2'(z) + \cdots + b_n'(z) = f'(z)$$

3.10 Using the formal language of Chapter 2, define the Groves–Ledyard mechanism as a privacy-preserving mechanism.

3.11 Assuming that marginal rates of substitution are everywhere defined, show that the vector q_i of a Lindahl equilibrium gives i's marginal rates of substitution: In other words, q_{ic}/p_1 is the maximum amount of the first private good that i would willingly sacrifice, at the margin, for an additional unit of public good c.

CHAPTER 4

Uncertainty

Uncertainty affects individual welfare in a variety of ways. This chapter deals with one of the most important consequences of the vicissitudes of nature, the randomness of initial endowments and of the input–output relationship in production. A career choice, for example, is a decision to acquire certain skills that become part of one's endowment and that can be more or less rewarding depending on occurrences that are random from the standpoint of the individual decision-maker. Bad weather can affect crops, and a farmer will not know with certainty the size of the harvest even though he or she knows how much seed was planted. Fire and flood can destroy homes. The first and last examples are consistent with a change in a person's preferences for commodities. However, we will simplify by supposing that individual preferences do not change as random events are realized even though a serious injury, say, can cause a change in preference because it affects one's ability to participate in some activities. Subject to this simplifying assumption, the Arrow–Debreu interpretation of the market mechanism is easily extended to accommodate uncertainty. All that is required is a reinterpretation of the notion of a commodity. Just as we distinguish an automobile delivered at one date from the same physical object at another date, insisting that they be identified as two different goods, so we also distinguish between an automobile delivered at one date when one specific random event is realized and the same automobile available at the same date under a different realization. There will be two different commodities and usually two different prices. Under this reinterpretation, an equilibrium of the market mechanism is Pareto optimal provided that a market exists for each of the newly defined goods. This would require an intolerably large number of markets in practice. The system is no longer informationally viable since an individual would spend all his time negotiating contracts in an astronomical number of markets. A new and closely related mechanism will be designed in order to reduce the number of markets. The new mechanism will include markets for securities, one for each possible random event, as well as markets for commodities in the usual sense. Pareto-optimal allocations once again emerge at equilibrium, but the *completeness of markets* condition is still suspect.

4.1   Preferences and uncertainty

There are k (private) goods when a commodity is characterized by its physical description and its delivery date. There are n individuals indexed by $i = 1, 2, \ldots, n$. If random event t is realized, then household i will have an endowment w_i^t, a k-vector, which may or may not be different from w_i^r, for $r \neq t$. Let T be the set of possible states of nature, or realizations of random events; we distinguish the event "1's house is destroyed by fire" from the event "2's house is destroyed by fire" and this from the event "all of the houses on Elm Street are destroyed by fire." There are τ different simple events and $T = \{1, 2, \ldots, \tau\}$. Let X_i be the set of conceivable consumption plans for individual (household) i.

Individuals will not necessarily agree on the likelihood of the various events. Let π_i^t be the probability that individual i ascribes to the event t. Of course, $\pi_i^t \geq 0$ and $\Sigma_{t \in T} \pi_i^t = 1$. A consumption plan x_i for household i assigns a k-vector x_i^t to i for each state t. If the plan x_i has been somehow determined by or for i, then exactly one event will be realized: If it is event t, then i will consume x_i^t. This will give i a utility level of $U_i(x_i^t)$, and if $x_i^r = x_i^t$, then $U_i(x_i^t) = U_i(x_i^r)$ even though the events t and r otherwise have a different impact upon i. The overall utility u_i that i gets from the plan x_i is $u_i(x_i) = \Sigma_{t \in T} \pi_i^t U_i(x_i^t)$. That is, i prefers the plan x_i to the plan $\hat{x}_i$ if and only if $\Sigma_{t \in T} \pi_i^t U_i(x_i^t) > \Sigma_{t \in T} \pi_i^t U_i(\hat{x}_i^t)$. This representation of preference under uncertainty is due to von Neumann and Morgenstern (1944).

Even though utility U_i ultimately depends only on the goods consumed and not on the random events giving rise to that consumption, the individual's perception of the different probabilities will influence his decision. In a private ownership market economy the price of land in a particular area will be low if almost everyone believes that flooding is likely in that area. If one individual believes that flooding is unlikely, he can be expected to take advantage of the low land prices and build a house there *unless* he regards others as more qualified to determine the likelihood of a flood, in which case the low price of land tells him something about their expert opinions. The situation in which an agent uses the prices to make inferences about the expectations of others is the theme of Section 4.10. In the other sections we examine the preliminary case in which individuals are guided only by their own initial beliefs about the likelihood of events. If these beliefs, the π_i^t's, differ across households, due to different expectations about flooding, for example, new opportunities for mutually advantageous trading arise. Individuals can trade across states of nature: Individual a takes an action that will result in some of his wealth being transferred to person b if event r, to which a attaches a low probability, is realized and b reciprocates by making some of his wealth available to a should event t be realized, an event considered by b to be highly unlikely. For example, if r is the event "flood" and t is the event "no flood" and a purchases land, at a low price, in an area others believe to be susceptible to flooding, then a will be wealthy relative to b if t occurs (since a will have a high net income even after purchasing land for a house), but a will be relatively poor if r occurs since he will have to rebuild his house on another site. (Person a will not be able to insure against flooding if everyone else believes that a flood is likely.) Of course, it is not necessary for individuals to barter with each other: The price system organizes the exchanges in a decentralized way.

An individual's attitude toward risk is reflected in the shape of his utility-of-goods-consumed function U_i. There are two common types. An individual exhibits *risk aversion* (or risk avoidance) if he is willing to pay a small fee in order to avoid risk. An individual is a *risk preferer* (or a risk seeker) if he is willing to pay a small fee to assume some risk. For example, a risk averter would pay a small insurance premium to ensure that he had a house of a certain quality whether or not the event "house destroyed by fire" occurred. On the other hand, some risk seekers have been known to mortgage their houses, considerably reducing their equity, in order to spend the proceeds on state lottery tickets, which on average return much less than the amount spent on tickets. In either case the purchase decision will not be made if the fee, the insurance premium or lottery ticket price, is too high. Therefore, the intuitive notions of risk aversion and risk preference must be made precise. To do this, we suppress the subscript identifying the individual and refer simply to U and π^t.

Set $\tau = 2$, $T = \{1, 2\}$, and $k = 1$. We can refer to the single commodity as money, or the market value of wealth. Let I^t (instead of x^t) denote an amount of the commodity consumed in state t. Consider two amounts of money, I^1 and I^2, with $I^1 < I^2$. Suppose ΔI is positive and small enough so that $I^1 + \Delta I < I^2$. These variables define the "lotteries" L and L^* (depicted in Figure 4.1), for which $\pi^1 = \pi^2 = \frac{1}{2}$. Now L offers a 50 : 50 chance of I^1 or $I^2 + \Delta I$ dollars and L^* offers a 50 : 50 chance of winning $I^1 + \Delta I$ or I^2. The two lotteries have the same expected monetary value, $\frac{1}{2}I^1 + \frac{1}{2}(I^2 + \Delta I) = \frac{1}{2}(I^1 + \Delta I) + \frac{1}{2}I^2$. This number is identified as the mean wealth in Figure 4.1. It is close to the average amount of money held if the individual were to participate in the lottery a large number of times: Half the time the larger amount of money would be won and half the time the smaller amount would be won. Obviously, L entails more risk than L^*; their average value is the same, but L^* promises a smaller devia-

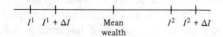

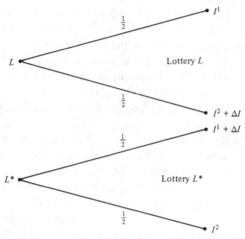

Figure 4.1

tion from that average. Therefore, we say that an individual is risk averse if he always prefers L^* to L for all combinations of I^1, I^2, and ΔI, as long as $I^1 < I^1 + \Delta I < I^2 < I^2 + \Delta I$. ($I^1$ is less than I^2 and ΔI is positive and relatively small.)

Suppose that U', the first derivative of U, exists for all values of I. If the individual is risk averse, we have

$$\tfrac{1}{2}U(I^1 + \Delta I) + \tfrac{1}{2}U(I^2) > \tfrac{1}{2}U(I^1) + \tfrac{1}{2}U(I^2 + \Delta I)$$

and this is equivalent to

$$U(I^1 + \Delta I) - U(I^1) > U(I^2 + \Delta I) - U(I^2)$$

Since $\Delta I > 0$, we can also state

$$\frac{U(I^1 + \Delta I) - U(I^1)}{\Delta I} > \frac{U(I^2 + \Delta I) - U(I^2)}{\Delta I}$$

By definition of U', we can make the left-hand side of the last expression as close as we like to $U'(I^1)$ by making ΔI small enough, and we can make the right-hand side as close as we like to $U'(I^2)$ in the same way. We conclude that $U'(I^1) \geq U'(I^2)$ whenever $I^1 \leq I^2$ if U pertains to a risk-averse individual.

In fact, if $U'(\alpha) \geq U'(\beta)$ whenever $\alpha < \beta$ and U is risk averse, then it must actually be the case that $U'(\alpha)$ is strictly greater than $U'(\beta)$ if α is strictly less than β. If $U'(\alpha) = U'(\beta)$ and $\alpha < \beta$, then $U'(\alpha) = U'(\lambda) = U'(\beta)$ for $\alpha \leq \lambda \leq \beta$ since U' can never increase as λ increases. But then L is indifferent to L^* if we set $I^1 = \alpha$, $\Delta I = \frac{1}{4}(\beta - \alpha)$ and $I^2 = \frac{1}{4}\alpha + \frac{3}{4}\beta$ contrary to the assumption of risk aversion.

Therefore, if U' always exists, risk aversion is equivalent to strictly diminishing marginal utility of wealth. Risk preference is defined so that L is always preferred to L^* and hence U' is strictly increasing. A risk-neutral individual is one whose choice depends exclusively on the expected monetary value: One lottery is preferred to another if and only if the first has a higher payoff on average. Therefore, a risk-neutral individual would be indifferent between L and L^*, and this leads to

$$\frac{U(I^1 + \Delta I) - U(I^1)}{\Delta I} = \frac{U(I^2 + \Delta I) - U(I^2)}{\Delta I}$$

whatever the value of ΔI. Hence $U'(I^1) = U'(I^2)$ for all values of I^1 and I^2. The only continuous function for which this holds at all points has the form $\alpha I + \beta$. It is safe to assume $\alpha > 0$ in an economic context. Set $\alpha = 1$ and $\beta = 0$: Any positive value of α and any value of β give rise to the same preference ordering as $U(I) = I$. Then $u(I^1, I^2) = \pi^1 I^1 + \pi^2 I^2$, and this is just the expected monetary value.

4.2   Production and uncertainty

Each firm is characterized by a technology set Y_j, a subset of R^{k_T}. A plan $y_j \in y_j$ specifies firm j's input–output vector y_j^t for each state $t \in T$. In addition to technological limitations, Y_j reflects the extent to which inputs must be committed prior to the resolution of uncertainty. If, for example, $y_{jc}^t < 0$ implies $y_{jc}^r = y_{jc}^t$ for all $r \in T$ (for arbitrary $y_j \in Y_j$), then input is committed before the realized state is known. In that case uncertainty concerns the amount of output that will be obtained. This would be the case with a farm: Seed must be planted before the weather conditions governing germination and maturation are known. A bakery, on the other hand, might not be directly affected by uncertainty at all, and Y_j would merely reflect technological limitations. If uncertainty affected the harvest of crops and no more, then the bakery could devise a production plan that employed less wheat and more rye in states that resulted in a relatively low yield of wheat. The bakery would not have to know the size of the harvest; this would be implicit in the relative price of wheat, which would be different for different states.

(In fact, there is no pure case. A farmer must plant the seed in advance, but as time passes and more is learned about the growing conditions, any adverse weather can be offset to some extent by means of additional inputs–irrigation, for example, if the rainfall is unusually low. The bakery can burn down: If t is an event in which the bakery is destroyed, we would have $y_j^t \leq 0$ for all $y_j \in Y_j$. The baker can insure against this, but society cannot; the building is destroyed and the productive capacity of the economy is diminished as reflected in the constraint $y_j^t \leq 0$.)

The technology set Y_j is *self-regarding* if each of its production plans is specified independently of the actions of other agents.

There are m firms, indexed by $j = 1, 2, \ldots, m$, and α_{ij} is the share of firm j owned by household i.

4.3   Allocations and uncertainty

An *allocation* (x, y) is a specification of a consumption plan x_i for each household i and a production plan y_j for each firm j. The allocation is feasible if $x_i \in X_i$ and $y_j \in Y_j$ for each household i and firm j and if the global feasibility condition, $\sum_{i=1}^n (x_i^t - w_i^t) \leq \sum_{j=1}^m y_j^t$, holds for each state of nature $t \in T$.

4.4   Pareto optimality and uncertainty

An allocation (x, y) is Pareto optimal if it is feasible and there is no other feasible allocation $(\hat{x}, \hat{y})$ such that $u_i(\hat{x}_i) > u_i(x_i)$ for each individual i. Strictly speaking, we should say that (x, y) is *ex ante* Pareto optimal in this case since it merely indicates that prior to the resolution of uncertainty it is impossible to increase everyone's *expected* utility by means of any other system of contingency plans. Once a particular state – call it r – is realized, society will regret having committed itself to the plan (x, y) if there is some other arrangement that, given r, would allow each household i to achieve a level of *ex post* utility greater than $U_i(x_i^r)$.

There are two reasons why this might be possible even though (x, y) is ex ante Pareto optimal. First, (x, y) may require a commitment of inputs (seed) that is wasted if event r (severe frost), though unlikely, actually occurs. Since this precommitment would be necessary and binding on any decision-maker in any resource allocation mechanism, it should be incorporated into the definition of feasibility when defining ex post Pareto optimality. This is implicit in the sets Y_j. Therefore, we will say that allocation (x, y) is *ex post Pareto optimal for event t* if there is no $(\hat{x}^t, \hat{y}^t)$ such that $U_i(\hat{x}^t) > U_i(x_i^t)$ for all i and $\sum_{i=1}^n (\hat{x}_i^t - w_i^t) \leq \sum_{j=1}^m \hat{y}_j^t$ and $(y_j^1, y_j^2, \ldots, y_j^{t-1}, \hat{y}_j^t, y_j^{t+1}, \ldots, y_j^\tau)$ belongs to Y_j for all j. The last condition ensures that irreversible decisions are not implicitly assumed to be reversible in defining ex post optimality. It is easy to show that every ex ante Pareto-optimal allocation (x, y) is ex post Pareto optimal for t if $\pi_i^t > 0$ for all i. If $U_i(\hat{x}_i^t) > U_i(x_i^t)$ for all i, then $u_i(\tilde{x}_i) > u_i(x_i)$ for all i, where allocation $(\tilde{x}, \tilde{y})$ is defined by setting $\tilde{x}_i^r = x_i^r$ and $\tilde{y}_j^r = y_j^r$ for all i, j, and $r \neq t$ and $\tilde{x}_i^t = \hat{x}_i^t$ and $\tilde{y}_j^t = \hat{y}_j^t$ for all i and j. Since (x, y) is feasible, the allocation $(\tilde{x}, \tilde{y})$ will be feasible if $(\hat{x}^t, \hat{y}^t)$ satisfies the two feasibility requirements of ex post optimality. This contradicts ex ante optimality since we now have a feasible allocation that gives each i more expected utility than x_i. Therefore, ex ante Pareto optimality implies ex post Pareto optimality.

The second reason why this conclusion might be invalid has to do with real-world considerations not incorporated into our model. In the real world uncertainty impinges on agents in stages over time. Let x_i^0 denote that part of household i's consumption that cannot be conditioned on uncertain events; x_i^0 must be delivered and consumed immediately. Let $V_i(x_i^0)$ be the derived utility. Then i's expected utility is $\Sigma_{t \in T} \pi_i^t [V_i(x_i^0) + U_i(x_i^t)]$, which equals $V_i(x_i^0) + \Sigma_{t \in T} \pi_i^t U_i(x_i^t)$. For ease of exposition suppose that the vectors x_i^0 and x_i^t are one-dimensional $(k = 1)$ and that every good is consumed by each household. If the functions are differentiable, then ex ante Pareto optimality requires the marginal rate of substitution

$$\rho_i^t = \frac{\pi_i^t \partial U_i(x_i^t)}{\partial x_i^t} \bigg/ \frac{\partial V_i(x_i^0)}{\partial x_i^0}$$

to be the same for all i given $t \in T$. If state r is realized, then ex post optimality in state r requires equality of the marginal rates of substitution γ_i^r defined with respect to the utility functions $V_i(x_i^0) + U_i(x_i^r)$. Clearly, $\gamma_i^r = \rho_i^r / \pi_i^r$. Ex ante optimality implies $\rho_1^r = \rho_2^r$, and this is consistent with $\gamma_1^r = \gamma_2^r$ if and only if $\pi_1^r = \pi_2^r$. In this setting ex ante optimality implies ex post optimality in each state if and only if all individuals have the same probability beliefs. [See Starr (1973).] Harris (1978) has devised a mechanism in which ex ante decisions lead to ex post optimal results. The planner determines personal prices $\pi_i^t p^t$ for each i. However, this requires each i to reveal π_i^t, and if $\pi_i^t = 1$, individual i has every incentive to report a very low π_i^t to reduce $\pi_i^t p^t$ and increase his purchasing power in state t.

Since divergence between ex post and ex ante optimality occurs only when some consumption must be fixed in advance and this decision could not be reversed under *any* economic system, it seems sensible to evaluate the performance of a mechanism in terms of the random component of utility, $\Sigma_{t \in T} \pi_i^t U_i(x_i^t)$. In that case ex ante optimality implies ex post optimality for any state t for which $\pi_i^t > 0$ for all i, as we have shown. Nonetheless, whenever the term Pareto optimality is employed in the rest of this chapter, ex ante optimality is intended.

The reader is encouraged to verify that all of the results and arguments of this chapter remain valid if the utility function depends upon the state, in which case expected utility would be $\Sigma_{t \in T} \pi_i^t U_i^t(x_i^t)$, where $U_i^t(x_i^t)$ is the utility from consuming x_i^t in state t.

## 4.5	The Walrasian mechanism and uncertainty

Instead of k commodities we now have $k\tau$ commodities. A price system p assigns a price vector p^t to each state t; p^t is a nonnegative k-vector. An allocation (x, y) gives i an expenditure limit, or income, of

$$\sum_{t \in T} p^t w_i^t + \sum_{t \in T} \sum_{j=1}^m \alpha_{ij} p^t y_j^t$$

where α_{ij} is i's share in firm j. Individual i is required to announce the consumption plan x_i that maximizes $u_i(x_i)$ subject to the budget constraint. This is identical to the individual's role in the Walrasian mechanism under certainty. The only difference is that the utility function belongs to a special class. Otherwise, we have just reinterpreted the notion of a commodity.

Each firm j is required to announce a production plan in Y_j that maximizes profit, $\Sigma_{t \in T} p^t y_j^t$. Just as consumers buy contingent claims to goods and pay in advance, firms sell output in advance, contingent on the realization of the state of nature. Shareholders receive their share of the profits from contingent sales before the state of nature is known.

Household i's consumption plan x_i specifies, for each commodity c and each event t, a demand for x_{ic}^t units of c contingent on the realization of state t, and i is required to pay $p_c^t x_{ic}^t$ units of "money" in this market before the uncertainty is resolved. If i wants to be certain of consuming one unit of c, he must set $x_{ic}^t = 1$ for all t and pay $\Sigma_{t \in T} p_c^t$ in total. For example, $T = \{1, 2\}$. Let 1 be the event "no fire" and 2 the event "fire." If c is the commodity "house," we would regard p_c^1 as the price of a house in the conventional sense and p_c^2 as a fire insurance premium, which must be paid whether there is a fire or not but which will ensure that the individual will have a house whether there is a fire or not. Overall, i will have to spend $\Sigma_{t \in T} p^t x_i^t$ on the plan x_i. Since endowments are also sold in advance of the resolution of uncertainty, i will have an income of $\Sigma_{t \in T} p^t w_i^t$ plus his share of profit income.

An equilibrium (p, x, y) of this extended Walrasian mechanism is a list of messages that satisfies conditions (4.1)—(4.3):

For each household i the plan $x_i \in X_i$ maximizes u_i subject to the budget constraint

$$\sum_{t \in T} p^t x_i^t \leq \sum_{t \in T} p^t w_i^t + \sum_{t \in T} \sum_{j=1}^{m} \alpha_{ij} p^t y_j^t \tag{4.1}$$

For each firm j the plan y_j maximizes profit,

$$\sum_{t \in T} p^t y_j^t, \text{ over all plans in } Y_j. \tag{4.2}$$

$$p^t \geq 0 \text{ and } \sum_{i=1}^{n} (x_i^t - w_i^t) = \sum_{j=1}^{m} y_j^t \text{ for all } t \in T \tag{4.3}$$

Except for the change in notation and interpretation, this definition of Walrasian competitive equilibrium agrees with the one given in Section 3.3. It is formally equivalent. (As a matter of convenience, this chapter ignores the possibility of excess supply at equilibrium even if the good in question has a zero price.) Therefore, we already have a proof of Pareto optimality of competitive equilibrium. To reinterpret Theorem 3.1 in the present context, think of the price vector p^* of Chapter 3 as the vector $p^* = (p^1, p^2, \ldots, p^\tau)$, where each p^t is a nonnegative k-vector, and replace k by $k\tau$. Then $p^* x_i = \Sigma_{t \in T} p^t x_i^t$, $p^* w_i = \Sigma_{t \in T} p^t w_i^t$, and $p^* y_j = \Sigma_{t \in T} p^t y_j^t$.

This extension of the Walrasian mechanism to accommodate uncertainty will be called the *contingent contracts economy*. The first welfare theorem is restated for reference.

Theorem 4.1. *If there is a market for each of the $k\tau$ commodities, if each household's utility depends exclusively on its own consumption, and if each firm's technology set is self-regarding, then a competitive equilibrium of the contingent contracts economy is Pareto optimal.*

4.6   Equilibrium with securities markets

The contingent contracts economy requires $k \times \tau$ markets, and an individual must participate in τ of these if he is to be certain of purchasing one unit of a particular commodity. He must demand and pay for one unit of good c contingent on every event t to complete the contract. The system is not informationally efficient: There is a much simpler way of establishing the same equilibrium.

The number of markets is reduced from $k \times \tau$ to $k + \tau$ with the introduction of τ *securities markets*. A security is a fiduciary asset that pays one monetary unit (one dollar) if, and only if, a specified state is realized; otherwise it pays nothing. Let I_i^t denote the amount of security t purchased by individual i at a price of s^t. This security pays one dollar if and only if state t is realized and it must be purchased before the state of nature is known. Once the state is known, the markets for goods open up and trading takes place according to the standard definitions of the Walrasian mechanism except that an individual's income comes exclusively from his holdings of securities. Let q^t denote the vector of prices that emerges when event t is realized. Since expenditure in state t is limited by $I^t_{i,}$ and this is determined prior to the resolution of uncertainty, the individual must choose a portfolio $I_i = (I^1_i, I^2_i, \ldots, I^\tau_i)$ that maximizes his expected utility. We can now define the Walrasian mechanism with securities (WMS).

The planner's message is a pair (s, q) where s assigns a price s^t to each security t and q assigns a vector q^t of "spot" prices for the k goods for each state t. Securities are sold by households, and each household i can sell S^t_i securities of type t, where S^t_i is the income to which i would be entitled, from the sale of w^t_i and from i's share of profits, were event t to be realized. This is defined by

$$S^t_i = q^t w^t_i + \sum_{j=1}^{m} \alpha_{ij} q^t y^t_j \tag{4.4}$$

Individual i's income, I^0_i, is derived from the sale of securities. Therefore, $I^0_i = \sum_{t \in T} s^t S^t_i$. Combining this with equation (4.4) yields

$$I^0_i = \sum_{t \in T} s^t S^t_i = \sum_{t \in T} s^t q^t \left(w^t_i + \sum_{j=1}^{m} \alpha_{ij} y^t_j \right) \tag{4.5}$$

Let I^t_i denote the amount of security t *purchased* by i. Therefore,

$$\sum_{t \in T} s^t I^t_i \leq I^0_i \tag{4.6}$$

must hold. Individual i will both buy and sell securities. In particular, i will sell securities for states in which he holds wealth but that he feels are unlikely to occur and will use the proceeds to purchase securities for states that he believes to have a high probability of realization.

Partition the set of events into two disjoint sets A and B and suppose that B is a compound event in which i's endowment is destroyed. If $w^t_i = w^0_i$, a constant, for each t in A and $w^t_i = 0$ for each t in B, and if $\alpha_{ij} = 0$ for all j, then i will have no wealth if event B is realized. If B is at all likely, i will have to use his income from the sale of securities, $\sum_{t \in A} s^t q^t w^0_i = I^0_i$, to purchase securities for events in B. If everyone agrees that the compound event A will occur with very low probability, there will be little demand for the corresponding securities and I^0_i will be very low. Household i will be poor and will not have much purchasing power when a state is realized. Given sufficient income, the existence of securities allows households to trade indirectly with each other across states of nature. The prices s^t determine the rates at which trade takes place. An individual expecting one dollar in the event t can give up his claim to this dollar in return for s^t/s^r dollars in state r. This will be very low if s^t is low and s^r is high. This is the same as the case of an individual in the certainty version of Walrasian system having an endowment consisting of goods that are not much desired. These goods will fetch a low price, and the individual will not have much purchasing power. The market system allows individuals to trade undesired units of a good for other goods but only at rates that reflect the desirability of goods in the aggregate, and this applies just as well when the goods refer to units of the same physical object available in different states of nature.

While individuals can trade with each other across states of nature, the community as a whole cannot do so after the resolution of uncertainty. The global feasibility condition, $\sum_{i=1}^{n}(x_i^t - w_i^t) \leq \sum_{j=1}^{m} y_j^t$, must hold for each state t. At equilibrium this will hold as a strict equality. Let $S^t = \sum_{i=1}^{n} S_i^t$ be the supply of security t, and let $D^t = \sum_{i=1}^{n} I_i^t$ be the demand for t. Then D^t must equal S^t at equilibrium.

To prove that D^t equals S^t, note that each household i must respect the budget constraint $q^t x_i^t \leq I_i^t$ if state t is realized and i chooses the commodity vector x_i^t at the spot prices q_c^t, $c = 1, 2, \ldots, k$. We will have $q^t x_i^t = I_i^t$ at equilibrium since i will optimize. Since $\sum_{i=1}^{n}(x_i^t - w_i^t) = \sum_{j \in J} y_i^t$ also holds at equilibrium, we have

$$D^t = \sum_{i=1}^{n} I_i^t = \sum_{i=1}^{n} q^t x_i^t = q^t \left(\sum_{i=1}^{n} w_i^t + \sum_{j=1}^{m} y_j^t \right) = \sum_{i=1}^{n} S_i^t = S^t$$

The WMS requires firms to maximize purchasing power for their shareholders, and because their purchasing power comes from the money received from the sale of securities, a firm j will maximize $\sum_{t \in T} s^t q^t y_j^t$. We will see that the security prices s^t can be interpreted as market-assigned probabilities for the states of nature. In particular, $\sum_{t \in T} s^t = 1$, and the more likely state t is considered to be, the greater will be the demand for security t and the higher will be s^t. According to this interpretation, we can think of $\sum_{t \in T} s^t q^t y^t$ as the expected profit from j's input commitment, and it is reasonable for the firm to maximize this. This will be the case whatever the nature of household attitudes to risk and however much π_i^t differs from s^t for j's shareholders since, whatever outcomes they consider to be likely, they prefer more purchasing power to less and a higher profit income in any state will enable more of the associated securities to be sold before the resolution of uncertainty.

An equilibrium (q, s, x, I, y) of the WMS is defined, as usual, in terms of individual utility maximization, firm profit maximization, and market clearance. Conditions (4.7)–(4.9) provide the details:

For each household i, $x_i = (x_i^1, \ldots, x_i^\tau) \in X_i$ and $I_i = (I_i^1, \ldots, I_i^\tau) \geq 0$ maximize $u_i(x_i)$ subject to the budget constraints

$$\sum_{t \in T} s^t I_i^t \leq \sum_{t \in T} s^t q^t w_i^t + \sum_{t \in T} \sum_{j=1}^{m} \alpha_{ij} s^t q^t y_j^t \tag{4.7}$$

and $q^t x_i^t \leq I_i^t$ ($\forall t \in T$).

For each firm j, $y_j \in Y_j$ and

$$\sum_{t \in T} s^t q^t y_j^t \geq \sum_{t \in T} s^t q^t \hat{y}_j^t \qquad \forall \hat{y}_j \in Y_j. \tag{4.8}$$

$$(q, s) \geq 0 \quad \text{and} \quad \sum_{i=1}^{n} (x_i^t - w_i^t) = \sum_{j=1}^{m} y_j^t \qquad \forall t \in T \tag{4.9}$$

Individual i does not enter into a contract with suppliers for each x_i^t, $t = 1, 2, \ldots, \tau$, specified by the plan x_i. Instead, i purchases a portfolio I_i of securities that will enable i to purchase x_i^t, whichever event t is realized, in spot markets under price regime q^t.

Rather than prove that every WMS equilibrium is Pareto optimal we will show that there is a one-to-one correspondence between these equilibria and those of the contingent contracts economy. Once this is established, Theorem 4.1 implies optimality of the WMS equilibria.

Theorem 4.2. *Configuration (p, x, y) is an equilibrium of the contingent contracts economy if and only if (q, s, x, I, y) is an equilibrium of the WMS for p, q, s, and I satisfying*

$$s^t = \sum_{i=1}^{n} p^t x_i^t \bigg/ \sum_{r \in T} \sum_{i=1}^{n} p^r x_i^r \tag{4.10}$$

$$q^t = p^t / s^t \tag{4.11}$$

$$I_i^t = q^t x_i^t \tag{4.12}$$

Proof: Both x_i and I_i are nonnegative for all i. Therefore, $p \geq 0$ if and only if $(q, s) \geq 0$, given equations (4.10)–(4.12). Therefore, (4.3) holds if and only if (4.9) does. If (4.11) holds, then (4.2) and (4.8) are equivalent. It remains to show that (4.1) and (4.7) are equivalent under the hypothesis of the theorem.

If (x_i, I_i) satisfies the budget constraint of (4.7), then x_i satisfies the budget constraint of (4.1). Therefore, (4.1) implies (4.7). Suppose, then, that (x_i, I_i) solves (4.7) but there exists $\hat{x}_i \in X_i$ such that $u_i(\hat{x}_i) > u_i(x_i)$ and

$$\sum_{t \in T} p^t \hat{x}_i^t \leq \sum_{t \in T} p^t w_i^t + \sum_{j=1}^{m} \alpha_{ij} p^t y_j^t$$

Set $\hat{I}_i^t = p^t \hat{x}_i^t / s^t$. Then

$$q^t \hat{x}_i^t = \hat{I}_i^t \quad \text{and} \quad \sum_{t \in T} s^t \hat{I}_i^t = \sum_{t \in T} p^t \hat{x}_i^t \leq \sum_{t \in T} s^t \left(q^t w_i^t + \sum_{j=1}^{m} \alpha_{ij} q^t y_j^t \right)$$

Therefore, $(\hat{x}_i, \hat{I}_i)$ satisfies the budget constraint of (4.7), and since that plan provides more utility than (x_i, I_i), we have a contradiction. Therefore, (4.7) implies (4.1). Therefore, (4.1)–(4.3) and (4.7)–(4.9) are equivalent, given (4.10)–(4.12).   Q.E.D.

The contingent contracts economy is formally identical to the Walrasian mechanism. Therefore, the former has all of the properties attributed to the latter in Chapter 3, in particular Pareto optimality. Theorem 4.2 allows us to claim these properties for the Walrasian mechanism with securities as well.

It was asserted that the security prices s^t can be interpreted as market-assigned probabilities. It is clear that the more likely the public believes state t to be, the greater will be the demand for security t and the higher will be its price. It is not so obvious that the security prices will sum to unity. This can be demonstrated if we assume that securities are sold for money that is then used to purchase other securities. When a particular state is realized, the relevant securities are exchanged for money, which is then used to buy commodities in the spot markets. Let I_0^0 be the supply of money (I_0^0 can be viewed as the planner's endowment). At equilibrium, the demand for security t, $\sum_{i=1}^{n} q^t x_i^t$, equals the supply of security t. The total value of securities supplied (before uncertainty is resolved) is therefore $\sum_{t \in T} \sum_{i=1}^{n} s^t q^t x_i^t$, and this must equal I_0^0 because a supply of one dollar's worth of a security is a demand for one monetary unit. When an event, say t, is realized, the market value of the demand for goods must also equal the supply of money: $\sum_{i=1}^{n} q^t x_i^t = I_0^0$. This follows from the fact that $\sum_{i=1}^{n} q^t x_i^t$ units of security t will be exchanged for money so that goods may be purchased in spot markets. Therefore, $s^t \sum_{i=1}^{n} q^t x_i^t = s^t I_0^0$. Summing over T yields

$$\sum_{t \in T} \sum_{i=1}^{n} s^t q^t x_i^t = I_0^0 \sum_{t \in T} s^t$$

or

$$\sum_{t \in T} s^t = \left(\sum_{t \in T} \sum_{i=1}^{n} s^t q^t x_i^t \right) \Big/ I_0^0$$

which equals unity.

It might strike the reader as odd that securities are issued by households and not firms. Household i will issue $q^t w_i^t + \sum_{j=1}^{m} \alpha_{ij} q^t y_j^t$ securities of type t. The second component of that sum is attributed to the activities of the firms in which i owns a share. Of course, we can think of these securities as being issued by the firm but held by the firm's owners, in proportion to their ownership shares, and exchanged by these owners for securities in other states, according to preference. The first component, $q^t w_i^t$, is approximated only roughly by real-world institutions. Think of an endowment consisting mainly of labor skills. Before entering the labor market, an individual takes some costly actions – training – in order to enhance the value of his endowment. Whether the end product will be valued by the market depends on how much competition the individual faces that will affect q^t and whether the training program that will affect the components of w_i^t is successful. Suppose that the individual were able to obtain a loan to finance his or her training on condition that the loan be paid back only if $q^t w_i^t$ turns out to be roughly as high as expected. This loosely corresponds to the individual in the WMS selling $q^t w_i^t$ securities of type t. The proceeds can be used to purchase securities in other states associated with the failure of i's training program. If i's training program fails – state t is not realized – then i can still cash in his other securities and maintain a reasonable standard of living. If i were forced to take out a loan that had to be repaid even if the training program failed, then i would be forced to divert most of his income in that event to the repayment of the loan, and his standard of living would be very low. This system, which is commonplace, discourages many individuals from acquiring productive skills even though there is no risk to society in spite of the risk to the individual: Some individuals will fail, but the proportion that succeed can be known with near certainty.

The fact that this sort of conditional loan is not readily available reflects an imperfection in capital markets. Owners of corporations can obtain such loans for the installation of physical capital: Their liability for default is limited. Investment in human capital usually cannot be financed in this way. One reason for this is the *moral hazard* phenomenon. Lenders could not determine whether an individual's failure occurred because of lack of effort on his or her part or because of random forces beyond the individual's control. Moral hazard refers to just this situation: One party to a contract cannot observe the actions of the other party and can only observe the joint effects of the state of nature and the decisions of the latter, but not the two separately. (Yale University offered a modified version of the plan to its students in the 1970s. The moral hazard problem is less serious in this case since a university has access to fairly reliable information about the work habits of its students. This information comes at zero *marginal* cost to the university since it is collected during the admission process.)

Finally, we note than even though $k + \tau$, the number of markets required by the WMS, is less than $k\tau$ (if k and τ exceed 1), it is still an astronomically large number.

4.7   Limitations of the Arrow–Debreu model

The two versions of the Walrasian mechanism presented in this chapter constitute what is commonly referred to as the Arrow–Debreu model: Markets are complete in either mechanism. All future plans are settled before any trade occurs. The plans are conditional on events, and although the true state is not known when plans are formulated, all prices for all events are known because trading does not take place until all equilibrium prices are determined. This assumption obviously does not conform to reality. Let us consider whether the Arrow–Debreu model glosses over important real-world institutions or even if Theorems 4.1 and 4.2 are misleading as an endorsement of actual market systems. There are two headings under which these considerations are discussed: (1) models with complete markets in which agents have different information about the likelihood of uncertain events, and (2) sequences of incomplete markets over time. Under heading 1 there are three subcases that deserve special attention.

(i) *The production and sale of information.* An individual with poor information relative to someone else will employ subjective probabilities that are relatively inaccurate. Nevertheless, the individual's expected utility and demands will be well defined. The Arrow–Debreu model explicitly allows for this. However, Theorems 4.1 and 4.2 established Pareto optimality in terms of the individual expected utility functions, which in turn are based on individual information that may be woefully inaccurate relative to the collective information of society. Radner (1968) prefers to say that Theorems 4.1 and 4.2 establish Pareto optimality relative to a given information structure.

If it were not for the fact that individuals can acquire information in several ways, and so revise their probability beliefs, these results could not be improved upon. In reality, an agent can increase the reliability of his probability assessments by devoting input, particularly labor, to research into the likelihood of events or by purchasing information from others who have. This is easily accommodated by the Arrow–Debreu model if we assume that the production of knowledge is reflected in one or more of the technologies (the Y_j's). However, the production of knowledge usually involves substantial setup costs that vitiate the nonincreasing returns to scale assumption on which *existence* of equilibrium depends. For example, research into the average quality of a particular model of automobile involves a substantial investment in testing apparatus. Once the results of the research and testing information have been provided to one household, they can be provided to additional households at close to zero marginal cost. Even if an equilibrium exists with this degree of increasing returns to scale, the assumption of price-taking behavior is in jeopardy.

(ii) *Learning from the market clearing prices.* Individual probability assessments affect individual expected utility and therefore influence demands and ultimately prices. As a result, the price of a commodity may hint at information possessed by expert traders. For example, a family moves to a new town and discovers some extremely attractive and very inexpensive land along a riverbank. The family considers it an ideal site for a house, but the low price prompts some nervous questions about the annual flooding conditions. In general, a complete system of market clearing prices may lead some individuals to change their plans based on what the prices suggest concerning the probability beliefs of others. If the revealed information causes a change in the π_i''s, then i's expected utility function will change and so will his demands. These new demands will result in new market clearing prices. When this process comes to an end, we have a rational expectations equilibrium (Section 4.10).

The first two difficulties can be fairly successfully circumvented by reinterpreting or extending the Arrow–Debreu model. The third phenomenon presents a more formidable obstacle.

(iii) *Moral hazard:* Individual i's probability values may depend in part on actions undertaken by i that cannot be observed by other agents. For example, the probability of fire depends in part on preventive measures undertaken by the homeowner, and some of these cannot be monitored by the insurer. It is not difficult to imagine situations in which each household has little incentive to exercise care, and as a result the total amount of property destroyed is large. This leaves the community with more labor (little is devoted to prevention) and less property, and this might not be a Pareto-optimal outcome since the private cost of carelessness is lower than the social cost (Helpman and Laffont, 1975).

There are classes of risk for which moral hazard makes a viable insurance contract impossible. A business can fail due to forces that are random from the standpoint of the firm in question. If an insurance company were to offer a contract that insured against the failure of a firm to make a profit, there would be very little incentive for an entrepreneur to strive for a successful business. One would expect the insurance premium to be just about equal to the loss against which insurance is provided.

There are four points under heading 2: In the real world uncertainty impinges on society in stages over time. At any one time there are future date–event possibilities for which futures markets are not open–due in part to the impossibly large number of markets that would be required. The proper way to model this is as a sequence of incomplete markets (Hahn, 1971). If some futures markets do not exist at each date, then the prices associated with some (future) date–event situations will not be known at the time that current plans–which will have a bearing on future consumption possibilities–are formulated. As a result, there are real-world phenomena that arise naturally in sequence models but not in the Arrow–Debreu model. We will discuss four of these.

(i) *Money as a store of value.* Agents must speculate about the future prices of goods for which there are no futures markets currently active. If storage is indicated, it may be more efficient for a speculator to store money rather than commodities. (See also Section 2.1.)

(ii) *Shareholder conflict.* If markets are incomplete, there is no natural way of comparing a firm's net revenue over alternative (future) date–event combinations. If, say, play y_j yields a high profit under future event r but a low profit under t and shareholder 1 places a high probability on r and 2 places a low probability on r, then 1 may favor y_j whereas 2 favors a plan that would yield a high profit under t. It may be possible for these individuals to hedge by trading in other commodities conditioned on other events (Ekern and Wilson, 1974; Radner, 1974), but this is by no means guaranteed. There may be fundamental disagreement among shareholders concerning the course that the firm should pursue. This can never arise in an Arrow–Debreu model since each household has an incentive to make the right-hand side of the budget constraint as large as possible, and this implies maximization of $\alpha_{ij}\Sigma_{t\in T}p^t y_j^t$ (or $\alpha_{ij}\Sigma_{t\in T}s^t q^t y_j^t$) for any shareholder of j, and this implies maximization of $\Sigma_{t\in T}p^t y_j^t$ (or $\Sigma_{t\in T}s^t q^t y_j^t$); there is complete agreement.

(iii) *Trading in shares.* Consider the component $\alpha_{ij}\Sigma_{t\in T}p^t y_j^t$ (or $\alpha_{ij}\Sigma_{t\in T}s^t q^t y_j^t$) of the right-hand side of i's budget constraint in the Arrow–Debreu model. Suppose that this number is $1000. If another individual a were to pay $999 for i's share α_{ij} of firm j, then the right-hand side of a's budget constraint would fall by $999 and rise by $1000, leading to an increase in u_a. Therefore, the equilibrium value of i's share of firm j cannot be less than $1000: At any lower value the demand would exceed the supply. If a were to pay more than \$1000 for i's share, then the right-hand side of a's budget constraint would diminish: No one would demand i's share at a price higher than \$1000. But i would attempt to sell his share at a price of \$1001 or more since his purchasing power would increase by at least one dollar. Hence, supply would exceed demand. Therefore, the equilibrium value if i's share of firm j is exactly $\alpha_{ij}\Sigma_{t\in T}p^ty_j^t$ (or $\alpha_{ij}\Sigma_{t\in T}s^tq^ty_j^t$). In other words, in a world of complete markets everyone agrees on the value of a share in firm j and there is no basis for trade in shares. In a sequence economy with incomplete markets at each date there is no natural way of comparing firm j's net revenues in different date–event situations. Therefore, individuals will not always agree on the value of a firm's production plan and stock markets will be active.

(iv) *Adverse selection*. If markets are not complete, then the fact that different agents have different information (about probabilities) can undermine the performance of competitive markets apart from moral hazard. If insurance companies, for example, do not have as much information about individual risks as the individuals themselves, then an equilibrium may fail to exist. Suppose that very little life insurance is available to individuals over sixty-five although many of these people will expect to live another fifteen years at least. One would expect the price (or premium) to rise to equate demand and supply. It may happen that the low-risk individuals who are over sixty-five withdraw their demand: The new contract is no longer attractive. But now the percentage of claims paid will rise since the insured population is riskier. This can cause a further increase in premium, which will lead to withdrawal of those remaining customers with the lowest risk, and so on. This is the adverse selection phenomenon; there may be no price at which demand equals supply. [See Akerlof (1970).] The next section investigates this problem in detail.

Although the Arrow–Debreu model has its limitations as a description of actual market systems, it remains central to economic theory. It provides a standard by which real institutions can be tested and also a blueprint for constructing more complex models.

4.8   Competitive insurance markets

This section highlights the difficulties of achieving a satisfactory outcome when traders differ with respect to the information they possess concerning the likelihood of events. To abstract from most of the other issues, assume that $k = 1$. There is only one basic commodity. Uncertainty concerns the status of an individual's endowment, which is either partially destroyed–by fire, say–or remains intact. The set T of events is the family of subsets of $\{1, 2, \ldots, n\}$, the set of individuals. For any $t \in T$ if $i \in t$, then i's endowment is partially destroyed, and if $i \notin t$, then i suffers no loss. Therefore, there are 2^n simple events. If there are ten million households in the economy–a modest number–and an individual entered into a contract every second, it would take the lifetime of 200,000 suns for him to negotiate 2^n contracts.

Obviously, both the contingent contracts economy and the Walrasian mechanism with securities are not informationally viable even though the number of potential contracts is finite. Real-world insurance markets do not require an individual to enter into more than a few contracts to ensure that his wealth will be fairly constant under all but the most bizarre circumstances. We will consider whether Pareto optimality is guaranteed nonetheless. The analysis follows Rothschild and Stiglitz (1976).

Insurance companies offer relatively few types of contracts. Each contract requires the purchaser to pay a stipulated fee–the premium–before the resolution of uncertainty. If i purchases a contract, he receives a stipulated payment from the insurance company if *any* of the events t for which $i \in t$ is realized. From i's point of view, only two compound events are of interest, $C^1 = \{t: i \notin t\}$ and $C^2 = \{t: i \in t\}$. It will be simpler to refer to events 1 and 2 instead of C^1 and C^2. We will further simplify by supposing that π_i^1 can have only one of two values over all households i. Even within this limited framework there are potential difficulties in terms of the satisfactory performance of competitive markets.

The number π_i^1 denotes the probability that i is not in t: the probability that i does not have an accident (or a fire in his house). If $\pi_i^1 > \pi_a^1$, we say that i is a low-risk individual. There are only two possible values of π_i^1 and hence only two types of individuals, low risk ($i = L$) and high risk ($i = H$), so we write π_L^1 and π_H^1. Of course, $\pi_i^2 = 1 - \pi_i^1$. Each individual i has the utility-of-wealth function $U(I^t)$. Individuals are assumed to be risk averse: $U''(I^t) < 0$ for all $I^t \geq 0$. Each i has the same endowment $w = (w^1, w^2)$ with $w^2 < w^1$. (An accident destroys wealth.) There are n_L low-risk individuals and n_H high-risk individuals. Although $U_H = U_L = U$, it is not the case that $u_H = u_L$ since $u_i(I) = \pi_i^1 U(I^1) + (1 - \pi_i^1) U(I^2)$ and $\pi_H^1 \neq \pi_L^1$. The crucial assumption is that insurance companies cannot identify L-types and H-types directly but can separate them only by employing conjectures about their preferences (u_H and u_L) for insurance contracts and by observing their contract choices.

An insurance contract $y = (y^1, y^2)$ specifies a premium y^1 and a net claim y^2. In case of accident the insured receives a claim check for $y^1 + y^2$ dollars but has to pay his premium in any case, so the net payment received from the insurance company is y^2. Specifying y is equivalent to specifying final wealth $I = (w^1 - y^1, w^2 + y^2)$. Therefore, we will think of a contract as a modified endowment $I = (I^1, I^2)$.

It will be assumed that n_H and n_L are both large in absolute value, although one number might be small relative to the other. If n_i is large, then the total number of accidents will be close to the expected number, $(1 - \pi_i^1)n_i$. In fact, it will be assumed that the total number of accidents is always equal to the expected number in order to avoid having to say that the results hold only approximately, or with high probability. It will also be assumed, for simplicity, that administration costs are constant and relatively small. This will permit us to assume zero administrative costs without affecting the results. In that case, competition among insurance companies will ensure that the value of premiums taken in at equilibrium equals the value of gross claims paid out at equilibrium.

Since the H-types are identical to each other, they will make the same choices, and for the same reason, the L-types will all choose the same contract. Therefore, if a contract has any buyers at all, it will have either n, or n_H, or n_L buyers. If we let $n_0 = n$, then we can say y will have n_i buyers for $i = 0, H$, or L. Similarly, π_0^1 denotes the probability that an individual randomly selected from the entire population will not have an accident:

$$\pi_0^1 = (n_H\pi_H^1 + n_L\pi_L^1)/n \tag{4.13}$$

The condition that all money taken in from a contract y_i is paid out is $n_iy_i^1 = (1 - \pi_i^1)n_i(y_i^2 + y_i^1)$, where n_i ($i = 0, H$, or L) is the number of individuals who purchase the contract. Since $I_i = (w^1 - y_i^1, w^2 + y_i^2)$, we can rewrite this as

$$n_i(w^1 - I_i^1) = (1 - \pi_i^1)n_i(I_i^2 - w^2 + w^1 - I^1)$$

and this can be simplified by grouping terms:

$$\pi_i^1 I_i^1 + (1 - \pi_i^1)I_i^2 = \pi_i^1 w^1 + (1 - \pi_i^1)w^2 \tag{4.14}$$

To establish a benchmark case, suppose that insurance companies are able to distinguish H-types from L-types. Assume, for instance, that each person can be relied on to answer truthfully when asked which risk group he belongs to. In addition, suppose that there is no cross-subsidization: All claims made by i-types are paid out of premiums contributed by i-types ($i = H$ or L). Then equation (4.14) must hold at equilibrium for $i = H$ and L. If the left side of equation (4.14) exceeds the right side, the contract is not feasible since the value of gross claims paid out will exceed the value of premiums collected. If the right side exceeds the left side, then insurance companies are earning excess profits and competition will force premiums to fall, indicating that the original state was not in equilibrium.

Under these conditions, the best contract to offer risk group i is the one that maximizes u_i subject to equation (4.14). Use equation (4.14) to solve for I_i^2: $I_i^2 = \delta - \beta I_i^1$ for $\beta = \pi_i^1(1 - \pi_i^1)^{-1}$ and $\delta = \beta w^1 + w^2$. Now maximize $u_i(I_i) = \pi_i^1 U(I_i^1) + (1 - \pi_i^1)U(\delta - \beta_i I_i^1)$. The first-order condition is

$$\pi_i^1 U'(I_i^1) - (1 - \pi_i^1)\beta U'(I_i^2) = 0$$

and this implies $U'(I_i^1) = U'(I_i^2)$. Risk aversion implies that U' decreases as wealth increases. Therefore, $U'(I_i^1) = U'(I_i^2)$ implies $I_i^1 = I_i^2$ $(= \delta - \beta I_i^1)$. The optimal consumption is

$$I_i = (\pi_i^1 w^1 + (1 - \pi_i^1)w^2, \pi_i^1 w^1 + (1 - \pi_i^1)w^2) \tag{4.15}$$

and the optimal contract is $y_i = (w^1 - I_i^1, I_i^2 - w^2)$, where I_i is given by equation (4.15). Since $I_i^1 = I_i^2$, we have what is known as *complete insurance*.

Now we can specify a simple mechanism for achieving these optimal insurance levels. Each individual i reports his risk parameter π_i^1. In plain words, when asked by the insurance agent which risk group he belongs to, the individual is assumed to respond truthfully. Insurance companies are required to offer feasible contracts that maximize profit, which is premium income minus claims paid out, given the reported risk parameters. Since insurers are able to classify individuals by risk, profit maximization may require them to offer different contracts to different risks. An individual is required to choose a utility-maximizing contract from among those offered to his risk category by insurers. There is no demand-equals-supply requirement since contracts are printed at zero cost and they are either accepted or not. (The real-world counterpart to demand-equals-supply is the requirement that a firm sell enough contracts to enable it to take advantage of the law of large numbers.)

The rest of this section – in particular, the next theorem – assumes that each U_i is weakly monotonic: if $M \geq M'$ then $U_i(M) \geq U_i(M')$. Therefore, u_i will be weakly monotonic as well.

Theorem 4.3 proves that an equilibrium is Pareto optimal if each individual discloses his risk category truthfully. This qualification is unnecessary if either n_H or n_L is zero. A problem arises only when there are two risk categories and the insurer does not know to which group a client belongs. To understand why this creates a problem, we first consider the performance of insurance markets when we assume, naively, that an individual voluntarily provides the insurer with the required information.

Theorem 4.3. *If each risk type i reports his risk parameter π_i^1 truthfully, then the contracts I_H and I_L of equation (4.15) ($i = H, L$) define a Pareto-optimal equilibrium.*

Proof: First, we show that equation (4.15) defines a Pareto-optimal allocation of wealth. Suppose that there is another outcome $\hat{I}$ such that $u_i(\hat{I}_i) > u_i(I_i)$ for all i. Then

$$\pi_i^1 \hat{I}_i^1 + (1 - \pi_i^1)\hat{I}_i^2 > \pi_i^1 w^1 + (1 - \pi_i^1)w^2 \tag{4.16}$$

This follows from the fact that I_i maximizes u_i subject to equation (4.14) and hence subject to

$$\pi_i^1 I_i^1 + (1 - \pi_i^1)I_i^2 \le \pi_i^1 w^1 + (1 - \pi_i^1)w^2 \tag{4.17}$$

since u_i is weakly monotonic.

Outcome $\hat{I}_i$ need not be the same for all individuals i in a particular risk category. Let $\hat{I}(H)$ be the sum of all $\hat{I}_i$'s over all i in risk category H. Define $\hat{I}(L)$ analogously. If we sum both sides of inequality (4.16) over all individuals in a particular risk category, we get

$$\pi_i^1 \hat{I}^1(i) + (1 - \pi_i^1)\hat{I}^2(i) > \pi_i^1 n_i w^1 + (1 - \pi_i^1)n_i w^2 \tag{4.18}$$

for $i = H, L$. Since $\pi_i^1 n_i$ and $(1 - \pi_i^1)n_i$ are, respectively, the number of i-types with an endowment of w^1 and the number that have an endowment of w^2, the right-hand side of equation (4.18) is the total amount of wealth held by i-types. The left-hand side is the total amount of wealth provided to i-types on average by $\hat{I}$. If we add both sides of inequality (4.18) for H and I, we conclude that the total amount of wealth provided to the community by the insurance scheme $\hat{I}$ exceeds the total amount available. Therefore, $\hat{I}$ is not feasible. We have proved that I is Pareto optimal.

Now let us see why equation (4.15) defines an equilibrium, assuming truthful revelation. It is implicit in equation (4.15) that each risk group is offered but a single contract. Given only one choice, each individual i trivially maximizes utility by choosing the contract y_i leading to I_i. (Remember, H-types are not allowed to choose y_L.) Is there a more profitable course of action for an insurer than offering y_H to H-types and y_L to L-types? If the insurance companies collude, the profit of each, which is zero by equation (4.15), can be increased. But we are assuming competitive behavior, and this means, among other things, that the insurance companies act independently. Therefore, we assume that the contracts y_H and y_L implicit in equation (4.15) continue to be offered by some insurance companies when others offer new contracts $\hat{I}_H$ and $\hat{I}_L$ (not necessarily different). Is there a choice of $\hat{I}$ that will yield positive profit given that y_H and y_L are still available? The new contracts will be chosen in preference to the original ones only if they provide more utility. Since I_i maximizes utility subject to constraint (4.17), the contract underlying $\hat{I}_i$ will be chosen only if inequality (4.16) holds and this yields a *negative* profit. It is conceivable that an insurer would lose money on, say, H-types, but more than make up for this with the profit earned on L-types. However, a contract offered to L-types will be profitable if and only if constraint (4.17) holds for $i = L$. But y_L already maximizes u_L subject to (4.17), and the L-types will not switch from this contract, which yields zero profit. Similarly, if original contracts are still available, an insurer cannot obtain a positive profit by designing contracts through which H-types subsidize L-types. Therefore, equation (4.15) is consistent with equilibrium.

Q.E.D.

The mechanism under discussion is successful if individuals behave sincerely, but H-types have no incentive to do so since $I_L \gg I_H$. If they masquerade as L-types, H-types will have much more wealth. Everyone will declare himself to be in risk category L and will purchase I_L. This outcome is not feasible since I_L yields zero profit only when H-types are excluded. If I_L is purchased by some H-types, who file more claims per dollar of premium than L-types, there will not be enough premium income to honor each claim. This is an instance of *adverse selection*. It is a consequence of asymmetric information: Insurance buyers know which risk category they belong to, but insurers do not, and some buyers have an incentive to misrepresent themselves. In other words, our mechanism is not even compatible with competitive behavior.

(To see why $I_L \gg I_H$, note that $w^1 > w^2$ and $\pi_L^1 > \pi_H^1$. Then $\pi_L^1(w^1 - w^2) > \pi_H^1(w^1 - w^2)$ and thus, using equation (4.15), $I_L^t = w^2 + \pi_L^1 (w^1 - w^2) > w^2 + \pi_H^1(w^1 - w^2) = I_H^t$ for $t = 1, 2$.)

Assume from now on that high-risk individuals will not directly reveal their identity. There are only two possible equilibria: Either the same contract is offered to both risk categories – this defines a *pooling equilibrium* – or the H-types are separated out by providing the L-types with a contract that is not preferred by the H-types to the one designed for them – this defines a *separating equilibrium*.

The constraint that incorporates feasibility and the zero profit condition for a pooling equilibrium is

$$\pi_0^1 I^1 + (1 - \pi_0^1)I^2 = \pi_0^1 w^1 + (1 - \pi_0^1)w^2 \tag{4.19}$$

[Parameter π_0^1 is defined by equation (4.13).] Consider any I satisfying equation (4.19). Let MRS_i denote type i's marginal rate of substitution at I:

$$\mathrm{MRS}_i = \frac{\pi_i^1 U'(I^1)}{(1 - \pi_i^1)U'(I^2)}$$

Now $\mathrm{MRS}_L > \mathrm{MRS}_H$ since $\pi_L^1 > \pi_H^1$. Then at the exchange rate $\lambda = \frac{1}{2}\mathrm{MRS}_L + \frac{1}{2}\mathrm{MRS}_H$ there is a number ε small enough in absolute value so that $u_L(I^1 + \varepsilon, I^2 - \lambda\varepsilon) > u_L(I)$ and $iu_H(I^1 + \varepsilon, I^2 - \lambda\varepsilon) < u_H(I)$. If an insurance company offered the contract $\hat{I} = (I^1 + \varepsilon, I^2 - \lambda\varepsilon)$, it would be preferred to I by L-types but not by H-types. The insurance company could offer $\hat{I}$ and be sure that L-types would purchase it in preference to I, but H-types would not. Even though the company would not be able to distinguish an L-type individual from an H-type, by judicious contract design a company could rely on the H-types to reveal themselves by their behavior.

An insurance company that catered exclusively to L-type risks would have to pay claims to the fraction π_L^2 of its policyholders. Before $\hat{I}$ was available, both types purchased I and the fraction π_0^2 of policyholders filed claims. If $\varepsilon > 0$ is small, then $\hat{I}$ and I are almost the same, but $\pi_L^1 > \pi_0^1$ and a company offering $\hat{I}$ will pay a smaller fraction of its premium receipts in claims, though the premium and net claim per person will be almost the same as for I. Therefore, $\hat{I}$ will yield a profit to the insurance companies offering it, and this means that the original situation in which each person purchased I is not in equilibrium. Companies would have an incentive to offer a new contract $\hat{I}$, and it would yield a profit if the individuals who preferred it in preference to I purchased it. (We still won't have an equilibrium when $\hat{I}$ is introduced since the viability of I depends, through equation (4.19), on its being purchased by L-types as well as by H-types, but the former will defect to $\hat{I}$ as soon as it is offered. The companies that continue to offer I will take a loss, and this is not consistent with equilibrium.)

What we have discovered is that an equilibrium must separate H-types from L-types by offering different contracts such that neither risk type would want to buy the contract designed for the other *and* the contracts satisfy equations (4.20) and (4.21):

$$\pi_L^1 I_L^1 + (1 - \pi_L^1) I_L^2 = \pi_L^1 w^1 + (1 - \pi_L^1) w^2 \qquad (4.20)$$

$$\pi_H^1 I_H^1 + (1 - \pi_H^1) I_H^2 = \pi_H^1 w^1 + (1 - \pi_H^1) w^2 \qquad (4.21)$$

There must be separate contracts at equilibrium. Individuals of the same risk type will buy the same contract: Given two contracts satisfying equation (4.20), the average of the two will also satisfy it and will be on a higher indifference curve than at least one of the original contracts, which cannot, therefore, be part of an equilibrium. The same argument applies to high-risk types. Therefore, only two contracts will be offered at equilibrium since there are two risk categories. It is possible that the contract I_L available to L-types is below the line representing equation (4.20). This will mean that the L-types are subsidizing the H-types. But this is inconsistent with equilibrium since a new firm could enter and obtain a positive profit by offering a contract close to I_L. This could be done in such a way that L-types prefer the new contract and H-types still prefer their original

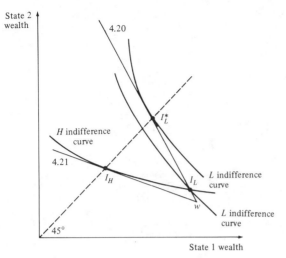

Figure 4.2

choice. Therefore, equation (4.20) must be satisfied at equilibrium by the contract designed for L-types. Similarly, equation (4.21) must be satisfied by the contract purchased by H-types.

Conditions (4.20) and (4.21) are represented geometrically as straight lines in Figure 4.2. Since w satisfies both equations, it is on both lines. Since the individuals are risk averse, we need not be concerned with any I_i for which $I_i^1 > w^1$. (Why?) Is there any reason why the H-types cannot have their most-preferred contract subject to condition (4.21)? No. If any other were offered, a company would have incentive to offer the most-preferred contract, I_H defined by equation (4.15) (for i = H), and this would be purchased by H-types in preference to the one originally offered. Both would give rise to the same profit (zero), but because I_H is preferred, a company could raise the premium slightly and make more profit than with the original contract, and H-types would still prefer the new contract to the original. Therefore,

$$I_H = (\pi_H^1 w^1 + (1 - \pi_H^1)w^2, \pi_H^1 w^1 + (1 - \pi_H^1)w^2)$$

is the only contract that H-types would be offered at equilibrium. Now this imposes a constraint on I_L, which must satisfy

$$u_H(I_H) \geq u_H(I_L) \tag{4.22}$$

At equilibrium I_L will maximize u_L subject to conditions (4.20) and (4.22). This means that L-types will not be offered their most-preferred contract subject to equation (4.20) (I_L^* in Figure 4.2) since that would be

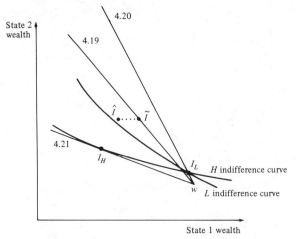

State 2 wealth

4.20

4.19

$\hat{I}$ ..... $\tilde{I}$

4.21

I_H

I_L H indifference curve

w   L indifference curve

State 1 wealth

Figure 4.3

preferred by H–types to I_H, and I_L is feasible if and only if it is purchased exclusively by L-types.

The contract I_L offered to L-types at equilibrium is depicted in Figure 4.2. The striking thing is that H-types are exactly as well off as if the L-types did not exist, but the L-types are worse off as a result of the presence of individuals with a higher risk of accident. Without the H-types the L-types would have I_L^* at equilibrium, but as it is, they wind up with I_L.

The pair (I_H, I_L) of Figure 4.2 is the only candidate for equilibrium, but even this may not *be* an equilibrium. Suppose that n_H is relatively small and that the line corresponding to equation (4.20) is close to the line depicting equation (4.19), as shown in Figure 4.3. Then there is a profitable contract $\hat{I} = \hat{I}_H = \hat{I}_L$ that both groups prefer to the contracts I_H and I_L. (Contract $\hat{I}$ is profitable because it provides the same claim as $\tilde{I}$ but requires a larger premium than $\tilde{I}$, which is on the zero profit line.) Therefore, (I_H, I_L) is not an equilibrium, and the following theorem has been proved.

Theorem 4.4. *If $\pi_H^1 < \pi_L^1$ and n_H/n is sufficiently close to zero, then there does not exist a competitive equilibrium in the insurance market.*

Return to the case for which a competitive equilibrium exists. Is the equilibrium (I_H, I_L) of Figure 4.2 Pareto optimal? Assuming knowledge of each individual's risk parameter π_i^1, it is not difficult to design a scheme

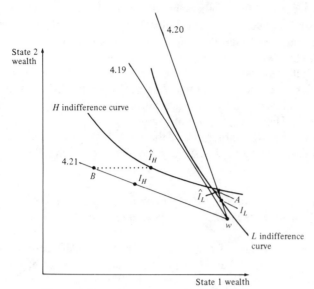

Figure 4.4

that would make everyone better off. If L-types consume I_L^* (Figure 4.2) and H-types continue to consume I_H, then we have a feasible allocation that makes the former better off without affecting the utility of the latter. (Can you modify this outcome slightly so that everyone is better off?) But how would a planner or a government offer I_L^* to low-risk individuals without the high-risk individuals purchasing the contract by masquerading as low-risk individuals? Even though (I_H, I_L^*) Pareto dominates (I_H, I_L), it would be impossible to implement the former. Is there a superior allocation that could be implemented? Such an allocation, denoted $\hat{I}$ in Figure 4.4, exists if n_H/n is not too large. Note first that H-types prefer $\hat{I}_H$ to I_H, but they also prefer $\hat{I}_H$ to $\hat{I}_L$ so they would choose $\hat{I}_H$; they would not choose to masquerade as low-risk individuals. Second, the low-risk individuals themselves prefer $\hat{I}_L$ to I_L and to $\hat{I}_H$. Third, $\hat{I}_L$ yields a positive profit since it requires a higher premium than A, which pays the same claim and yields a zero profit. Finally, $\hat{I}_H$ entails a loss since it requires a lower premium than B while paying the same claim as B, which breaks even. But the planner could offer $\hat{I}_H$ and $\hat{I}_L$ to the community as long as $n_L(A^1 - \hat{I}_L^1) \geq n_H(\hat{I}_H^1 - B^1)$, and this will be possible if n_H/n is not too large. [Note that $A^1 - \hat{I}_L^1$ will be very small since $\hat{I}_L$ must be near I_L to ensure $u_H(\hat{I}_H) > u_H(\hat{I}_L)$.] The allocation $\hat{I}$ could not be a competitive equilibrium since competition would lead some insurance companies to attract low-risk customers away from others by offering $\lambda \hat{I}_L + (1 - \lambda)A$ for some real number λ between zero and unity. Since $\lambda < 1$, this contract will provide the same coverage as $\hat{I}_L$ at a lower premium. If λ is sufficiently close to 1, the new contract will provide almost the same profit per customer as $\hat{I}_L$, but the total profit will be greater since the insurer will have only low-risk customers. Although $\hat{I}$ is not a competitive equilibrium, it could be implemented by a planner since each risk group i would rationally choose $\hat{I}_i$. Therefore, (I_H, I_L) of Figure 4.2 is not Pareto optimal if n_H/n is not too large; the larger is n_H, the more high-risk individuals there are to be subsidized by the low-risk group. This is the final theorem of this section:

Theorem 4.5. *If $\pi_H^1 < \pi_L^1$ and n_H/n is not too large, then a competitive equilibrium of the insurance market is not Pareto optimal.*

In the model we have just discussed an individual can be certain of owning a house – that is, of having the same wealth in any event – by entering into two contracts. He buys a house conditional on $t = 1$ (no fire) and pays an insurance premium that leads to his receiving a gross payment equal to the initial value of his house in the case of fire. In effect, he buys a house conditional on $t = 2$. The probability that the event 2 is realized is low, but the price of the house (the insurance premium) will also be low. Since there is a manageable number of contracts to negotiate, the competitive insurance markets economy is informationally viable whereas the WMS is not. However, in satisfying one criterion of performance, we have violated another. Even when an equilibrium exists, the corresponding allocation is not guaranteed to be Pareto optimal.

[Wilson (1977) points out that existence of a pooling equilibrium is assured if we modify the assumption of competitive behavior. Let I_0 maximize u_L subject to equation (4.19). There is a contract $\hat{I}$ close to I_0 such that each L-type prefers $\hat{I}$ to I_0 and each H-type prefers I_0 to $\hat{I}$. Although $\hat{I}$ lies to the right of the line (4.19) (why?), it will generate a positive profit if it is close enough to the line since it will be purchased exclusively by low-risk types. Only the high-risk individuals will buy I_0, which breaks even only when it is purchased by both types. Now I_0 will be unprofitable and it will be withdrawn. Wilson assumes that insurance companies anticipate this when contemplating the introduction of $\hat{I}$. If they do, they will realize that I_0 will be withdrawn and everyone will buy $\hat{I}$, which will then lead to losses since $\hat{I}$ is to the right of the line (4.19). Hence, I_0 is an equilibrium if insurance companies anticipate – to some extent – the reaction to the introduction of new contracts.]

As an introduction to the treatment of rational expectations equilibrium in Section 4.10 we consider, in the next section, why an equilibrium in the Arrow–Debreu model is Pareto optimal regardless of how individual probability beliefs differ, while in the Rothschild–Stiglitz model the presence of even two distinct subjective probabilities can undermine Pareto optimality.

4.9   Pareto optimality reconsidered

Continue to assume that there are $\tau = 2^n$ simple events corresponding to the subsets of $\{1, 2, \ldots, n\}$. Again, T is the family of all such subsets. The compound event "i has an accident" is the event $\{t: i \in t\}$. Let this event be donoted A_i. Let π^{A_i} be the probability that i has an accident. We are assuming that this is objectively defined and is known by i. The Rothschild–Stiglitz treatment of uncertainty (Section 4.8) assumes that i can purchase a contract that has a payoff to i conditional on event A_i only. This allows one to define i's expected utility exclusively in terms of π^{A_i}:

$$u_i(I^1, I^2) = \pi^{A_i}U_i(I_i^2) + (1 - \pi^{A_i})U_i(I_i^1) \tag{4.23}$$

where I_i^2 is i's wealth when A_i is realized and I_i^1 is i's wealth when A_i is not realized. Expression (4.23) does not involve the accident probabilities of other individuals because in the Rothschild–Stiglitz model and for insurance contracts as actually written individual i cannot purchase a contract that has a payoff conditional on someone else having an accident.

This limitation on the nature of the contract that one can purchase affects the way that Pareto optimality is defined. A set of contracts is Pareto optimal if it is feasible and there is no other feasible set of contracts that gives each individual i more expected utility according to definition (4.23). We would probably wish to impose the additional constraint that the probabilities π^{A_i} are revealed only through individual contract choices and are not assumed to be known in advance by the planner. The thing to note at this point is that Pareto optimality is defined in terms of the objective probabilities π^{A_i} via equation (4.23). [In the case of exactly two risk categories, H (high) and L (low), π^{A_i} is expressed as π_i^2 in Section 4.8 with $i = H$ and L, respectively.]

The Arrow–Debreu model, with or without securities, requires each individual i to form a probability assessment π_i^t for each of the simple events t in T. This will be determined in part by the probability that i has an accident, and this will be known by i. But for all t, π_i^t will depend also on all of the other objective probabilities π_j^t. Let us suppose that each individual i estimates the probability distribution π_i^t ($t = 1, 2, \ldots, \tau$) in some way. The subjective probability distributions influence individual decisions, but an equilibrium of either the contingent contracts economy or the Walrasian mechanism with securities is bound to be Pareto optimal. However, Pareto optimality is defined in terms of individual expected utility, which is in turn defined in terms of the subjective probabilities since $u_i(x_i) = \Sigma_{t \in T} \pi_i^t U_i(x_i^t)$. In the present context this is specious. Suppose, for example, that the objective probabilities π^{A_i} have only two possible values, high (π_H^2) and low (π_L^2). Suppose further that each person assumes that all others are in the same risk category as himself. Then i will set π_i^t equal to $(\pi_H^2)^{\#t}(1 - \pi_H^2)^{n-\#t}$ if he is a high-risk type and will set π_i^t equal to $(\pi_L^2)^{\#t}(1 - \pi_L^2)^{n-\#t}$ if he is a low-risk type. (Here $\#t$ is the number of individuals in t.) A low-risk person will expect to observe only $\pi_L^2 n$ accidents but will in fact observe $\pi_L^2 n_L + \pi_H^2 n_H$ accidents, a larger number. His expectations are not rational and they will be revised. [If an individual knows that there are only two risk types, he can determine π_0^2, the probability of a randomly selected individual having an accident. This will simply be the number of observed accidents divided by n. Each individual can employ π_0^2 and can set $\pi_i^t = (\pi_0^2)^{\#t}(1-\pi_0^2)^{n-\#t}$. However, if π_H^2 is much different from π_L^2, this will not be a good estimate of the true probability of event t even though π_0^2 will predict accurately the expected number of accidents.]

An Arrow–Debreu equilibrium – an equilibrium of either the contingent contracts economy, or the WMS, with complete markets – is Pareto optimal with respect to individual preferences determined by the respective individual probability distributions, however these are arrived at. But the individual probability distributions might be quite misleading relative to some objective standard. We should employ a criterion of performance that gives more weight to the objective probabilities. (Section 4.8 is really a discussion of the way that the information required to determine the objective probability distribution can be uncovered by the planner when individuals reveal information through their choices.)

Strictly speaking, the Arrow–Debreu models are not privacy preserving in the presence of uncertainty. If there is a sense in which probabilities are objective, a demanding test of Pareto optimality would require a definition of individual expected utility in terms of the objective probabilities. However, the proof that an Arrow–Debreu equilibrium is Pareto optimal assumes that individual behavior is conditioned by the same probabilities that are used to define expected utility. This implicitly assumes that each individual knows a good deal about other individuals' characteristics. In other words, if it is claimed that an Arrow–Debreu competitive equilibrium is Pareto optimal, and Pareto optimality is defined in terms of the objective probabilities, then it is implicit that each individual is aware of more than just his own specific characteristic. Although knowledge is dispersed initially, and it is a mistake to assume that individuals are aware of the characteristics of others at the outset, it may be the case that enough of the private information is revealed in prices to rescue the first welfare theorem. This is certainly the case when there is no uncertainty. The next section shows how prices also reveal information about agents' beliefs concerning the likelihood of events.

In order to accept the proof of the Pareto optimality of equilibrium (in either the contingent contracts economy or the Walrasian mechanism with securities) as a confirmation of satisfactory performance by the market system in the real world, one must verify that markets are complete and that the probabilities that enter individual utility functions and demands are meaningful. The completeness of markets assumption requires the existence of a futures market for every commodity in every event in the case of the contingent contracts mechanism and a securities market for every event in the case of the Walrasian mechanism with securities. As has been pointed out already, one fact standing in the way of the existence of a complete set of markets is the astronomical number of logically possible events. There are ways of simplifying, as in the case of the competitive insurance markets model, which reduces the number of markets from 2^n to 2, but, as we have seen, existence and Pareto optimality of competitive equilibrium is not necessarily preserved.

4.10 Rational expectations equilibrium

The contingent contracts mechanism will be used to show how prices can transmit information to uninformed agents about the beliefs of agents who are well informed about the likelihood of particular events.

The distinction between objective probabilities and subjective probabilities is not as clear-cut as suggested in the previous section. Individuals will have access to two types of objective evidence that shed light on the probability distribution from which the states of nature, or simple events, are drawn. One type of objective evidence concerns quantitative signals, such as atmospheric pressure, that an individual can use to refine his estimate of the probability of good weather for planting crops. Let σ_i be the signal observed by individual i. The vector $\tilde{\sigma} = (\tilde{\sigma}_1, \tilde{\sigma}_2, \ldots, \tilde{\sigma}_n)$ is a list of random variables $\tilde{\sigma}_i$, one for each individual. A realization of $\tilde{\sigma}_i$ is a signal σ_i observed by trader i. The random vector σ is correlated with the random variable we have called the state of nature and that has τ possible realizations. Let $\pi_i(\sigma)$ be the probability distribution assumed by individual i to govern the random selection of a state of nature conditional on the realization σ of the signal vector $\tilde{\sigma}$. A particular trader i will know only

σ_i, not the entire vector, and therefore i cannot immediately determine $\pi_i(\sigma)$, which is the counterpart to the objective probability distribution discussed in the previous section. If the signal σ_i were the only source of information available to i concerning the probability distribution of the states of nature, then i would use the "subjective" probability distribution $\pi_i(\sigma_i)$, which is the distribution conditional on the realization σ_i of $\tilde{\sigma}_i$.

There is a second kind of evidence that can be used by i to make an inference concerning $\pi_i(\sigma)$. The signals actually observed by traders will influence their assessment of the probability distribution over states of nature, and the individual trader's estimate of the probability distribution will be used to define individual expected utility, which, of course, influences individual demands. Hence, there is a relationship between the signals received by individuals and the market clearing prices that emerge. An individual trader's signal affects that individual's probability assessment, which is incorporated into individual utility, which governs individual demands. Since the configuration of individual demands is reflected in the market clearing prices, there is a sense in which the prices observed by i embody information concerning the signals observed by other traders.

The link between the vector of signals σ and the prices that emerge might appear to be a nebulous one. However, one can imagine situations in which traders could be informed in a rough way of the signals observed by others by observing prices. Suppose that σ is realized and that $\pi_i^t(\sigma)$ is very very small. Suppose also that $\pi_a^t(\sigma_a)$ is also very small for all $a \neq i$. That is, each trader a, other than i, receives a signal σ_a that is correlated with the probability distribution of states of nature in a way that allows each $a \neq i$ to conclude that the probability of event t (given σ_a) is almost zero. Suppose that individual i's signal σ_i provides no information about the specific event t and i concludes that event t is reasonably likely. The *initial* market clearing prices p^t will be very low since almost no one will demand commodities in event t because almost no one believes that there is any chance that t will be realized. If individual i knows that other traders are "experts" in predicting the likelihood of t – their signals provide good information concerning the probability of event t – individual i can conclude from his observation of the low prices p^t that t is in fact very unlikely. *Then i will revise his demands.* We will not be at equilibrium after all even though we began with a Walrasian equilibrium price system that cleared all markets *given* the individual expected utility functions. The individual expected utility functions will change as individual probability distributions are revised in the light of the new information embodied in prices. When this process of revising individual traders' estimates of probabilities based on traders' observations of prices comes to an end, we have a *rational expectations equilibrium*. At a rational expectations equilibrium configuration of prices not only do all markets clear but the equilibrium prices when observed by traders are consistent with each individual's probability distribution π_i in the sense that an individual knowing the mechanism by which market clearing prices are determined would expect to see these prices when the signal vector σ was transmitted and each i used the probability distribution $\pi_i = \pi_i(\sigma)$ to guide his behavior.

Radner (1979) was the first to show that the relationship between signals and prices is not at all nebulous but is, on the contrary, one-to-one (except in exceedingly rare cases). An example will clarify the notion of agents learning about the signals transmitted to other agents by observing prices.

There are two states of nature ($\tau = 2$), two commodities ($k = 2$), and two households ($n = 2$). There is no production. Let x_i^t be individual i's consumption of the first good in state t and let y_i^t be individual i's consumption of the second good in state t. For each i, $U_i(x_i^t, y_i^t) = \ln x_i^t + \ln y_i^t$ so that expected utility is

$$u_i = \pi_i^1(\ln x_i^1 + \ln y_i^1) + \pi_i^2(\ln x_i^2 + \ln y_i^2)$$

Of course, $\pi_i^1 + \pi_i^2 = 1$. Now π_i is a function of the signal σ_i received by i. For simplicity, suppose that $\sigma_1^1 = \sigma_1^2 = 0$. That is, individual i receives signal σ_i^t if state t is realized, but since $\sigma_1^1 = \sigma_1^2$, individual 1 learns absolutely nothing from his signal. On the other hand, $\sigma_2^1 = 1$ and $\sigma_2^2 = 2$; individual 2's signal reveals the state that has been realized. In general, individual i enters into contracts after he observes σ_i but before the realized state is known to him. The present example is an extreme case of this phenomenon. Trader 1's signal tells him nothing, so we assume that $\pi_1^1 = \pi_1^1(\sigma_1) = \frac{1}{2}$, and that trader 2's signal tells him everything, so we assume that $\pi_2^1(\sigma_2) = 1$ when $\sigma_2 = 1$ and $\pi_2^1(\sigma_2) = 0$ when $\sigma_2 = 2$. Obviously, 2's demands for commodities conditional on $t = 1$ will be quite different under the different signals received by 2. We will show how trader 1 can learn from this. (The zealous reader can verify that the following argument does not depend on the specification of π_1^1.)

Uncertainty is assumed to affect the economy through the individual endowments. Specifically, set $w_1^1 = w_1^2 = (1, 0)$ and $w_2^1 = (0, 1)$ and $w_2^2 = (1, 1)$. Let us compute the equilibrium.

First, assume that $\pi_1^1 = \frac{1}{2}$. Let p^t be the price of good 1 in state t and let q^t be the price of good 2 in state t. Individual 1's wealth will be $p^1 + p^2$ and 2's wealth will be $q^1 + p^2 + q^2$. (A complete set of markets is assumed.)

(*i*) $\sigma = (0, 1)$; that is, event 1 is realized and trader 2 knows it. The individual demands are as follows:

$$x_1^1 = \frac{p^1 + p^2}{4p^1} \qquad y_1^1 = \frac{p^1 + p^2}{4q^1}$$

$$x_2^1 = \frac{q^1 + p^2 + q^2}{2p^1} \qquad y_2^1 = \frac{q^1 + p^2 + q^2}{2q^1}$$

$$x_1^2 = \frac{p^1 + p^2}{4p^2} \qquad y_1^2 = \frac{p^1 + p^2}{4q^2}$$

$$x_2^2 = 0 \qquad y_2^2 = 0$$

To verify these demand functions, show that for every pair of goods individual 1's marginal rate of substitution as determined by the utility function $\frac{1}{2} \ln x_1^1 + \frac{1}{2} \ln y_1^1 + \frac{1}{2} \ln x_1^2 + \frac{1}{2} \ln y_1^2$ equals the associated price ratio and that the total value of 1's demands equals his wealth. Then show that individual 2's marginal rate of substitution for state 1 goods only equals the state 1 price ratio and that the value of individual 2's demands equals his wealth. Individual 2 will not devote any of his wealth to the purchase of state 2 commodities since he knows that state 2 is impossible when $\sigma_2 = 1$. Now, equate demand and supply in order to solve for the market clearing price ratios:

$$x_1^1 + x_2^1 = 1 \quad \text{and} \quad y_1^1 + y_2^1 = 1 \qquad (4.24)$$

$$x_1^2 + x_2^2 = 2 \quad \text{and} \quad y_1^2 + y_2^2 = 1 \qquad (4.25)$$

Arbitrarily setting $p^1 = 1$ yields $p^1 = 1$, $q^1 = 1$, $p^2 = \frac{1}{7}$, and $q^2 = \frac{2}{7}$, which we write as $p^*(0, 1) = (1, 1, \frac{1}{7}, \frac{2}{7})$, where $(0, 1) = \sigma$ in this case.

(*ii*) $\sigma = (0, 2)$: State 2 is realized and trader 2 knows it. This time, trader 2 will not devote any of his wealth to state 1 goods. The demands, which are verified as in case (i), are as follows:

$$x_1^1 = \frac{p^1 + p^2}{4p^1} \qquad y_1^1 = \frac{p^1 + p^2}{4q^1}$$

$$x_2^1 = 0 \qquad y_2^1 = 0$$

$$x_1^2 = \frac{p^1 + p^2}{4p^2} \qquad y_1^2 = \frac{p^1 + p^2}{4q^2}$$

$$x_2^2 = \frac{q^1 + p^2 + q^2}{2p^2} \qquad y_2^2 = \frac{q^1 + p^2 + q^2}{2q^2}$$

Employ equations (4.24) and (4.25) to equate demand and supply. With $p^1 = 1$, we have $q^1 = 1$, $p^2 = 3$, and $q^2 = 6$, which we write as $p^*(0, 2) = (1, 1, 3, 6)$.

Since $p^*(0, 1)$ is different from $p^*(0, 2)$, individual 1 can accurately determine the state of nature by observing prices. If $p = (1, 1, \frac{1}{7}, \frac{2}{7})$ is observed, trader 1 will want to recontract because he will know that event 1 was realized and he will not want to devote any part of his wealth to the purchase of state 2 goods. If $p = (1, 1, 3, 6)$ is observed, trader 1 will also want to recontract; specifically, he will want to reallocate to state 2 goods that part of his wealth that he had used to order state 1 goods. Therefore, $p*$ is not a rational expectations equilibrium. Note that person 1 only needs enough economic horse sense to infer that state 2 prices will be relatively high when trader 2 has information that state 1 is impossible.

Let $p**$ denote a rational expectations equilibrium. It is straightforward to show that $p**(0, 1) = (1, 1, 0, 0)$ and $p**(0, 2) = (0, 0, 1, 2)$. We have $p^2 = q^2 = 0$ when $\sigma = (0, 1)$ is realized because there is no market for the state 2 endowments; no one has anything to gain by offering them for sale. Analogously, $p^1 = q^1 = 0$ when $\sigma = (0, 2)$. Now verify that $p**$ is an equilibrium when trader 1 uses observed prices to determine the realized state of nature.

Since $p**(0, 1) \neq p**(0, 2)$, individual 1 can determine the true state of nature when these prices are observed. Let us check that these would be the market clearing prices when both traders know which state has been realized.

(*i*) $\sigma = (0, 1)$: Each trader would spend all his wealth on state 1 goods. Since $p^2 = q^2 = 0$, individual 1's wealth is p^1 and 2's wealth is q^1. Equating marginal rates of substitution and price ratios, assuming that all wealth is devoted to state 1 goods, yields

$$x_1^1 = \tfrac{1}{2} \quad \text{and} \quad y^1 = \frac{p^1}{2q^1}$$

$$x_2^1 = \frac{q^1}{2p^1} \quad \text{and} \quad y_2^1 = \tfrac{1}{2}$$

Arbitrarily setting $p^1 = 1$ and equating demand and supply yields $q^1 = 1$. We cannot yet conclude that $p**(0, 1)$ is an equilibrium until we verify that $p**(0, 2)$ would be an equilibrium and the two states would be distinguished.

(*ii*) $\sigma = (0, 2)$: Each trader would spend all his wealth on state 2 goods. Since $p^1 = q^1 = 0$, individual 1's wealth is p^2 and 2's is $p^1 + q^2$. We have

$$x_1^2 = \tfrac{1}{2} \quad \text{and} \quad y_1^2 = \frac{p^2}{2q^2}$$

$$x_2^2 = \frac{p^2 + q^2}{2p^2} \quad \text{and} \quad y_2^2 = \frac{p^2 + q^2}{2q^2}$$

Set demand equal to supply and $p^2 = 1$. This yields $q^2 = 2$, as claimed.

For completeness, we can set $(x_i^2, y_i^2) = w_i^2$ when $\sigma = (0, 1)$ and $(x_i^1, y_i^1) = w_i^1$ when $\sigma = (0, 2)$.

Both the regimes $p^*(\sigma)$ and $p^{**}(\sigma)$ allow uninformed traders to determine the entire vector σ of signals received by the expert or informed traders, but the former is not consistent with equilibrium when traders use a model of the relationship between $\tilde{\sigma}$ and prices to infer something about the information possessed by other traders. In the example trader 1 discovers the realized state of nature σ by observing prices $p^*(\sigma)$ and then revises his demands; they are no longer the demand functions that led to the original market clearing price regime $p^*(\sigma)$. A new price system will emerge as a result of the modifications in the demand functions of the uninformed traders, individual 1 in this case. Although $p^*(\sigma)$ can be used to determine σ, it is not the price regime that will prevail when σ is generally known.

To find the proper rational expectations equilibrium regime p^{**} as a function of σ, assume that each trader i knows the entire signal vector σ as soon as it is transmitted. This is not the case (i observes only σ_i) but the assumption is merely the first step in a thought experiment that will clarify the definition. If $\sigma \neq \sigma'$, we assume that $\pi_i(\sigma) \neq \pi_i(\sigma')$ for some i. Otherwise, we would not bother to distinguish the signal vectors σ and σ'. Assuming that σ is known as soon as it is realized, each i will use the probability distribution $\pi_i(\sigma)$ to define his expected utility function, which in turn defines the individual's demand functions. We define $p^{**}(\sigma)$ to be the Walrasian equilibrium configuration of prices that emerges when σ is realized and individual behavior is governed by the probability distributions $\pi_i(\sigma)$, $i = 1, 2, \ldots, n$. Radner has shown that, except in very rare cases, $p^{**}(\sigma)$ will be distinct from $p^{**}(\sigma')$ if $\pi_i(\sigma)$ is different from $\pi_i(\sigma')$ for some i. Ruling out the rare cases, it follows that traders *can* use the price relationship p^{**} to identify the realized signal vector σ. But we cannot be sure that $p^{**}(\sigma)$ is consistent with equilibrium unless we believe that $p^{**}(\sigma)$ would emerge when traders do acquire knowledge of the entire signal vector *and* place orders for goods on the basis of this knowledge. Since $p^{**}(\sigma)$ is defined on the assumption that each i has knowledge of σ, it does meet both of the requirements of a rational expectations equilibrium: (1) it serves to distinguish different signal vectors and (2) once the signal vector is generally known, all markets clear under the price system specified by p^{**} and no trader would wish to recontract after discovering that $p^{**}(\sigma)$ is an equilibrium. The function p^* satisfies the first condition but not the second.

Let $f^{**}(\sigma)$ denote the allocation that emerges along with the rational expectations equilibrium $p^{**}(\sigma)$ when the signal vector σ is transmitted.

When σ is transmitted, the appropriate probability distribution to use in defining individual expected utility in order to test for Pareto optimality of $f^{**}(\sigma)$ is $\pi_i(\sigma)$ for each trader i. At the outset individual i has knowledge only of the component σ_i of σ. In other words, knowledge is dispersed. When knowledge is dispersed, we require an economic system to transmit information concerning the relevant properties of one agent's characteristic to other agents. By the same token, everything that is known about the economic environment enters into the characterization of a Pareto-optimal allocation, whether or not there is *general* knowledge. Now, $p^{**}(\sigma)$ is by definition the equilibrium price system that emerges in the contingent contracts economy when each agent i's decisions are governed by the probability distribution $\pi_i(\sigma)$. Therefore, we can apply Theorem 4.1 and claim that $f^{**}(\sigma)$ is Pareto optimal. Furthermore, agents eventually will employ the probability distributions $\pi_i(\sigma)$ given σ because the market clearing prices will inform them of the signals received by other agents. The rational expectations equilibrium allocation is plausible and Pareto optimal.

4.11 The theory of teams

One of the most striking theorems in modern economics is the informational efficiency theorem. If $\mathcal{M}$ is a privacy-preserving Pareto-satisfactory resource allocation mechanism that responds in a continuous way to changes in agent characteristics, then the dimension of $\mathcal{M}$'s message space is at least as large as that of the Walrasian mechanism. This is part of the claim of the private ownership market system to information processing economy. The efficiency theorem is very important, but it is concerned with just one type of informational cost involved in the operation of an economic system.

Not only can mechanisms differ with respect to (1) the dimension of the message an agent is required to transmit, but they can also differ with respect to (2) the amount of internal computation required in order for the agent to determine the appropriate message to transmit and (3) the amount of time that passes before the sequence $\{m^1, m^2, \ldots, m^t, \ldots\}$ of messages converges to a stationary point – that is, the amount of external information processing. They also differ with respect to (4) the extent of communication among the agents.

Team theory, a term coined by J. Marschak (1955) in a seminal paper, addresses the last two of these informational issues. It seeks to determine procedures for generating desirable outcomes after only a few iterations and to uncover the terms on which society can devote additional resources to extend the communication network among agents in order to obtain a more desirable outcome. Team theory is equally well suited to the design of an optimal decision structure for a single firm attempting to maximize expected profit. In either case, subunits of the organization possess private information not known to other units or even to the center. Some of this information can be transmitted to the center (or planner), which then makes a decision affecting the activities of the subunits. Part of the center's decision may be to communicate to each subunit the private information gleaned from all units. This adds to the cost of running the organization or mechanism, and it is part of the objective of team theory to determine conditions under which such costs are warranted.

Treatments of resource allocation in the team theory vein usually assume that the agents agree on the organization's goals, or payoff function, and are committed to playing their part in the maximization of the payoff, hence the word *team*. But team theory is not in principle incompatible with the assumption that the subunits also have private incentives – the desire to avoid hard work, for example – that may conflict with the maximization of the organization's payoff. In fact, this problem is central to Groves (1973), a paper that inspired one of the most important developments in public finance of this century. (See Section 3.9.)

Even if the team members are assumed to suppress their private incentives, the success of the organization is problematic because of the dispersion-of-knowledge phenomenon. (The reader might benefit from a review of Chapter 2 at this point.)

The two most distinctive features of the team theory approach are the assumption that there is some a priori knowledge about individual characteristics that is known to all agents, a possibility that is not exploited, or even recognized, in conventional general equilibrium theory, and the willingness to consider resource allocation mechanisms that possess a memory. A resource allocation mechanism depends on a memory if the rules require an agent at time t to relate his message not only to his own characteristic and the messages of other agents transmitted at the same time but also to the messages transmitted during the previous period. It is customary in team theory to assume that the process terminates after two rounds, so we can define a mechanism merely by specifying how m^1 and m^2 are to be selected. This certainly allows us to claim that the mechanism is economical in terms of criterion 3.

The shared a priori information is usually assumed to be the functional form of the production functions. Knowledge is dispersed in the sense that the specific parameters of a firm's production function are known only to that firm's manager. Communication between agents takes place through agent 0, the planner, or center, who then reports some or all of the information received by an agent to all other agents. Much of team theory is concerned with the issue of improving the utility of the outcome at the cost of additional communication among agents (via the center).

For example, suppose that there are three commodities Q, K, and L and that each consumer has the utility function $Q + \lambda L$, where $\lambda > 0$. Consumers are endowed with L and nothing else. Let L_0 denote the total amount held by households. Each firm j uses K and L to produce Q, and $Q_j = F_j(\theta_j, K_j, L_j)$ is the amount of output produced by j when it uses K_j units of K, a resource, and L_j units of L if its production parameter is θ_j. Pareto optimality requires the maximization of $\Sigma F_j(\theta_j, K_j, L_j) + \lambda(L_0 - \Sigma L_j)$, which is equivalent to maximizing

$$\sum F_j(\theta_j, K_j, L_j) - \lambda \sum L_j = \sum Q_j - \lambda \sum L_j \qquad (4.26)$$

Summation is taken over all firms j. There are r firms in total. The total amount of the resource available is K_0, and this is initially known to the planner. Here K_0 may be a random variable. The production parameter θ_j is random, and the θ_j are assumed to be independently and identically distributed. Hence it is necessary to maximize the expectation of the sum (4.26).

To define a mechanism with minimal communication, set $m_0^1 = 0$ and $m_j^1 = (\theta_j, L_j)$ for firm j. Then L_j is a decision taken by firm j dependent on the realization of θ_j, which it alone can observe. Firm j can observe only m_j^1 in period 1, but the planner observes the entire configuration m since the messages are reported to the planner. In period 2 the planner allocates resources to the firms, so $m_0^2 = (K_1, K_2, \ldots, K_r)$, and hence each firm's output is $F_j(\theta_j, m_{0j}^2, m_{j2}^1) = F_j(\theta_j, K_j, L_j)$. For each firm j, $m_j^2 = F_j(\theta_j, K_j, L_j)$. Assume that $F_j(\theta_j, K_j, L_j) = \min\{\theta_j K_j, L_j\}$. Suppose that 1 is the largest possible value of θ_j and that π, a positive real number, is the probability that $\theta_j = 1$. A mechanism of this form is called a CEC mechanism: complete exchange of information with the center. Each firm discloses all of its private information to the center.

Define a specific CEC mechanism $\mathscr{E}_1$:

$$m_j^1 = (\theta_j, 0) \quad \text{if } \theta_j < 1 \quad \text{and} \quad m_j^1 = (\theta_j, K_0/\pi r) \quad \text{if } \theta_j = 1$$
$$m_{0j}^2 = 0 \quad \text{if } \theta_j < 1 \quad \text{and} \quad m_{0j}^2 = K_0/\pi r \quad \text{if } \theta_j = 1$$

In words, all of the resource is allocated, in equal measure, to the firms realizing the maximum output per unit of input. Since each firm manager knows this allocation rule and each wishes to cooperate in maximizing expected utility, arbitrary firm j will not hire any labor of $\theta_j < 1$ and will hire its share of labor otherwise.

The mechanism $\mathscr{E}_1$ is not the only possible CEC mechanism. We could define a new mechanism by specifying alternative decision rules m_j^1 and m_0^2, but $\mathscr{E}_1$ would appear to yield the highest expected utility of all CEC mechanisms. We will establish this claim indirectly by comparing it to a mechanism, which we will call $\mathscr{E}_2$, that requires a full exchange of information.

The expected utility of the ultimate outcome can be improved by having the planner report the results of the first round of communication to each firm. Accordingly, we set $m_0^1 = 0$, $m_j^1 = (\theta_j)$, and $m_0^2 = (K, \theta)$, where $K = (K_1, \ldots, K_r)$ and $\theta = (\theta_1, \ldots, \theta_r)$. In period 2 the firm is allowed to observe the production parameters of the other firms so L_j is not determined until then: $m_j^2 = (L_j, F_j(\theta_j, K_j, L_j))$. Such a mechanism is called a full exchange of information (FEI) mechanism.

Specify the FEI mechanism $\mathscr{E}_2$

$$m_{0j}^2 = K_j = \begin{cases} 0 & \text{if } \theta_j < \max\{\theta_1, \theta_2, \ldots, \theta_r\} = \theta^* \\ K_0/\#\{j: \theta_j = \theta^*\} & \text{if } \theta_j = \theta^* \end{cases}$$

($\#\{j: \theta_j = \theta^*\}$ is the number of firms j for which θ_j equals the maximum of the realized values of the production parameters.)

$$m_{j1}^2 = L_j = \begin{cases} 0 & \text{if } \theta_j < \theta^* \\ \theta_j K_j & \text{if } \theta_j = \theta^* \end{cases}$$

FEI mechanisms permit the achievement of a higher level of expected utility since each firm has more information about the production processes of other firms when it makes its employment decision. Such mechanisms are more costly to operate because of the more extensive information transmission. Whether such a trade-off would be in consumers' interests is hard to determine since it is very difficult to properly model the way that information processing consumes scarce resources. We can circumvent this difficulty by demonstrating that if the number r of firms is large, then the mechanisms $\mathscr{E}_1$ and $\mathscr{E}_2$ give almost the same expected utility. In that case the additional costs of information transmission required by $\mathscr{E}_2$ do not yield enough additional expected utility for $\mathscr{E}_2$ to represent a net improvement over $\mathscr{E}_1$. This is proved in Arrow and Radner (1979) for the general case.

For any realization $\theta_1, \theta_2, \ldots, \theta_r$ the mechanism $\mathscr{E}_2$ yields a total utility level of $\theta^* K_0 + \lambda(L_0 - \theta^* K_0)$. Therefore, the expected utility of $\mathscr{E}_2$ is

$$\lambda L_0 + K_0 (1 - \lambda)E(\max\{\theta_1, \theta_2, \ldots, \theta_r\})$$

where E is the expectation operator.

For a particular realization the mechanism $\mathscr{E}_1$ provides the following level of utility:

$$(K_0/\pi r)\#\{j: \theta_j = 1\} + \lambda(L_0 - K_0/\pi r)\#\{j: \theta_j = 1\})$$

If r is very large, then the probability that $\#\{j: \theta_j = 1\} = \pi r$ is almost 1 so that the expected utility of $\mathscr{E}_1$ is close to $(K_0/\pi r)\pi r + \lambda[L_0 - $

$(K_0/\pi r)\pi r]$, which equals $\lambda L_0 + (1 - \lambda)K_0$. Similarly, $E(\max\{\theta_1, \ldots, \theta_r\})$ will be close to 1 if r is very large. Therefore, the expected utility of $\mathscr{E}_2$ is close to $\lambda L_0 + K_0(1 - \lambda)$. Hence, both mechanisms yield roughly the same total utility if r is large; the additional communication costs of $\mathscr{E}_2$ are not offset by an increase in expected utility.

An intuitive explanation for this result and its generalization is not difficult to find. If each firm manager knows the distribution from which every firm's production parameter is drawn, then if the number of firms is large, this known probability distribution can be used as a good approximation to the unknown sample distribution, obviating the need for an exchange of information among firms to determine which firms have which production parameters.

The above argument has shown that under certain conditions the mechanism $\mathscr{E}_2$ is unnecessarily complex; it is defined only for the purpose of establishing an ideal against which the performance of other mechanisms can be compared. It plays the same role as the definition of Pareto optimality. It is a standard that, arguably, society would insist on if information processing were costless and computation were instantaneous. If that standard can be realized by means of an organization that requires only a partial exchange of information and limited computation, then one can make a case that the organization serves society well.

4.12   Summary

The central phenomenon with which a resource allocation mechanism must cope is dispersion of knowledge. The vector e of characteristics underlies the determination of Pareto-optimal outcomes, but no single agent has enough knowledge to specify e in any detail. We must assume that each agent i knows only the component e_i, called i's characteristic. Uncertainty introduces a special instance of dispersion of knowledge. Part of agent i's special information is the signal σ_i, which is correlated with the state of nature, but the state itself cannot be known before decisions are taken. However, individual preference depends on the entire vector σ of signals. From a formal standpoint nothing new appears to have been added by the incorporation of uncertainty. There is in fact an interesting difference.

Uncertainty apart, any application of a mechanism is concerned with a single environment, or vector of characteristics, e. One begins with a much larger set of environments E and requires the mechanism to perform satisfactorily with respect to every e in E for two reasons. First, the fundamental data of the economy are not immutable, and the mechanism must be able to cope with a variety of preferences and production recipes.

Second, insisting that the mechanism perform well over a wide range E of environments is a simple way of incorporating the notion that knowledge is dispersed and e is not known in advance. However, all of the results of Chapter 3 go through a fortiori if we assume that preferences and production recipes are unique and permanent. This is not the case with the notion of rational expectations equilibrium, which depends crucially on variability. Unless the signal vectors σ vary over time, agents cannot learn the relationship between prices and signal vectors and will be unable to use the former to determine the latter, which enter into individual preferences via the probability distribution. If there is variability, the relationship will be discovered and the dispersion of knowledge problem will be overcome. No planner could improve on the rational expectations equilibrium allocation to the satisfaction of all even if he or she knew e in great detail, including signal components.

There remains one great difficulty with the Walrasian mechanism in this setting: A market is required for each possible state of nature and contracts must be negotiated conditional upon states. Not only does this imply an extraordinary number of markets but it also runs into the difficulty of state verification or moral hazard. It will often be impossible to determine whether the state on which a contract is conditioned has occurred.

Even without a complete set of markets, traders can discover the relationship between private signals and market clearing prices. In other words, a rational expectations equilibrium can be defined just as well when markets are incomplete. The difficulty in the incomplete markets case is that competitive equilibria are unlikely to be Pareto optimal. To verify this, one can specify a conventional two-person, two-commodity exchange economy for which the endowment point is far from Pareto optimal but is, however, a competitive equilibrium allocation if there is no market for commodity 2.

4.13   Background

Probability theory was founded in the seventeenth century by the Swiss mathematician Jacques Bernoulli. His nephews Nicholas and Daniel Bernoulli made further advances. Daniel Bernoulli, in particular, provided an insight that is absolutely fundamental to the study of decision making under uncertainty. His resolution of the *St. Petersburg paradox* rested on the distinction between expected utility and expected monetary value, which he was the first to recognize. The St. Petersburg game requires a coin to be tossed repeatedly and pays the player 2^n dollars if the first occurrence of heads is on the nth toss. The player's expected monetary value is infinite, but few individuals would pay more than a small fee to play this game. Bernoulli posited diminishing marginal utility and showed how this would impose a limit on the fee that one would willingly pay. Bernoulli applied his argument to conventional business risks such as the transport of merchandise in ships. Two centuries passed before expected utility was given an axiomatic rationale in terms of individual preference for lotteries (von Neumann and Morgenstern, 1944). Herstein and Milnor (1953) provide a streamlined version of their result. The connection between risk-averse behavior and individual preference was formalized by Arrow and Pratt in the early 1960s [Pratt (1964) and the essay on risk aversion in Arrow (1971)].

The extension of the Walrasian model to a complete set of contingent claims markets in the face or uncertainty was accomplished by Arrow and Debreu in the early 1950s. Their work appeared in separate articles in French. English versions may be found in Arrow (1971) and Debreu (1959). The seminal paper on competitive insurance markets is Rothschild and Stiglitz (1976).

Radner (1968) began the task of refining general equilibrium theory to require individual plans to be consistent with the private information revealed by prices. Kreps (1977) and Green (1977), among others, provided examples to show that continuity and convexity of preference are not sufficient to ensure continuity of demands and existence of a rational expectations equilibrium. Difficulties caused by boundary endowments aside, continuity and convexity of preference imply continuity of demands in the certainty version of the Walrasian model or in the contingent contracts economy when individual beliefs are not informed by observed prices. However, if expectations are rational in the sense that individual beliefs are consistent with observations, then demands may be discontinuous even if preferences are continuous. As two price regimes converge to a common price vector, any slight difference between the two regimes suffices to allow an uninformed agent to infer that others have different private information in the two cases. In the limit this information is lost to the uninformed traders who may then make a radical change in their demands. Most of the subsequent work on the existence of a rational expectations equilibrium is designed to determine whether nonexistence is rare. Radner (1979) was the first to establish conditions under which nonexistence would be exceedingly unlikely. Grossman (1981) analyzes the case of complete markets. For the incomplete markets case, in which traders cannot order goods conditional on the realization of particular events, papers by Allen (1982) and Jordan (1982a) together with Radner (1979) establish that nonexistence is rare as long as the space of private information parameters does not have the same dimension as the price space. Otherwise, there are economies in which a rational expectations equilibrium does not exist and nonexistence is preserved under slight perturbations of individual preferences. In other words, the nonexistence example is not balanced precariously on a knife edge. The example was developed by Jordan and Radner and is discussed in Jordan and Radner (1982). That paper and Radner (1982) provide good introductions to rational expectations theory.

As explained in Section 4.10, the team theory approach to resource allocation was developed in Marschak (1955).

EXERCISES

4.1 Assume one commodity and two states of nature. The individual's endowment is w^t in state t and $0 < w^2 < w^1$. Let $U(I) = \ln I$ be the utility derived from I units of wealth. A consumption plan $x = (x^1, x^2)$ specifies wealth in each state and π is the probability of state 1. The individual can insure against a drop in wealth from w^1 to w^2 by buying insurance at a price of p: If y^2 units of insurance are purchased, the individual pays a premium of py^2 dollars and will receive a net claim – net of the premium paid – of y^2 dollars if state 2 occurs. Let $u(x)$ be the expected utility of plan x. (i) Show that $U'(I) > 0$ and $U''(I) < 0$ for all $I > 0$. (ii) Define the individual's optimization problem. (iii) Compute the marginal rate of substitution as a function of x and explain how and why it varies with π. (iv) Compute the demand functions $x^t(p)$, $t = 1, 2$. Compute $\partial x^t / \partial p$ and interpret. (v) Under what conditions would $x^1(p)$ equal $x^2(p)$?

4.2 For the competitive insurance markets model of Section 4.8 set $w_H = w_L = (24, 8)$, $U_H(I) = U_L(I) = 2I^{1/2}$, and $\pi_L^1 = \frac{1}{2}$, $\pi_H^1 = \frac{1}{4}$. (i) Compute the marginal rates of substitution for the two groups and explain their relative magnitudes. (ii) Show why a pooling contract cannot be a competitive equilibrium. (iii) Compute the equilibrium allocation, assuming that a separating equilibrium exists. (iv) Determine the conditions under which an equilibrium exists.

4.3 Construct a simple example of an economy in which preferences are self-regarding but the Walrasian competitive equilibrium is not Pareto optimal because one of the markets is missing.

4.4 The proof of Theorem 4.3 implicitly assumes that the contract that maximizes u_i subject to a convex constraint set is unique. Prove that this is implied by $U'' < 0$ and weak monotonicity of U.

CHAPTER 5

Incentive compatibility

This chapter presents three important results on the possibility of designing a resource allocation mechanism that gives each agent the incentive to follow the rules in every situation.

The proof that a Walrasian competitive equilibrium is Pareto optimal does not assume a large number of agents. It does assume that agents take prices as given. Section 5.1 shows that this assumption is suspect: *Any* mechanism that improves the well-being of each agent and yields Pareto-optimal outcomes can be manipulated. Someone, in some situation, will have an incentive to violate the rules governing the behavior of agents. Section 5.2 proves that any gain from a violation of the rules of the Walrasian mechanism will be miniscule if each commodity has a large number of suppliers. Therefore, it will not be worth anyone's while departing from prescribed behavior in that case. The last section shows that manipulation – a rule violation that cannot be detected – is inevitable in mechanisms that determine the Pareto-optimal supply of a public good and, unlike the case of the Walrasian mechanism, the difficulties do not fade as the number of agents increase, whatever mechanism is used.

The phenomenon on which to focus attention is the ability of an agent to influence prices by taking into consideration the effects of his decision on demand or supply. The most easily understood instance is that of a monopoly. The monopoly will optimize by producing at the point where marginal revenue equals marginal cost. By definition, no other firm supplies a product that is considered a close substitute for the monopolist's output. Therefore, the demand curve confronting the monopoly is downward sloping, and price will exceed marginal cost if the latter equals marginal revenue. Let p be a price regime at which all markets clear. Suppose that the monopoly produces y_1 units of commodity 1. Then p_1 will exceed the marginal cost of producing good 1. *If* the monopoly were able to sell any amount it produced, then y_1 would not be its optimal supply *given p_1.* A larger level of output, where marginal cost equals p_1, is profit maximizing given p_1. However, the monopoly realizes that if demand is y_1 under price regime p, then an increase in its output would result in a decline in

p_1 since there would be excess supply. The monopoly can provide its shareholders with more profit at equilibrium by violating the Walrasian rule "optimize given prices" and instead exploiting the relationship between its own supply and the price of its output.

Even a simple numerical illustration of this phenomenon would require specification of the ownership shares in the monopoly so that the utility of each shareholder is shown to be lower when the firm takes prices as given. There is, however, a simple way of showing that price taking is not always to an agent's advantage in the Walrasian mechanism. The activities of the OPEC oil cartel have made a commonplace phenomenon, that of a group of producers withholding or destroying part of their output, even better known. We will show that a single agent can do this in a way that influences prices to his advantage. The example was devised by Aumann and Peleg (1974). It is a two-person, two-commodity economy. There is no production: The "crops" have already been harvested and no further production takes place.

Person 1's endowment is (2, 0) and 2's is (0, 1). Each person has the utility function u_i:

If $y \leq \frac{2}{3}x$ then $u_i(x, y) = x + 8y$
If $y \geq \frac{2}{3}x$ then $u_i(x, y) = 19(x + y)/5$

We can make this more meaningful by referring to Figure 5.1. The indifference curves are two line segments that meet at the ray $y = \frac{2}{3}x$ and have slope -1 to the left of that ray and slope $-\frac{1}{8}$ to the right of that ray. In fact, any utility function u_i that gives rise to indifference curves with slope equal to $-\frac{1}{8}$ at $(\frac{2}{5}, \frac{1}{5})$ and slope equal to -1 at $(\frac{1}{2}, \frac{1}{2})$ suffices for this example. The broken curves provide an illustration.

With the endowments as specified $x^* = ((\frac{2}{5}, \frac{1}{5}), (\frac{8}{5}, \frac{4}{5}))$ is a Walrasian competitive equilibrium for the price system $p^* = (1, 8)$: Each person's marginal rate of substitution equals the price ratio, the value of 1's demand is $(\frac{2}{5} \times 1) + (\frac{1}{5} \times 8)$, which equals 2, the value of 1's endowment at p^*, and 2's demand has a value of $(\frac{8}{5} \times 1) + (\frac{4}{5} \times 8) = 8$, which is 2's income. If 1 destroys half of his endowment, we have a new equilibrium allocation $\hat{x} = ((\frac{1}{2}, \frac{1}{2}), (\frac{1}{2}, \frac{1}{2}))$ at prices $\hat{p} = (1, 1)$ since the endowments are now $w_1 = (1, 0)$ and $w_2 = (0, 1)$. By destroying half of the good that he supplies, agent 1 finds his consumption increasing from $(\frac{2}{5}, \frac{1}{5})$ to $(\frac{1}{2}, \frac{1}{2})$ at equilibrium and this certainly increases his utility. Of course, if 1 merely withholds one unit of the first good, either storing it or consuming it, he will still gain.

In principle, an individual's endowment can be verified by direct observation, but preferences cannot. Therefore, it is more important to investigate the potential for manipulation by misrepresenting preferences. (If i's

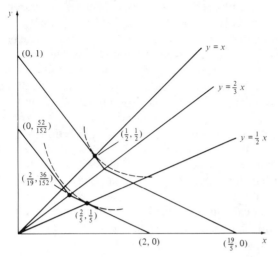

Figure 5.1

endowment consists of a certain type of labor skill, it may not be that easy for an outside observer to evaluate it, however.)

In the context of the Walrasian mechanism misrepresentation of preference occurs if the individual employs a demand correspondence, which maps prices into commodity bundles, that is different from the correspondence generated by utility maximization subject to the budget constraint. It is as if the individual were maximizing some false utility function. We will see that there are many situations in which this sort of departure from the rule "optimize given prices" leads to a higher level of utility using the individual's true utility function to evaluate the outcome. We will see that this is also true of *any* mechanism that yields Pareto-optimal and individually rational outcomes at equilibrium. Recall that an allocation is *Pareto optimal* if it is feasible and there is no other feasible allocation that would give everyone a higher level of utility. An allocation is *individually rational* if it provides each individual i with at least as much utility as afforded by his initial endowment w_i. In both cases the true utility functions must be used in the evaluations. A utility function is *self-regarding* if it depends only on the private goods consumption of the individual in question.

A *dominant strategy mechanism* is one for which no agent ever has an incentive to depart from prescribed behavior, regardless of the actions of others. Since mechanisms require complex organizations of individual actions, it will not necessarily be easy for an individual to predict how a change in his behavior will affect the outcome. There is one special kind of strategy that can be easily followed through, at least formally.

Suppose that an equilibrium is reached by some adjustment process, perhaps involving the planner. Suppose that for each assignment e of utility functions to individuals there is a unique equilibrium allocation f and the adjustment process converges to that allocation. If individual i applies the rules of the mechanism, not to his true utility function u_i, but to a false utility function $\hat{u}_i$, then the adjustment process will converge to the allocation $\hat{f}$ that is associated with $\hat{e}$ for which i's utility function is $\hat{u}_i$ and the utility function of agent $a \neq i$ is u_a, the same as for e. If $u_i(\hat{f}) > u_i(f)$, then individual i prefers the outcome that results when he departs from prescribed behavior in this specific way (by applying the mechanism's rules to the false utility function $\hat{u}_i$). We say that agent i can *manipulate* the mechanism in that case. If a mechanism can be manipulated by some agent, then it certainly cannot be a dominant strategy mechanism.

5.1   Private goods

The proof of Hurwicz (1972) will be used to show that there does not exist a dominant strategy mechanism that always yields equilibrium allocations that are Pareto optimal and individually rational. The theorem is true even within a family E^H of environments of very modest scope. To simplify, assume two commodities and two households. Production has already taken place and is incorporated in the individual endowments, $w_1 = (0, 1)$ and $w_2 = (1, 0)$. Let E^H be rich enough so that it includes all self-regarding utility functions that are continuous and that generate indifference curves exhibiting a diminishing marginal rate of substitution everywhere.

Suppose initially that $u_i(x_i) = (x_{i1})(x_{i2})$, for $i = 1, 2$. Consider first the Walrasian mechanism. The competitive equilibrium allocation is $x^* = ((\frac{1}{2}, \frac{1}{2}), (\frac{1}{2}, \frac{1}{2}))$, and $p^* = (1, 1)$ is the equilibrium price vector (Figure 5.2). One could solve for x^* by equating marginal rates of substitution, locating x_1^* on 1's budget line, and setting $x_2^* = (1, 1) - x_1^*$, yielding four equations in four unknowns. It will be more instructive to use the demand functions as the route to the equilibrium. Maximize $u_i(x_i)$ subject to $px_i = p_c$ for $c \neq i$. The first-order condition is $x_{i2}/x_{i1} = p_1/p_2$, and together with the budget constraint we can solve for x_i as a function of p:

$$x_1(p) = (p_2/2p_1, \tfrac{1}{2}) \quad \text{and} \quad x_2(p) = (\tfrac{1}{2}, p_1/2p_2) \tag{5.1}$$

Market clearance requires $p_2/2p_1 + \frac{1}{2} = 1$ and $p_1/2p_2 + \frac{1}{2} = 1$. Solve for $p_1 = p_2$, which implies $x_i(p) = x_i^*$.

If individual 1 employs a different demand function than equation (5.1), the market clearing price vector will change, perhaps in a way that leaves

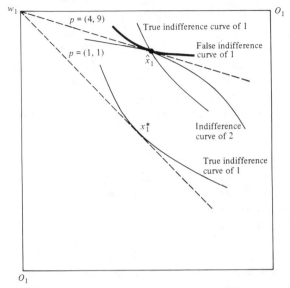

Figure 5.2

1 with a higher level of utility. Suppose that 1 uses a false demand function $\hat{x}_1(p)$ satisfying

$$\hat{x}_1(4, 9) = (\tfrac{1}{2}, \tfrac{7}{9}) \tag{5.2}$$

Then (i) $\hat{x}_i(4, 9)$ satisfies 1's budget constraint for $p = (4, 9)$; (ii) demand, $\hat{x}_1(p) + x_2(p)$, is $(1, 1)$, which equals supply when $p = (4, 9)$; and (iii) *if* 1 could get the planner to announce $p = (4, 9)$, then 1 would be better off using a strategy that implies equation (5.2) since $u_1(\tfrac{1}{2}, \tfrac{7}{9}) > u_1(\tfrac{1}{2}, \tfrac{1}{2})$.

How could 1 get the planner to work the prices around to $p = (4, 9)$? The planner adjusts prices whenever demand is unequal to supply. Suppose the price adjustment process always leads to the competitive equilibrium allocation when each agent's behavior is governed by a utility function. Then if 1 can find a utility function $\hat{u}_1$ for which the demand function satisfies equation (5.2) *and* the unique equilibrium for economy $\hat{e}$ is the allocation $\hat{x} = ((\tfrac{1}{2}, \tfrac{7}{9}), (\tfrac{1}{2}, \tfrac{2}{9}))$, 1 can be sure of steering the system to $\hat{x}$ since that is where the adjustment rule is bound to lead when the economy is $\hat{e}$ (see Figure 5.2; $\hat{e}$ is defined by the utility functions $\hat{u}_1$ and u_2). Since knowledge is dispersed, the planner or the mechanism cannot distinguish between the true and the false economy if the observable aspects of individual behavior are identical in both cases. Define

$$\hat{u}_1(x_1) = \tfrac{1}{2} + x_{12} - (1 + x_{11})^{-1} \tag{5.3}$$

on $\{x_1 \geq 0 : x_1 \leq (1, 1)\}$. An indifference curve is characterized by $x_{12} = (1 + x_{11})^{-1} + c$, where c is a constant. Then the marginal rate of substitution, $-dx_{12}/dx_{11}$, diminishes as x_{11} increases: $\hat{u}_1$ is admissible. Confirm that equation (5.2) is implied by $\hat{u}_1$: The marginal rate of substitution is $(1 + x_{11})^{-2}$, which equals the price ratio p_1/p_2. Add the budget constraint, $p_1x_{11} + p_2x_{12} = p_2$, to solve for $\hat{x}_1$ as a function of p: $\hat{x}_{11}(p) = (p_2/p_1)^{1/2} - 1$, which is nonnegative if and only if $p_2 \geq p_1$. (If $p_2 < p_1$, the marginal rate of substitution is smaller than the price ratio even for $x_{11} = 0$. Therefore, $\hat{x}_{11}(p) = 0$ if $p_2 < p_1$.)

$$\hat{x}_1(p) = ((p_2/p_1)^{1/2} - 1, 1 + p_1/p_2 - (p_1/p_2)^{1/2}) \quad \text{if } p_2 \geq p_1 \qquad (5.4)$$

Equation (5.4) implies equation (5.2), and we have found a strategy for 1 that leads to the equilibrium allocation $\hat{x}$ if 2 announces his true utility-maximizing vector given the announced price vector. Since 1 prefers $\hat{x}_1$ to x_1^*, according to his true utility function, he can manipulate the Walrasian mechanism. Individual 1 violates the rules of the Walrasian game, but the violation cannot be detected because his strategy can be rationalized by *some* utility function and no one knows his true utility function. (If the utility functions were known, a mechanism would not be needed.) The first theorem proves that this vulnerability to manipulation is ubiquitous.

Theorem 5.1. *Let $\mathcal{M}$ be a mechanism defined on E^H, the family of pairs of self-regarding utility functions that exhibit diminishing marginal rates of substitution everywhere. If for every environment e in E^H the mechanism $\mathcal{M}$ generates equilibrium allocations that are Pareto optimal and individually rational, then it can be manipulated.*

Proof: Let e be the environment specified by $u_i(x_i) = (x_{i1})(x_{i2})$, $i = 1, 2$. As above, $w_1 = (0, 1)$ and $w_2 = (1, 0)$. Pareto optimality requires equality of marginal rates of substitution and $x_1 + x_2 = (1, 1)$. Therefore, x is Pareto optimal if and only if

$$x_{11} = x_{12}, \quad 0 \leq x_{11} \leq 1, \quad \text{and} \quad x_2 = (1, 1) - x_1 \qquad (5.5)$$

[Verify that statement (5.5) must hold even if $x_{ic} = 0$ for some i and some c.]

Suppose that x^* is an equilibrium allocation for e. We have $x_{i1}^* \leq \frac{1}{2}$ for some i. Without loss of generality, assume that $x_{11}^* \leq \frac{1}{2}$. Then $x_{12}^* \leq \frac{1}{2}$ by statement (5.5), and therefore $u_1(x_1^*) \leq \frac{1}{4}$. Let $\hat{e}$ be the environment with utility functions $\hat{u}_1$ [equation (5.3)] and u_2. If 1 applies the mechanism's rules to the false utility function $\hat{u}_1$, whereas 2 is governed by u_2, the outcome will be an equilibrium of $\hat{e}$. Let $\hat{x}$ be an individually rational Pareto-optimal allocation for $\hat{e}$.

Individual rationality implies

$$\hat{u}_1(\hat{x}_1) \geq \hat{u}_1(w_1) = \hat{u}_1(0, 1) = \tfrac{1}{2}$$

Then $\hat{x}_{12} - (1 + \hat{x}_{11})^{-1} + \tfrac{1}{2} \geq \tfrac{1}{2}$, which simplifies to $\hat{x}_{12} \geq (1 + \hat{x}_{11})^{-1}$. Since $\hat{x}$ is Pareto optimal for $\hat{e}$, the two individuals must have identical marginal rates of substitution with respect to $\hat{u}_1$ and u_2. Therefore,

$$\frac{1}{(1 + \hat{x}_{11})^2} = \frac{\hat{x}_{22}}{\hat{x}_{21}} = \frac{1 - \hat{x}_{12}}{1 - \hat{x}_{11}} \tag{5.6}$$

If $\hat{x}$ also satisfies $\hat{u}_1(\hat{x}_1) = \hat{u}_1(w_1)$, then $\hat{x}_{12} = (1 + \hat{x}_{11})^{-1}$ and, substituting this into equation (5.6), we have $(\hat{x}_{11})^2 + 2\hat{x}_{11} - 1 = 0$. The relevant solution of this quadratic is $\hat{x}_{11} = -1 + \sqrt{2}$. Then $\hat{x}_{12} = 1/\sqrt{2}$ since $\hat{x}_{12} = (1 + \hat{x}_{11})^{-1}$. We have $u_1(\hat{x}_1) = 0.29 > 0.25 \geq u_1(x_1^*)$.

To summarize, if $\hat{x}$ is Pareto optimal for $\hat{e}$ and $\hat{u}_1(\hat{x}_1) = \hat{u}_1(w_1)$, then $u_1(\hat{x}_1) > u_1(x_1^*)$. Let x be *any* Pareto-optimal and individually rational allocation for $\hat{e}$. Then $\hat{u}_1(x_1) \geq \hat{u}_1(w_1) = \hat{u}_1(\hat{x}_1)$. This implies that $x_1 = \hat{x}_1$ if $x_1 \leq \hat{x}_1$. If $x_{1c} > \hat{x}_{1c}$ for some commodity c, we have $x_{1c} > \hat{x}_{1c}$ for $c = 1, 2$ since x must equate the marginal rates of substitution of persons 1 and 2. (If, say, $\hat{x}_{11}$ increases and $\hat{x}_{12}$ decreases, then $1/(1 + \hat{x}_{11})^2$ decreases and $(1 - \hat{x}_{12})/(1 - \hat{x}_{11})$ increases and equation (5.6) cannot hold. Similarly, equation (5.6) cannot hold if $\hat{x}_{11}$ decreases and $\hat{x}_{12}$ increases.) Therefore, if x is an equilibrium allocation for $\hat{e}$, we have $x_1 \geq \hat{x}_1$. Then

$$u_1(x_1) \geq u_1(\hat{x}_1) > u_1(x_1^*). \qquad \text{Q.E.D.}$$

The proof of Theorem 5.1 assumes that one person manipulates whereas the other person behaves sincerely. We have shown that the former can realize a higher level of utility than when he also behaves sincerely. We are not assuming that in the real world when one person attempts to exploit a strategic advantage, he naively assumes that others do not. Our assumption that one person manipulates whereas everyone else behaves sincerely is part of a proof by contradiction. If we suppose that every individual is motivated to follow the rules implicitly, we are led to a contradiction: With all but one individual behaving sincerely the remaining person can gain by deviating from the rules.

5.2 Private goods economies with many consumers

For any finite number n of households one can find an example in which a single agent is able to increase his utility by manipulating the Walrasian mechanism. However, one would expect that the resulting utility gain would be very tiny if n were realistically large: The demand behavior of a single agent should not be able to deflect the price vector by more than a tiny degree from its equilibrium value. The argument of Roberts and Postlewaite (1976) will be used to prove this conjecture. As with many important results, the proof is very easy. The difficulty lies in stating the theorem in a meaningful way. What do we mean by a "large" value of n? How can one tell when an increase in utility is "small"? The best way to deal with the second problem is to require the gain in utility that results from manipulation to be closer and closer to zero as n gets larger and larger. This also settles the first issue but raises a new one: We do not have to decide in advance which values of n are large but merely to follow what happens as n increases without limit. But now we have to decide what we mean by an economy with an increasing number of consumers.

The simplest way to cause the economy to expand is to *replicate it*. One starts with an n-person exchange economy e. The economy, or environment, e specifies a utility function u_i and an initial endowment w_i for each consumer $i = 1, 2, \ldots, n$. The m-fold replica economy (m, e) is an economy with nm consumers in which there are m consumers identical to consumer i $(1 \le i \le n)$ of the economy e, which we can now denote as the economy $(1, e)$. In other words, (m, e) is an economy in which m consumers have the utility function u_i and the endowment w_i for each i from 1 through n. Let a denote any integer between 1 and n inclusive. We will think of a as a single agent who belongs to every economy (m, e), $m = 1, 2, \ldots$. For any value of m, trader a will likely be able to influence the equilibrium price regime p. We will show that any departure from equilibrium will be arbitrarily small for m arbitrarily large and that any utility gain resulting from manipulation will be arbitrarily small for arbitrarily large m.

The argument will be more transparent if we assume that for each strictly positive price vector p there is a unique commodity vector, $x_i(p)$, that maximizes u_i subject to $px_i \le pw_i$. We also assume that each commodity is desirable: If $p_c = 0$, then the demand for commodity c is arbitrarily large and hence p is inconsistent with equilibrium.

We say that trader a can *ratify* price vector p in economy (m, e) if there is some possible demand y_a by a, not necessarily satisfying $y_a = x_a(p)$, such that demand equals supply for every good when a demands y_a and all other agents demand their utility-maximizing bundles. Then a can ratify p in (m, e) if and only if

$$m\sum_{i \ne a} x_i(p) + (m - 1)x_a(p) \le m\sum_{i=1}^{n} w_i \tag{5.7}$$

The total supply of commodity c is $m\sum_{i=1}^{n} w_{ic}$ since there are m consumers i each with an endowment of w_{ic} units of good c. The total demand for c by all agents other than a at price regime p is

$$m\sum_{i \neq a} x_{ic}(p) + (m - 1)x_{ac}(p)$$

and if this exceeds the total supply, including a's endowment of c, there is nothing that a can do to disguise the fact that p does not clear all markets. Hence inequality (5.7) is necessary if a is to be able to ratify p in (m, e). It is also sufficient since

$$y_a = m\sum_{i=1}^{n} w_i - m\sum_{i \neq a} x_i(p) - (m - 1)x_a(p) \qquad (5.8)$$

has the three properties necessary to give p the appearance of a Walrasian competitive equilibrium: It will obviously be the case that demand equals supply in each market if a demands y_a and every other agent demands $x_i(p)$ if he is of type i. And y_a is feasible since $y_a \geq 0$. Finally, $py_a = pw_a$ so y_a is affordable for a. The last statement is a consequence of budget exhaustion, $px_i(p) = pw_i$, and equation (5.8). Now we show that the set of price vectors that agent a can ratify in (m, e) shrinks monotonically to the set of true Walrasian competitive equilibrium price regimes for (m, e) as m increases without limit. The theorem assumes budget exhaustion for all agents as well as the existence and uniqueness of the budget-constrained utility maximizer $x_i(p)$ for all $p \gg 0$, $i = 1, 2, \ldots, n$. It is also assumed that there is no affordable utility maximizer if $pw_i > 0$ and $p_c = 0$ for some commodity c. This will ensure that $p \gg 0$ at equilibrium.

Theorem 5.2. (i) *If agent a can ratify p in (m, e), then a can ratify p in (t, e) for all $t \leq m$. (ii) If for each positive integer t there is some $m \geq t$ such that a can ratify p in (m, e), then p is a Walrasian competitive equilibrium price vector in (m, e) for every positive integer m.*

Proof: (i) Suppose that inequality (5.7) holds. Since $(m/t)(t - 1) \leq (m - 1)$ if $t \leq m$, we have

$$t\sum_{i \neq a} x_i(p) + (t - 1)x_a(p) = (t/m)\left[m\sum_{i \neq a} x_i(p) + (m(t-1)/t)x_a(p)\right]$$

$$\leq (t/m)\left[m\sum_{i \neq a} x_i(p) + (m - 1)x_a(p)\right]$$

$$\leq (t/m)\left(m\sum_{i=1}^{n} w_i\right) = t\sum_{i=1}^{n} w_i$$

Therefore, a can ratify p in (t, e).

(ii) If for every t there is some $m \geq t$ such that inequality (5.7) holds, then $p \gg 0$ [since $x_i(p)$ is defined] and

$$\sum_{i \neq a} x_i(p) + [(m - 1)/m]x_a(p) \leq \sum_{i=1}^{n} w_i \tag{5.9}$$

for any m for which equation (5.7) is true. If $\sum_{i \neq a} x_{ic}(p) + x_{ac}(p) > \sum_{i=1}^{n} w_{ic}$ for some commodity c, then

$$\sum_{i \neq a} x_{ic}(p) + [(m - 1)/m]x_{ac}(p) > \sum_{i=1}^{n} w_{ic}$$

$$\forall m > x_{ac}(p)\left[\sum_{i \neq a} x_{ic}(p) + x_{ac}(p) - \sum_{i=1}^{n} w_{ic}\right]^{-1}$$

This contradicts inequality (5.9), which must hold for an infinite number of positive integers m by hypothesis. Therefore,

$$\sum_{i \neq a} x_i(p) + x_a(p) \leq \sum_{i=1}^{n} w_i \tag{5.10}$$

Budget exhaustion implies $p\sum_{i=1}^{n} x_i(p) = p\sum_{i=1}^{n} w_i$, and this along with $p \gg 0$ and inequality (5.10) implies $\sum_{i=1}^{n}[x_i(p) - w_i] = 0$. Therefore, p is a Walrasian competitive equilibrium price vector in $(1, e)$. Obviously, $m\sum_{i=1}^{n}[x_i(p) - w_i] = 0$ also holds so p is an equilibrium price regime in (m, e) for all m.   Q.E.D.

Suppose that we claim that there is a strategy available to agent a that yields more utility than the sincere strategy of reporting the true demand $x_a(p)$ at each p and that the resulting utility gain does not go to zero as m increases without limit. Then there is a positive number $\varepsilon > 0$ such that for each integer t there is some $m \geq t$ such that a can ratify some p^m in (m, e) and

$$u_a(y_a^m) \geq u_a(x_a) + \varepsilon \tag{5.11}$$

for all Walrasian competitive equilibrium allocations x, where

$$y_a^m \leq m\sum_{i=1}^{n} w_i - m\sum_{i \neq a} x_i(p^m) - (m - 1)x_a(p^m) \tag{5.12}$$

Then we have an infinite sequence $\{p^m\}$ of price vectors defined on some infinite set M of integers. For each m in M the first part of Theorem 5.2 assures us that a can ratify p^m in (t, e) for all $t \leq m$. Then the sequence

$\{p^m: m \geq t$ and $m \in M\}$ is contained in the set H_a^t of all price vectors that a can ratify in (t, e). Modest assumptions are required in order to ensure that this sequence, or a subset of it, converges to some price vector $p*$ in H_a^t. But this means that $p*$ is in H_a^t for all t in M and the second part of Theorem 5.2 proves that $p*$ is a Walrasian equilibrium price vector. If u_a is continuous, we are led to the conclusion that $u_a(x_a(p^m))$ can be made arbitrarily close to $u_a(x_a(p*))$ since p^m can be made arbitrarily close to $p*$. But (5.11) and (5.12) are inconsistent with this fact if we take $x_a = x_a(p*)$ in (5.11). This follows from the fact that $u_a(y_a^m) \leq u_a(x_a(p^m))$ by definition of the demand function $x_a(p)$ and the fact that (5.12) implies that y^m satisfies a's budget constraint for price system p^m. If $u_a(x_a(p^m))$ can be made arbitrarily close to $u_a(x_a(p*))$ by taking m large enough, we can ensure that $u_a(x_a(p^m)) \leq u_a(x_a(p*)) + \frac{1}{2} \varepsilon$ holds for m large enough. Since we also have $u_a(y_a^m) \leq u_a(x_a(p^m))$ and $p*$ is a Walrasian equilibrium price system, (5.11) is contradicted.

Therefore, if the number of consumers is large, any sort of misrepresentation of demand would yield such a small increase in utility that it would be more than offset by the costs of acquiring enough information about the demand behavior of others to permit the individual to influence prices in a way that affects his utility favorably. Sincere behavior is optimal for any individual if others are expected to behave sincerely and the number of households of each type is large. We can claim that the Walrasian mechanism is incentive compatible in the case of exchange economies with a large number of agents of each type. If the total number of agents is large but there is no other agent whose endowment is the same as a's, then we cannot rule out the possibility that a is the sole supplier of a particular good, in which case a has much to gain by not being a price taker.

5.3 Public goods

Incentive difficulties are more serious in models featuring public goods, but it is only when the number of agents is very large that this conclusion emerges from a formal treatment of the subject. In the case of a small economy there is the same vulnerability to manipulation in economies with public goods as there is in purely private goods economies. We now demonstrate this by proving the counterpart to Theorem 5.1. The proof is based on Roberts (1979).

We begin by defining a minimal family E^R of environments over which a mechanism is expected to perform successfully. There is one public good and one private good. There are two consumers and one firm, which is assumed to follow sincerely whatever rules are laid down. It suffices to study the strategic behavior of households. Let (x, y, z) denote an allocation: $x = (x_1, x_2)$ specifies the private goods consumption of consumers 1 and 2 and (y, z) is the production plan of the firm. The plan (y, z) employs $-y$ (≥ 0) units of the private good as input to produce z (≥ 0) units of the public good as output according to the recipe $z = \sqrt{-y}$. The technology set, $Y = \{(y, z): 0 \leq z \leq \sqrt{-y}$ and $y \leq 0\}$ is constant over E^R as are the individual endowments $w_1 = w_2 = (\frac{5}{2}, 0)$: Each individual has an endowment of $2\frac{1}{2}$ units of the private good and zero units of the public good. An environment e in E^R is specified by a pair of positive utility parameters (β_1, β_2) that define the utility functions $u_i(x_i, z) = x_i + \beta_i \ln(z + 1)$ for $i = 1, 2$. Consumer i's utility depends only on his consumption of the private good and the amount of the public good provided.

Theorem 5.3. *Let $\mathcal{M}$ be a mechanism defined on E^R. If, for every environment e in E^R, $\mathcal{M}$ generates equilibrium allocations that are Pareto optimal and individually rational, then it can be manipulated.*

Proof: In most cases there is a unique Pareto-optimal level, z^*, of the public good:

$$z^* = \tfrac{1}{2} \sqrt{1 + 2\beta_1 + 2\beta_2} - \tfrac{1}{2} \tag{5.13}$$

To prove this, maximize the function $V(z) = 5 - z^2 + (\beta_1 + \beta_2)$ $\ln (z + 1)$, which equals $u_1(x_1, z) + u_2(x_2, z)$ for $x_i = w_i - \lambda_i z^2$, where λ_i is the fraction of the cost of the public good contributed by i. ($\lambda_i \geq 0$ and $\lambda_1 + \lambda_2 = 1$. Verify that Pareto optimality implies $x_1 + x_2 = w_1 + w_2 - z^2$.) Any feasible allocation that maximizes $u_1 + u_2$ will be Pareto optimal.

Now, $V''(z) < 0$ for all $z \geq 0$. Therefore, z maximizes V if $V'(z) = -2z + (\beta_1 + \beta_2)/(z + 1) = 0$. Then z^* is the nonnegative solution of this quadratic.

Let (x, y, z) be any allocation for which $z \neq z^*$. If dz is sufficiently small in absolute value, the production of $z + dz$ units of the public good will require close to $z^2 + 2z\,dz$ units of input. The change in cost is close to $2z\,dz$ and if i pays the fraction $\lambda_i = \beta_i/(\beta_1 + \beta_2)$ of this, then i's consumption of the private good, x_i', will now be close to $x_i - \lambda_i(2z\,dz)$. The change in i's utility will be close to

$$du_i = -\lambda_i(2z\,dz) + \beta_i\,dz/(z + 1)$$

Since $V'' < 0$, we have $V'(z) > 0$ if $z < z^*$ and $V'(z) < 0$ if $z > z^*$. Choose $dz > 0$ if $z < z^*$ and $dz < 0$ for $z > z^*$. Then

$$[(\beta_1 + \beta_2)/\beta_i]\,du_i = [-2z + (\beta_1 + \beta_2)/(z + 1)]\,dz = V'(z)\,dz > 0$$

Therefore, $du_i > 0$ and the utility of both individuals can be increased as long as $x_i' = x_i - \lambda_i(2z\,dz) \geq 0$, $i = 1, 2$. This will certainly be the case if $dz < 0$. Therefore, Pareto optimality requires $z \leq z^*$. If $x_1 > 0$ and $x_2 > 0$, then $dz > 0$ can be made small enough so that $x' \geq 0$. Therefore, Pareto optimality requires $z \geq z^*$ if $x \gg 0$, and in that case we must actually have $z = z^*$ since $z \leq z^*$ holds in general.

Specify environment e in E^R by setting $\beta_1 = \beta_2 = 2$. Then $z^* = 1$. Suppose that (x, y, z) is Pareto optimal and $x_i = 0$. Since $z \leq 1$, we have

$$u_i(x_i, z) \leq 2 \ln(1 + 1) < 1.4 < 2.5 = u_i(w_i, 0)$$

Therefore, $x \gg 0$ if (x, y, z) is Pareto optimal and individually rational, and this in turn implies $z = z^* = 1$. After producing one unit of the public good, there are four units of the private good available for consumption. Therefore, if (x, y, z) is an equilibrium allocation for e, then either $x_1 \leq 2$ or $x_2 \leq 2$. Suppose, without loss of generality, that $x_1 \leq 2$.

Now consider the environment $\hat{e}$ specified by $\hat{\beta}_1 = \frac{2}{9}$ and $\hat{\beta}_2 = \beta_2 = 2$. This corresponds to the case where 1 manipulates and governs his behavior according to the false utility function $\hat{u}_1(x_1, z) = x_1 + \frac{2}{9} \ln (z + 1)$ whereas 2 continues to play sincerely and is guided by u_2. Let $(\hat{x}, \hat{y}, \hat{z})$ be an equilibrium allocation for $\hat{e}$. Equation (5.13) implies $\hat{z}^* = \frac{2}{3}$. Pareto optimality implies $\hat{z} \leq \hat{z}^*$. Individual rationality implies

$$\tfrac{5}{2} = \hat{u}_1(w_1, 0) \leq \hat{u}_1(\hat{x}_1, \hat{z}) \leq \hat{x}_1 + \tfrac{2}{9} \ln (\tfrac{5}{3})$$

and this in turn implies $\hat{x}_1 \geq \frac{5}{2} - \frac{2}{9} \ln \frac{5}{3} > 0$. Now, $\hat{x}_1 > 0$ implies $\hat{z} = \hat{z}^* = \frac{2}{3}$. (Since $\hat{\beta}_2 = \beta_2$, we have already shown that $\hat{x}_2$ must be positive.) Finally, $\hat{z} = \frac{2}{3}$, and $\hat{x}_1 \geq \frac{5}{2} - \frac{2}{9} \ln \frac{5}{3}$ implies

$$u_1(\hat{x}_1, \hat{z}) \geq \tfrac{5}{2} - \tfrac{2}{9} \ln \tfrac{5}{3} + 2 \ln \tfrac{5}{3} > 3.40$$

Since $x_1 \leq 2$, $u_1(x_1, z) \leq u_1(2, 1) = 2 + 2 \ln 2 < 3.39$. Therefore, $u_1(\hat{x}_1, \hat{z}) > 3.40 > 3.39 > u_1(x_1, z)$ and 1 can manipulate the mechanism.   Q.E.D.

There are two reasons why the incentive difficulties are more serious in the public goods realm than in the case of private goods. On the one hand, an individual requires less information in order to misrepresent his preferences for public goods in an advantageous way, unless the relationship between his tax burden and the messages of others is very complex. This is illustrated by the example of Section 1.5: In that case, as long as one's marginal utility for the public good at zero is less than the aggregate of everyone else's marginal utility at zero, reporting a marginal utility of zero is a dominant strategy. On the other hand, the temptation to misrepresent does not fade as the number of households increases in the public goods case. If the relative size of the public sector is fairly constant as the economy grows, then the per capita tax burden will be fairly constant and taxes will claim a substantial portion of one's gross income. There will be much to be gained from a strategy of misrepresentation that reduces one's tax burden, and if the number of households is large, the loss in utility from a change in the supply of public goods will be small since the individual effect on aggregate output of *any* good will be tiny. Therefore, there will be a significant net gain in utility. [See Roberts (1976).]

5.4   Summary

Whether public goods must be accommodated or not, it is possible to design a resource allocation mechanism that always yields Pareto-optimal equilibria if each agent takes the messages of other agents as given. In other words, each agent is assumed to behave competitively. With or without public goods, there will be some departure from competitive behavior that will be to some agent's advantage. Whether such a strategy is still beneficial after deducting the costs of acquiring the information necessary to ensure that a departure from the rules changes one's utility in the desired direction is the real question. In the case of an agent's demands for and supplies of private goods in the private ownership market economy, the net gain will not be positive unless the agent is a supplier of some commodity for which there are few rival suppliers. In that case and in the case of public goods – and consumption externalities in general – the incentive compatibility problem remains a central one.

5.5   Background

Hurwicz (1972) first proved that every mechanism that yields Pareto-optimal and individually rational outcomes can be manipulated. Only private goods were incorporated into the model. Curiously, the impossibility theorem for public goods allocation came later (Ledyard and Roberts, 1974; Roberts, 1979). These impossibility theorems require Pareto optimality only over environments with utility functions having convex upper contour sets and that are not sensitive to the private goods consumption of agents other than the one in question. In the early 1970s two scholars independently discovered that with unrestricted preferences every nondictatorial mechanism can be manipulated (Gibbard, 1973; Satterthwaite, 1975). A dictatorial mechanism is one that allows a single individual to control the outcome in all situations. Nondictatorship is the only normative restriction in the hypothesis of the Gibbard–Satterthwaite theorem; neither Pareto optimality nor individual rationality are imposed. It is also assumed that three or more alternatives are available. (The simple majority rule mechanism cannot be manipulated if there are only two alternatives: Individuals are required to vote for their most-preferred candidate and this is a dominant strategy. Ties are broken in a particular way, and this tie-breaking rule provides room for strategic maneuvering when there are more than two alternatives.)

Assuming that agents manipulate, one can ask if the Nash equilibria of the *manipulation game* will be as satisfactory as the outcome would have been if the agents had behaved sincerely. Agents are treated as if they reported their characteristics to a referee who then works out the equilibrium by applying the mechanism's rules to the reported characteristics. The reported characteristics constitute a Nash equilibrium of the manipulation game if no agent can secure a better outcome in terms of his true characteristic by reporting a different characteristic. Hurwicz (1979c) and Otani and Sicilian (1982) have solved for the equilibria of the Walrasian manipulation game: Many of them will be far from Pareto optimal. For example, the endowment point is always an equilibrium in the pure exchange context.

Although it is logically possible for individual households to manipulate the Walrasian mechanism, it has long been understood that an individual household has virtually no market power and any utility gain, although mathematically positive, would be practically zero. It has not been until relatively recently that this notion has been given formal expression in a tractable economic model. Aumann (1964) used the expedient of a continuum of traders. The absence of individual market power is captured by the mathematical fact that addition – Lebesgue integration – over a continuum is not affected by a change in a value at a single point. Brown and Robinson (1972) brought this technique closer to our intuitive understanding by employing a model in which the number of agents is an "infinite integer."

Ostroy (1980) and Makowski (1980) show that a model with a large number of agents is required if no single agent is to have significant market power, and Roberts and Postlewaite (1976) show that this construct is sufficient to capture the idea that agents will have an incentive to take prices as given.

Campbell (1984) considers the optimality properties of mechanisms in which households behave sincerely but some firms manipulate. If this manipulating behavior is accepted as a constraint on the system, one can ask if sincere behavior on the part of all other agents is welfare optimal subject to this constraint. For virtually any definition of optimality the answer is affirmative, provided that the mechanism is welfare optimal when all agents behave sincerely.

EXERCISES

5.1 Consider a two-person, two-commodity exchange economy e with $u_i(x_i) = x_{i1}x_{i2}$ and $w_1 = (0, 1)$, $w_2 = (0, 1)$. Let (t, e) be the t-fold replication of this economy. Normalize and set $p_2 = 1$. (i) Determine the Walrasian equilibrium for (t, e). (ii) Suppose that all but one individual behaves sincerely. Compute the range of values of p_1 that the remaining agent can ratify in (t, e). Show that for all such values p_1' in the range, $\lim_{t \to \infty} u_i(x_i^t)$ does not exceed the level of utility enjoyed by i at the Walrasian equilibrium for any choice of x_i^t such that $p'x_i^t \leq p'w_i^t$.

5.2 For any n-person, k-commodity exchange economy define the *manipulation game* in which each individual i reports a utility function $\hat{u}_i$ that is then used to compute the associated Walrasian competitive equilibrium for the (known) initial endowments $w_1, w_2, \ldots, w_n$. The configuration $(\hat{u}_1, \hat{u}_2, \ldots, \hat{u}_n)$ is a Nash equilibrium of this game, with respect to the true utility functions $u_1, u_2, \ldots, u_n$, if for each i there is no utility function that would give rise to an outcome that gives more utility according to u_i than does $\hat{u}_i$, given that each $a \neq i$ reports $\hat{u}_a$. Prove that $(\hat{u}_1, \ldots, \hat{u}_n)$ is a Nash equilibrium for

$$\hat{u}_i(x_i) = \min\{x_{ic}/w_{ic} > 0\}$$

for any assignment of true utility functions. Use this result to explain why a Nash equilibrium of the manipulation game will usually be far from Pareto optimal.

5.3 Let

$$E_1 = E_2 = \{\lambda = (\lambda_1, \lambda_2) \in R^2 : 0 \leq \lambda_c < 1, c = 1, 2\}$$

Each $((\alpha_1, \beta_1), (\alpha_2, \beta_2)) \in E = E_1 \times E_2$ defines a two-person, two-commodity exchange economy with $u_i(x_i) = (x_{i1} + \alpha_i)(x_{i2} + \beta_i)$, $i = 1, 2$, and $w_1 = (1, 0)$, $w_2 = (0, 1)$. Now define a specific mechanism (M, μ, g): M_i, i's message set is E_i. For any $(e_1, e_2) \in E$, $\mu_i(e_i) = \{e' \in E : e_i' = e_i\}$ is i's equilibrium correspondence. Finally, the outcome function $g: M \to R^4$ is defined: For any $e = (e_1, e_2) = ((\alpha_1, \beta_1), (\alpha_2, \beta_2)) \in E$ set $g(e) = x = (x_1, x_2)$, where $x >> 0$ satisfies (i) $x_1 + x_2 = (1, 1)$, (ii) $(x_{11} + \alpha_1)(x_{12} + \beta_1) = (x_{21} + \alpha_2)(x_{22} + \beta_2)$, and (iii) x is Pareto optimal in economy e. Show that there is a unique $x >> 0$ satisfying (i)–(iii). If $e = ((\frac{1}{2}, \frac{1}{2}), (\frac{1}{2}, \frac{1}{2}))$ is the true economy, show that i can benefit by misrepresenting his preferences assuming that $a(\neq i)$ behaves sincerely. Now, find a Nash equilibrium configuration of utility parameters for the manipulation game. That is, find an $e' \in E$ such that $u_1(g(e_1', e_2')) \geq u_1(g(e_1'', e_2'))$ for all $e_1'' \in E_1$ and $u_2(g(e_1', e_2')) \geq u_2(g(e_1', e_2''))$ for all $e_2'' \in E_2$. [Here, $u_i(x_i) = (x_{i1} + \frac{1}{2})(x_{i2} + \frac{1}{2})$.] Is a Nash equilibrium of the manipulation game Pareto optimal in terms of the true preferences? Is Pareto optimality necessarily violated?

5.4 This question concerns the economy of Exercise 3.6 for the particular values $\varepsilon = \frac{3}{4}$ and $\beta = \frac{1}{2}$. (i) Determine the Walrasian competitive equilibrium allocation. (ii) Suppose that firm 1, which produces A, manipulates by demanding the amount of input that would be profit maximizing if the firm's production coefficient were $\frac{5}{8}$ instead of $\frac{3}{4}$, which it actually is. Show that this strategy would provide firm 1 with more profit at equilibrium than would sincere behavior. (When firm 1 demands t_1 units of input, it produces $\frac{5}{8}t_1$

units, of output, in order to keep its price high, instead of $\frac{3}{4}t_1$ units, which it would be capable of producing with t_1 units of input.) (iii) Suppose that the planner attempts to neutralize the manipulation of firm 1 by altering the behavior of firm 2. Specifically, the planner instructs firm 2 to behave as though its production parameter were δ: If the firm demands t_2 units of input, it will produce t_2^{δ} units of output. Since β is actually $\frac{1}{2}$, the planner must respect the constraint $t_2^{\delta} \leq t_2^{1/2}$ in selecting a value of δ that improves the utility of the outcome. Is there a $\delta \neq \frac{1}{2}$ that will accomplish this?

CHAPTER 6

Existence of a competitive equilibrium

Under ideal conditions an equilibrium of the Walrasian model of a private ownership market economy is Pareto optimal. The fact that these ideal conditions are not met without qualification in the real world does not vitiate the Walrasian approach to welfare economics, if only because Walrasian competitive equilibrium can be viewed as a standard to which policy-makers can aspire. The results of this book would be of little value, however, if it turned out that an equilibrium rarely exists. This chapter examines the conditions under which existence of equilibrium is assured.

Competitive behavior is assumed throughout. Other notions of equilibrium are more plausible in certain situations, but competitive behavior is important enough for a study of competitive equilibrium to constitute a useful introduction to the subject of existence of equilibrium. By assuming competitive behavior, we can be more specific about the features of a resource allocation mechanism. Accordingly, attention will be confined to mechanisms that require each agent to transmit a best response to the messages announced by others. A best response is one that would produce the best outcome for the decision-maker if the messages of others were to remain unchanged. If an agent's strategy has this property, his behavior is said to be competitive.

It is often claimed that proofs of existence of equilibrium constitute a mere mathematical flourish and are not worthy of study by anyone whose interest in economics stems from a desire to understand and prescribe for real-world phenomena. To dispel this notion, our treatment of the existence question begins with six examples of situations in which an equilibrium does not exist *for economic reasons*.

6.1 Counterexamples

Increasing returns to scale

Suppose that one firm can more than double its output every time it doubles its input. If the firm's output is desired by consumers, it will have

126

a positive price since a zero price would lead to a halt in production but give rise to a positive demand. (If the firm's input also had a zero price, it may produce and take a zero profit so we will assume that the input is desired in production elsewhere and has a positive price at equilibrium.) The firm uses t units of input to produce $f(t)$ units of output, which it sells at a price of P dollars. Input costs W dollars per unit. The firm's profit is $Pf(t) - Wt$. Now, $f(2t) > 2f(t)$ by the increasing returns-to-scale assumption. Therefore,

$$Pf(2t) - W2t > P2f(t) - W2t = 2[Pf(t) - Wt]$$

If there is a value of t for which the firm obtains a positive profit, there can be no Walrasian equilibrium since the firm can more than double its profit by doubling its scale, ad infinitum, and there is no point at which it reaches its maximum profit, given P and W.

For example, if $f(t) = t^2$ and P and W are positive, then as long as t exceeds W/P, profit will be positive and hence unbounded.

It is unlikely that a firm can continue doubling its scale without affecting prices. At least one firm can be expected to increase its output to the point where its own supply has an appreciable effect on market price. This is a consequence of the fact that if market prices do *not* change, average cost falls as output increases and the largest firm will be in a position to drive out many of its rivals with low but profitable prices. Therefore, one firm will be in a position where its own activities have an appreciable affect on market prices after all. If, on the one hand, the range of increasing returns to scale is unbounded, then a competitive equilibrium does not exist. If, on the other hand, the range of increasing returns is finite but large, even if a competitive equilibrium exists, it will not be realized since firms in the industry will not behave competitively.

Boundary endowments

Consider an exchange economy with two goods and two consumers. Let $u_i(x_i) = x_{i1}x_{i2}$ be i's utility function. The endowments are $w_1 = (1, 0)$ and $w_2 = (0, 1)$. Individual 2's commodity space, X_2, is $R_+^2 = \{x_2 \in R^2: x_2 \geq 0\}$. Individual 1's commodity space is $X_1 = \{x_1 \in R_+^2 : 2x_{11} + x_{12} \geq 2\}$. The fact that w_1 is on the boundary of X_1 will cause difficulties. *If* 1's commodity space were also R_+^2, then the Walrasian competitive equilibrium would be $p^* = (1, 1)$, $x_1^* = x_2^* = (\frac{1}{2}, \frac{1}{2})$. Because $x_1^* \notin X_1$, this cannot be an equilibrium for the economy as defined. In this economy there is no price system at which both markets clear, nor is there a price regime at which excess demand is small relative to the total supply.

The demonstration that markets cannot even clear in an approximate sense will be easier to follow if we normalize and fix the price of commodity 2 at unity. Let P denote the price of commodity 1. Now, compute the demand functions.

Individual 2's demand function, $x_2(P)$, is easily obtained by setting the marginal rate of substitution equal to the price ratio and using the budget equation to solve for x_2 as a function of P:

$$x_2(P) = (1/2P, \tfrac{1}{2}) \quad \text{if } P > 0$$

(Verify that utility maximization implies that all income will be exhausted, that demand will far exceed supply in the case of a zero price, and that individual 2 will consume a positive amount of both goods.) The same technique applied to u_1 and w_1 yields $x_1(P) = (\tfrac{1}{2}, \tfrac{1}{2}P)$. This will belong to X_1 if and only if $P \geq 2$. If $P < 2$, then $(P, 1)x_1 \leq (P, 1)w_1$ and $x_1 \in X_1$ implies $x_1 = w_1$. Therefore, $x_1(P) = (1, 0)$ if $P < 2$. Individual 1's demand function is not continuous:

$$x_1(P) = \begin{cases} (\tfrac{1}{2}, \tfrac{1}{2}P) & \text{if } P \geq 2 \\ (1, 0) & \text{if } P < 2 \end{cases}$$

As P approaches 2 from below, $x_1(P)$ remains constant at $(1, 0)$, but $x_1(2) = (\tfrac{1}{2}, 1)$.

If $P \geq 2$, then the total demand for good 2 is $\tfrac{1}{2}P + \tfrac{1}{2}$ and, subject to $P \geq 2$, this is minimized when $P = 2$. The excess demand for good 2 is $\tfrac{1}{2}$ when $P = 2$. If $P < 2$, then the demand for good 1 is $1 + 1/2P$ and this is minimized (subject to $P \leq 2$) when $P = 2$. The excess demand, $1 + 1/2P - 1$, must be at least $1 + \tfrac{1}{4} - 1 = \tfrac{1}{4}$ when $P < 2$.

There is no price system under which excess demand is less than $\tfrac{1}{4}$ for every good. For any even number n of agents, however large, we can construct an economy in which excess demand is always at least $\tfrac{1}{8}n$ times the total supply for some good. An economy in which half the agents are identical to individual 1 (above) and the other half are identical to individual 2 has this property.

The difficulty cannot be attributed to any discontinuity in individual preference; there is no sudden change in taste as a result of a small change in consumption. This is easy to verify in the present example since the utility functions are continuous. Individual 1's demand discontinuity results from a discontinuity in the budget set as prices vary. For all $P < 2$ the budget set, the set of affordable commodity bundles in X_1, is the singleton $(1, 0)$, but when P reaches 2, it explodes to become the line segment $\{x_1 \geq 0: 2x_{11} + x_{12} = 2\}$. This type of discontinuity cannot occur if there is some vector x_1 in the consumption set such that $w_1 \gg x_1$, as the reader can verify by experimenting with a diagram. In other words, if i's endowment is interior to his consumption set, the budget set will change continuously as prices change. If preferences are also continuous, then demands will vary continuously as prices change. If, as in the example of this section, demands do not vary continuously as prices change, an equilibrium may not exist. If the supply of good 1 exceeds the demand and P falls as the economy attempts to adjust to equilibrium, then demand increases as P declines. But if there is a sudden jump in the demand for good 1, the economy can find itself in a situation where the demand for good 1 exceeds supply for all prices less than, say, 2 and supply exceeds demand at all other prices. And in no case is the difference relatively small.

Rational expectations

This example features a two-person exchange economy with two states of nature, R (rain) and S (sunshine). The market mechanism is used to allocate commodities, but the traders do not have access to a complete set of markets. Specifically, they cannot order commodities conditional on the state of nature. There are two basic goods, $c = 1, 2$, and orders for these must be placed before everyone has direct knowledge of the state. Individual 2, however, receives an advance signal that is perfectly correlated with the realized state, and when he places his orders for goods, he will know which state has occurred. Individual 1 has no direct knowledge of the state until after he places his orders. Let us see if he can infer which state has been realized by observing market prices.

The endowments are not uncertain, but utility is because the contribution of each good to utility depends on whether R or S occurs: Let $u_i^t(x_i)$ be the utility of individual i when x_i is consumed and state t occurs ($t = R, S$). For $i = 1, 2$ $u_i^R(x_i) = (x_{i1})^{1/4}(x_{i2})^{1/4}$. If S occurs, then 1 places more weight on commodity 2, with $u_1^S(x_1) = (x_{11})^{1/4}(x_{12})^{1/2}$, and 2 places more weight on commodity 1, with $u_2^S(x_2) = (x_{21})^{1/2}(x_{22})^{1/4}$. One plausible interpretation is that commodity 2 is leisure, and individual 1 is more interested in consuming leisure when S occurs, for obvious reasons, but 2, who likes gardening, will devote more leisure to his hobby when R occurs. Let the endowments be $w_1 = (0, 1)$ and $w_2 = (1, 0)$, which do not depend on the state. Normalize and set the price of good 2 equal to unity. Let P be the price of commodity 1.

Let $x_{11}(P)$ be 1's demand for good 1 as a function of its price. We are assuming that 1 does not have any knowledge of the state when he places his demands. Individual 2 will demand $\frac{1}{2}$ a unit of good 1 if R occurs. (Maximize u_2^R subject to $Px_{21} + x_{22} = P$.) Therefore, if P^R clears both markets when R occurs, we will have $x_{11}(P^R) = \frac{1}{2}$. If S occurs, then 2 will demand $\frac{2}{3}$ of a unit of good 1. (Maximize u_2^S subject to the budget constraint.) Therefore, $x_{11}(P^S) = \frac{1}{3}$ if P^S clears both markets when S occurs. Since $x_{11}(P^R) \neq x_{11}(P^S)$, we have $P^R \neq P^S$.

If 2 is the informed trader and 1 is completely uninformed, then 2's knowledge will be revealed to 1 by means of the market prices. As a result, the prices P^R and P^S will not constitute a (rational expectations) equilibrium after all since 1 will want to revise his demands after observing market prices. Therefore, a rational expectations equilibrium pair of prices P^{*R} and P^{*S} will equate supply and demand when *both* agents are assumed to have advance knowledge of the state. If R occurs and 1 knows it, he will demand 1/2P units of good 1. Trader 2 will demand $\frac{1}{2}$ a unit. Therefore, $1/2P^{*R} = \frac{1}{2}$ or $P^{*R} = 1$ if P^{*R} is to clear both markets. Now, suppose that S occurs and both know it. Trader 1 will demand $\frac{1}{3}P$ units of good 1, and 2 will demand $\frac{2}{3}$ of a unit. Both markets will clear only if $P^{*S} = 1$ when S occurs and both traders are aware of this. But $P^{*R} = P^{*S}$, contradicting the supposition that trader 1 can discover what 2 has learned by means of the market clearing prices. Therefore, there is no rational expectations equilibrium.

This example is taken from Anderson and Sonnenschein (1982), who in turn credit Kreps (1977).

Competitive insurance markets

As explained in Section 4.8, an equilibrium set of insurance contracts does not exist if there is a relatively small number of high-risk individuals and insurance companies cannot distinguish the high-risk types from the low-risk types, except through their responses to various contract proposals. In general, a single contract proposal is not consistent with equilibrium since it will pay insurance companies to change the terms, offering slightly less coverage at a lower premium, in a way that will not be attractive to the high-risk types but will be preferred by the low-risk individuals to the original contract. And if a company has only low-risk customers, it will have fewer claims and can make more profit if the new terms are judiciously chosen. If the number of high-risk types is low, a situation in which the two risk types buy different contracts cannot be consistent with equilibrium either since insurance companies are forced to design a contract with very low coverage and premium for the low-risk group in order to prevent high-risk customers, who cannot be identified directly, from buying it. A single contract with higher premium and coverage would be more attractive to both groups than their respective current contracts, and since it is more valuable to individuals, terms could be struck so that insurance companies would receive more profit. Hence, there is no equilibrium.

Average cost taxation

If one is determined to ignore the question of the existence of equilibrium, a mechanism that computes an optimal provision level for public goods can be designed quite easily; simply charge each household i some constant fraction λ_i of the cost of the public goods provided. Individuals can request changes in the vector of public goods, and these changes will result in a different mix of public goods and different tax burdens. The system is in equilibrium when all firms, including suppliers of public goods, are maximizing profit, demand equals supply in the usual sense in private goods markets, and no one proposes a change in the mix of public goods provided. Any such equilibrium is Pareto optimal as proved in Section 3.7. Obviously, there would have to be an unusual coincidence of preference for an equilibrium to exist since there would have to be a provision level of the public good at which i's marginal rate of substitution was λ_i/λ_a times a's marginal rate of substitution for *all* i and a with the λ's being predetermined fractions.

Majority rule

Any equilibrium of a majority rule voting process must be Pareto optimal: If everyone preferred outcome x to outcome y, then y could not survive a majority vote. If we could be sure that a majority equilibrium always exists, majority rule would be the obvious way to determine the optimal mix of public goods. However, counterexamples are not hard to find. Suppose there are three groups of voters of equal size and three alternatives x, y, and z. Group 1 prefers x to y to z. Group 2 prefers y to z to x. Group 3 prefers z to x to y. Then no alternative could survive a majority contest with every other alternative: z would defeat x, x would defeat y, and y would defeat z.

Fortunately, there are some simple and plausible conditions under which equilibrium is assured.

6.2   An abstract economy

There are N agents. Agent a chooses an action, or message, m_a from the *message set* M_a, a subset of R^k, k-dimensional Euclidean space. Then $M = M_1 \times M_2 \times \cdots \times M_N$ is the universal set of message N-tuples m, which specify a message m_a for each agent a. Agent a's message may be constrained by the messages announced by other agents. This is expressed by the *constraint correspondence* $B_a : M \to M_a$. If $m = (m_1, m_2, \ldots, m_N)$ is the N-tuple of currently transmitted messages, then agent a may revise his message, but his new message must belong to $B_a(m)$. An equilibrium message N-tuple m must be individually feasible in the sense that $m_a \in B_a(m)$, $a = 1, 2, \ldots, N$. Each agent a has a *preference correspondence* $P_a : M \to M_a$. If $m'_a \in P_a(m)$, then a prefers the outcome that results from the message N-tuple $(m_1, m_2, \ldots, m_{a-1}, m'_a, m_{a+1}, \ldots m_N)$ to the outcome that results from $(m_1, m_2, \ldots, m_{a-1}, m_a, m_{a+1}, \ldots, m_N)$. This reflects the competitive assumption: If a switches from m_a to m'_a, in order to precipitate a preferred outcome, he takes the messages of the other agents as given.

A *competitive equilibrium* of the abstract economy is a message N-tuple $m \in M$ such that $m_a \in B_a(m)$ and $P_a(m) \cap B_a(m) = \emptyset$ for each agent a. In words, m_a is feasible for agent a, given the messages of others, and there is no feasible message that generates an outcome preferred by a to the one associated with m, given the messages of others. If both hold true for all agents at once, then m is a competitive equilibrium.

It is worth remarking at this point that there is no logical reason why P_a need be based squarely on household a's preferences. Indeed, $P_a(m)$ can reflect whatever response the planner wishes a to make to the announced configuration m of messages, whether or not this would change the outcome in a way that coincides with a's self-interest. However, if P_a does not reflect a best response in terms of a's true utility function, there is little likelihood that a will follow the rules implicit in P_a. An equilibrium might exist for the abstract economy, but it would not be the one that emerges in a particular application of the mechanism.

6.3   The Walrasian mechanism as an abstract economy

We are interested in the existence of a Walrasian competitive equilibrium for a particular environment e. Let I be the set of households and J be the set of firms. For each $i \in I$, e specifies a consumption set $X_i \subset R^k_+$, an endowment $w_i \in X_i$, a utility function $u_i : X_i \to R^1$, and the share α_{ij} of firm j owned by i. (Of course, $\alpha_{ij} \geq 0$ and $\Sigma_{i \in I} \alpha_{ij} = 1$.) For each $j \in J$, e specifies a technology set $Y_j \subset R^k$. We will show how e induces a specification of an abstract economy with equilibria that are Walrasian competitive equilibria for e.

Set $N = 0 + n + r$, where n is the number of households and r is the number of firms. One of the agents in the abstract economy is the planner, who will be agent 0. $M_0 = \{p \in R^k : p \geq 0 \text{ and } p_1 + p_2 + \cdots + p_k = 1\}$: The planner announces a price vector p. If $a \in I$, set $M_a = X_a$, and if $a \in J$, set $M_a = Y_a$. For both $a = 0$ and $a \in J$ the constraint correspondence is constant: $B_a(m) = M_a$ for all $m \in M$. If $m \in M$, set $m = (p, x, y)$: $m_0 = p$, x_i is the message, or demand, of the ith household, and y_j is the message, or input–output plan, of the jth firm. For all $m = (p, x, y) \in M$ and $a \in I$

$$B_a(m) = \left\{ x'_a \in M_a : px'_a \le pw_a + \sum_{j \in J} \alpha_{aj} py_j \right\}$$

(By convention, $y_{jc} < 0$ if and only if the plan y_j requires commodity c as input. Therefore, py_j is the profit realized by j and $pw_a + \sum_{j \in J} \alpha_{aj} py_j$ is a's total income.)

Finally, we specify the preference correspondences. Choose arbitrary $m = (p, x, y) \in M$.

$$P_0(m) = \left\{ q \in M_0 : (q - p) \left(\sum_{i \in I} x_i - \sum_{i \in I} w_i - \sum_{j \in J} y_j \right) > 0 \right\}$$

For any $i \in I$

$$P_i(m) = \{ x'_i \in M_i : u_i(x'_i) > u_i(x_i) \}$$

For any $j \in J$

$$P_j(m) = \{ y'_j \in M_j : py'_j > py_j \}$$

In words, the planner prefers q to p if the former places a higher value on excess demand. This reflects an adjustment rule under which the planner, observing that p does not clear all markets, raises the price of any good for which there is excess demand. The other preference correspondences reflect agent decisions in a market economy in the obvious way. (Note that P_a, for $a \in I$, can be defined without a utility function: $P_a(m)$ is the set of x'_a that a strictly prefers to x_a.)

Suppose that $m = (p, x, y)$ is an equilibrium of the abstract economy. Since $x_i \in B_i(m)$ and $P_i(m) \cap B_i(m) = \varnothing$, the consumption plan x_i maximizes u_i subject to the budget constraint given prices and firm profits. Since $y_j \in B_j(m)$, the input–output plan is feasible for firm j. It is also profit maximizing since $B_j(m) \cap P_j(m) = \varnothing$. It remains to show that demand equals supply. First, we show that there is no excess demand. Since $x_i \in B_i(m)$ for all $i \in I$, we have

$$p\sum_{i \in I} x_i \le p\sum_{i \in I} w_i + \sum_{i \in I}\sum_{j \in J} \alpha_{ij} py_j$$

(Sum the budget inequality over all i.) This inequality simplifies to

$$p\sum_{i \in I}(x_i - w_i) \le p\sum_{j \in J} y_j \tag{6.1}$$

This means that

$$p\left(\sum_{i \in I}(x_i - w_i) - \sum_{j \in J} y_j \right) \le 0$$

If $\sum_{i \in I}(x_{ic} - w_{ic}) > \sum_{j \in J}y_{jc}$ holds for some commodity c, then

$$(q - p)\left[\sum_{i \in I}(x_i - w_i) - \sum_{j \in J}y_j\right] > 0$$

if we set $q_c = 1$ and set all other prices equal to zero. But this contradicts $B_0(m) \cap P_0(m) = \emptyset$. Therefore,

$$\sum_{i \in I}(x_i - w_i) \le \sum_{j \in J}y_j \qquad (6.2)$$

must hold.

This is actually as far as we can go without an additional assumption on household preferences. Suppose that each u_i satisfies *budget exhaustion:* If x_i maximizes u_i subject to the budget constraint (given p), then px_i equals i's total income. Budget exhaustion (for each household) implies that (6.1) holds as a strict equality. This, along with inequality (6.2), implies that any good in excess supply has a zero price. Therefore, (p, x, y) is a Walrasian competitive equilibrium.

(Budget exhaustion is usually obtained by assuming *local nonsatiation:* For any commodity vector x_i any neighborhood of x_i, however small, contains a commodity vector that is strictly preferred to x_i.)

6.4   The Shafer–Sonnenschein existence theorem

The theorem is stated, and its hypothesis explained, in this section. The role of each of the conditions of the hypothesis is elucidated in the next section. The proof itself is relegated to Appendix 3. (It requires much more than intermediate calculus, which suffices for the rest of this book.)

Theorem 6.1. *An abstract economy has a competitive equilibrium if for each agent a:*

M_a *is bounded, closed, and nonempty.*	(6.3)
M_a *is a convex set (in R^k).*	(6.4)
B_a *is a continuous correspondence.*	(6.5)
$B_a(m)$ *is a convex set for each m in M.*	(6.6)
P_a *has an open graph in $M \times M_a$.*	(6.7)
$P_a(m)$ *is a convex set for each m in M.*	(6.8)
For any m in M, $P_a(m)$ does not contain m_a.	(6.9)

As usual, R^k is k-dimensional Euclidean space: the set of all k-tuples $x = (x_1, x_2, \ldots, x_k)$ of real numbers, with $\|x\| = (x_1^2 + x_2^2 + \cdots +$

$x_k^2)^{1/2}$ defining the length of the vector x. A subset A of R^k is said to be *bounded* if there is some real number β such that $\|x\| \leq \beta$ for all $x \in A$. Set A is *closed* if it contains all of its boundary points. The vector $b \in A$ is a *boundary point* of A if for every real number $\varepsilon > 0$ there is some $x \in A$ such that $\|x - b\| < \varepsilon$ *and* some $y \notin A$ (and in R^k) such that $\|y - b\| < \varepsilon$. Since $\|z - b\|$ is the distance between z and b, a vector is a boundary point of A if it is in A (in which case we can set $x = b$) and arbitrarily close to points y not in A *or* it is not in A (in which case we can set $y = b$) and arbitrarily close to points x in A. If $k = 1$ and $A = \{\lambda \in R^1 : 0 \leq \lambda < 1\}$, then A is bounded (set $\beta = 1$); it is not closed since 0 and 1 are boundary points of A but 1 does not belong to A.

A set A in R^k is *convex* if for all a and b in A the vector $\lambda a + (1 - \lambda)b$ belongs to A for any real number λ such that $0 \leq \lambda \leq 1$. (See Appendix 1 for a brief discussion of convexity.)

A *function* $f : R^{Nk} \rightarrow R^k$ is continuous if for every pair of sequences $\{x^t : t = 1, 2, \ldots\}$ and $\{y^t : t = 1, 2, \ldots\}$ in R^{Nk} and R^k (respectively) converging to x and y (respectively) we have $f(x) = y$ if $f(x^t) = y^t$ for $t = 1, 2, \ldots$. A *correspondence* $B_a : M \rightarrow M_a$ for $M \subset R^{Nk}$ and $M_a \subset R^k$ is continuous if (i) for any $x \in M$ and $y \in M_a$, if the sequences $\{x^t : t = 1, 2, \ldots\}$ and $\{y^t : t = 1, 2, \ldots\}$ converge to x and y, respectively, and $y^t \in B_a(x^t)$ for all t, then $y \in B_a(x)$ and (ii) if $y \in B_a(x)$ and the sequence $\{x^t : t = 1, 2, \ldots\}$ converges to x, then there exists a sequence $\{y^t : t = 1, 2, \ldots\}$ converging to y and such that $y^t \in B_a(x^t)$ for all t.

A preference correspondence has an open graph if when one state is preferred to another, then anything sufficiently close to the former is preferred to anything sufficiently close to the latter. That is, the preference scheme is continuous; there are no large changes in preference resulting from small changes in the outcome. Formally, P_a has an open graph if, given $m_a' \in P_a(m)$, there is a real number $\varepsilon > 0$ such that $m_a'' \in P_a(\hat{m})$ whenever $\|m_a'' - m_a'\| < \varepsilon$, $\|\hat{m} - m\| < \varepsilon$, and m_a'' and $\hat{m}$ belong to M_a and M, respectively. This is equivalent to the requirement that the set $\{(m, m_a') : m_a' \in P_a(m)\}$, which is the graph of P_a, is an open set in $M \times M_a$.

Now we consider the economic significance of the various elements of the hypothesis of Theorem 6.1.

It is difficult to quarrel with assumption (6.9). It simply says that agent a does not prefer m_a to itself, given the messages of the other agents. This is really a defining property, indicating that strict preference is being represented. Condition (6.7), continuity of preference, is rarely questioned.

Convexity of $P_a(m)$ is, however, problematic. In the private ownership market economy $m_i' \in P_i(m)$ if and only if $u_i(x_i') > u_i(x_i)$ for $x_i' = m_i'$ and $x_i = m_i$, where i is a household. When is the set $U_i = \{x_i' \in$

$X_i:u_i(x_i') > u_i(x_i)\}$ likely to be convex? A counterexample is easily constructed by supposing that the consumer places a premium on extremes: If $u_i(x_i) = x_{i1}^2 + x_{i2}^2$, then $u_i(1, 0) = u_i(0, 1) = 1$, but

$$u_i[\tfrac{1}{2}(1, 0) + \tfrac{1}{2}(0,1)] = u_i(\tfrac{1}{2}, \tfrac{1}{2}) = \tfrac{1}{2}$$

The average of the two commodity bundles gives lower utility than either of the extreme bundles. Obviously, U_i is not convex for $x_i = (\tfrac{1}{2}, \tfrac{1}{2})$ since both $(1, 0)$ and $(0, 1)$ belong to that set but the average of the two, $(\tfrac{1}{2}, \tfrac{1}{2})$, does not. In short, $P_a(m)$ will be convex for household a if preferences are such that weighted averaging of commodity bundles is always utility enhancing and $P_a(m)$ will not be convex if preferences are such that a premium is sometimes placed on extremity. Section 6.6 demonstrates that an *approximate* equilibrium exists if the number of agents is large, even if $P_a(m)$ is not convex.

The set $P_a(m)$ is convex without restriction if a is a firm in a market economy; if $m = (p, x, y)$ and $py_a' > py_a$, $py_a'' > py_a$, then $p[\lambda y_a' + (1 - \lambda)y_a''] > py_a$ for any real number λ between zero and unity.

A preference correspondence is general enough to admit household preferences that are not self-regarding and also preferences that depend on announced prices. In fact, a firm in the Walrasian mechanism is nothing but an agent with price-dependent preferences. Because $P_a(m)$, the set of messages that a prefers to m_a, can depend on the messages announced by other agents, the abstract economy admits message-dependent preferences for any and all agents. For the same reason, household i's preference scheme need not be self-regarding: It can be sensitive to the consumption of other agents. Household i's preferences need not be representable by a utility function or even transitive under conditions (6.7)–(6.9). Utility functions are used in this chapter merely as an expositional convenience.

Finally, we consider the other elements of the hypothesis of Theorem 6.1. For any household i in a market economy, $B_i(m)$ is convex as the budget set. If $px_i \le \beta_i$ and $px_i' \le \beta_i$, then $px_i'' \le \beta_i$ for $x_i'' = \lambda x_i + (1 - \lambda)x_i'$ and for $0 \le \lambda \le 1$.

For any firm j, $B_j(m) = Y_j$ will not be convex (in the case of a private ownership market economy) if the technology set is not convex. If Y_j exhibits increasing returns to scale, there will be some $y_j \in Y_j$ such that $\tfrac{1}{2}y_j$ is not in Y_j. In words, y_j is a feasible input–output plan, but not when it is operated at half scale. If $0 \in Y_j$, then $\tfrac{1}{2}y_j = \tfrac{1}{2}(y_j) + \tfrac{1}{2}(0)$, and therefore Y_j is not convex. Return to the example at the beginning of this chapter to see why increasing returns to scale can prevent the existence of a competitive equilibrium.

Debreu (1959:64) proves that the budget correspondence B_i is continuous if the endowment vector is not on the boundary of the consumption set X_i. The second example of Section 6.1 shows why a discontinuity can result otherwise: $X_1 = \{x_1 \in R^2: 2x_{11} + x_{12} \geq 2\}$. Since $w_1 = (1, 0)$ and the example pertains to a pure exchange economy, we have

$$B_1(m) = B_1(p) = \{x_1: 2x_{11} + x_{12} \geq 2 \text{ and } p_1x_{11} + p_2x_{12} \leq p_1\}$$

Set $p' = (2 - 1/t, 1), t = 1, 2, \ldots$. This sequence of prices converges to $p^* = (2, 1)$, and $x_1^* = (\frac{1}{2}, 1)$ belongs to $B_1(p^*)$. However, for no value of t does $B_1(p')$ contain a vector close to x_1^*. In fact, $B_1(p') = \{(1, 0)\}$ for all t. There is a discontinuity at p^* where B_1 explodes.

We can usually assume with impunity that each message set M_a is convex since most mechanisms require it to be the nonnegative orthant, R_+^k, or Euclidean space for some finite k. This ensures that M_a is closed as well, but it is certainly at odds with boundedness since $(\lambda, \lambda, \ldots, \lambda) \in R_+^k$ for all positive real numbers λ. However, in proving that an equilibriums exists for some specific environment e, we can determine the maximum amount β_c of commodity c that the economy is capable of providing and set

$$M_i = \{x_i \in X_i: 0 \leq x_i \leq (\beta_1 + 1, \beta_2 + 1, \ldots, \beta_k + 1)\}$$

for each household i. It can be shown that an equilibrium of the truncated economy is an equilibrium of the original economy. Convexity is essential in proving this; one shows that if in the original economy an agent can do better for himself than by signaling his message as specified by the equilibrium of the truncated economy, then something like a convex combination of the two messages will lie inside the truncated message set and be better for the agent than his equilibrium message, contrary to the hypothesis that the truncated economy is in equilibrium. A similar technique will work for firms.

6.5   The role of the assumptions

To show that each of the requirements of the Shafer–Sonnenschein hypothesis is crucial to the proof of existence, we reduce the scope of the exercise so that there is only one agent ($N = 1$) and one commodity ($k = 1$). An equilibrium in this setting is simply a real number from M that produces the best outcome for the agent out of all those available. In other words, we will prove the existence of an optimal choice for the agent. The definition of equilibrium is not entirely satisfactory in this context, however. For example, suppose that $M = [0, 1] = \{\lambda \in R^1: 0 \leq \lambda \leq 1\}$, $B(m) = \{m\}$ for all m, and m is strictly preferred to m' if and only if $m > m'$. Every $m \in M$ is an equilibrium since, trivially, there is no $m' \in B(m)$ that is strictly preferred to m. But surely the individual would choose $m = 1$. This shortcoming of the definition of equilibrium need not distract us in this section for two reasons. First, we are merely concerned with technicalities at this point. Second, optimality of the equilibrium outcomes is addressed elsewhere in this book.

For each of the conditions in the Shafer–Sonnenschein hypothesis an example will be presented to show why the general existence theorem cannot be proved without it. Each example will satisfy every condition but one and an equilibrium will not exist.

Example 1 (*M* is not bounded)

$$M = R^1_+ = \{\lambda \in R^1: \lambda \geq 0\}$$
$$B(m) = M \text{ for all } m \in M$$
$$P(m) = \{m' \in M: m' > m\}$$

Here, *B* allows the agent to choose from all of *M* no matter which *m* is first picked, *P* reflects the notion that more is preferred to less, and *M* is closed since 0 is its only boundary point and that belongs to *M*. But *M* is obviously not bounded and for any $m \in M$ there is some $m' \in M$ such that $m' > m$. Therefore, no equilibrium exists.

Example 2 (*M* is not closed)

$$M = \{\lambda \in R^1: 0 \leq \lambda < 1\}$$

Correspondences *B* and *P* are defined in Example 1. The set *M* is bounded (by 1) but is not closed since 1 is a boundary point that does not belong to *M*. And, again, for every $m \in M$ there exists an $m' \in M$ such that $m' > m$; no equilibrium exists.

Example 3 (*M* is not convex)

$$M = \{\lambda \in R^1: 0 \leq \lambda \leq 1 \text{ or } 2 \leq \lambda \leq 3\}$$

Set *M* is bounded and contains all four of its boundary points. It is not convex since $\frac{3}{2} = \lambda(1) + (1 - \lambda)(2)$ for $\lambda = \frac{1}{2}$ but $\frac{3}{2} \notin M$. Again we set $B(m) = M$ for all *m*.

$$P(m) = [0, 1] = \{\lambda: 0 \leq \lambda \leq 1\} \quad \text{if } 2 \leq m \leq 3$$

and

$$P(m) = [2, 3] = \{\lambda: 2 \leq \lambda \leq 3\} \quad \text{if } m \in [0, 1]$$

Then *P* has an open graph in $M \times M$. We have $2 \in P(1)$, and for any $\varepsilon > 0$ there will be numbers $\lambda < 2$ such that $|2 - \lambda| = 2 - \lambda < \varepsilon$ and $\lambda \notin P(1)$. But these λ will not belong to *M*.

Nothing in [0, 1] can be an equilibrium since everything in [2, 3] is better, and vice versa.

Example 4 (*B* is not continuous)

$$M = [0, 1] = \{\lambda: 0 \le \lambda \le 1\}$$

Here *M* is closed, bounded, and convex.

$$P(m) = \{m' \in M: m' > m\}$$

Again, more is preferred to less. Finally,

$$B(m) = [0, 1) = \{\lambda: 0 \le \lambda < 1\}$$

This time $B(m)$ is not closed since it does not contain its right-hand boundary point. This means that it is not continuous. The sequence $\{1 - 1/t: t = 1, 2, \ldots\}$ converges to 1, which belongs to *M*, the sequence $\{m^t = 0: t = 1, 2, \ldots\}$ converges to 0, $1 - 1/t \in B(m^t)$ for all *t* but 1 $\notin B(0)$. And, of course, there is no equilibrium since for any $m \in [0, 1)$ there is some $m' > m$ in that set.

Example 5 [$B(m)$ is not convex]

$$M = [0, 1]$$

Set $B(m) = \{0, 1\}$ for all *m*. [Only zero and unity belong to $B(m)$.] Clearly, $B(m)$ is not convex.

$$P(m) = \{m': 0 \le m' < \tfrac{1}{4}\} \text{ if } m \in (\tfrac{3}{4}, 1] = \{\lambda: \tfrac{3}{4} < \lambda \le 1\}$$
$$P(m) = \{m': \tfrac{3}{4} < m' \le 1\} \text{ if } m \in [0, \tfrac{1}{4}) = \{\lambda: 0 \le \lambda < \tfrac{1}{4}\}$$

If *m* is an equilibrium, then $m \in B(m)$, and this implies $m = 0$ or $m = 1$. But $0 \in P(1)$ and $1 \in P(0)$, so neither can be an equilibrium.

Example 6 (*P* is not continuous)

$$M = [0, 1], B(m) = M \quad \text{for all } m$$
$$P(m) = \{m' \in M: m' > m\} \quad \text{if } m < 1$$
$$P(1) = \{0\}$$

Here *P* does not have an open graph since there are no points close to 0 that are better than points close to 1, even though 0 is better than 1. There is no equilibrium since each number in *M*, including 0, is inferior to some other number.

Example 7 [$P(m)$ is not convex]

$$M = [0, 1] \qquad B(m) = M \quad \text{for all } m$$

and

$$P(m) = \{m' \in M: m' \ne m\}$$

There is no equilibrium here since every point is worse than every other point. Of course, $P(m)$ is not a convex set for $0 < m < 1$ since $m = \lambda(0) + (1 - \lambda)1$ for $\lambda = 1 - m$ but $m \notin P(m)$ although $0 \in P(m)$ and $1 \in P(m)$.

Example 8 [$P(m)$ contains m]

$$M = [0, 1] = B(m) = P(m) \quad \text{for all } m$$

This section concludes with a demonstration that the Shafer–Sonnenschein theorem implies the existence of a best message (or demand) for agent a in $B_a(m^*)$ for arbitrary m_b^* ($b \neq a$), as long as B_a is independent of m_a. To obtain this corollary, define a one-agent abstract economy (M_a^*, B_a^*, p_a^*) with message set $M_a^* = M_a$. Set $B_a^*(m_a) = B_a(m^*)$ for all $m_a \in M_a^*$. Set $P_a^*(m_a) = \{m_a' \in M_a : m_a' \in P_a(m)$ where $m_b = m_b^*$ for all $b \neq a\}$ for $m_a \in M_a^*$. If m_a' is an equilibrium of this abstract economy, we have $m_a' \in B_a^*(m_a') = B_a(m^*)$ and $\emptyset = P_a^*(m_a') \cap B_a^*(m_a')$. Therefore, there is no $m_a \in B_a(m^*)$ that is better for a than m_a' given m_b^* for $b \neq a$. (When is $B_a(m^*)$ bounded?)

6.6   Nonconvexity

Consider an n-person, two-commodity exchange economy in which each consumer chooses to spend all of his income on whichever good is cheaper, and if the two prices are equal, he will still devote all of his income to the purchase of one good but will not care which good is consumed. Set $X_i = R_+^k$. If $w_i = (\frac{1}{2}, \frac{1}{2})$ for $i = 1, \ldots, n$, we must have $p_1 = p_2 > 0$ if (p, x) is an equilibrium. If not, each person will spend all of his income, $pw_i = \frac{1}{2}(p_1 + p_2)$, on the cheaper good and the total demand for this good will exceed n, which is far greater than the total supply of this good. If $p_1 = p_2$ and n is even, we can set $x_i = (1, 0)$ for half of the households and $x_i = (0, 1)$ for the other half. Then $\Sigma x_i = (\frac{1}{2}n, \frac{1}{2}n) = \Sigma w_i$ and (p, x) is a competitive equilibrium. If n is an odd number, however, one of the goods will be purchased by an even number of consumers and the total demand will be an integer although the supply is $\frac{1}{2}n$, which is not an integer when n is odd. If n is a very large odd number, we can set $x_i = (1, 0)$ for $\frac{1}{2}(n + 1)$ consumers and $x_i = (0, 1)$ for $\frac{1}{2}(n - 1)$ consumers. There will be excess demand for good 1 of $\frac{1}{2}$, but it will be a tiny fraction of the total supply if n is large. In that case we can take comfort in the notion of an approximate equilibrium; there is a price regime at which all markets approximately clear and any excess demand can be met through inventory reduction.

The reason an equilibrium may not exist in this case is that the demands are generated by nonconvex preferences. Verify that $u_i(x_i) = (x_{i1})^2 + (x_{i2})^2$ gives rise to the demand behavior described at the beginning of the previous paragraph. In this case, $u_i(1, 0) = u_i(0, 1) = 1 > \frac{1}{2} = u_i(\frac{1}{2}, \frac{1}{2})$, but $u_i [\frac{1}{2}(1, 0) + \frac{1}{2}(0,1)]$ does not exceed $u_i(\frac{1}{2}, \frac{1}{2})$. Because there are no discontinuities, however, there is a price regime under which markets clear in an approximate sense if the number of agents is large.

The same result holds true when nonconvexities arise on the production side and the range of increasing returns to scale is limited. To see why increasing returns and convexity of the technology set are in conflict, let $f(t)$ be the maximum amount of output a firm can produce with t units of input. Increasing returns to scale implies $f(2) > 2f(1)$. To simplify, suppose that $f(0) = 0$. Then $y^0 = (0, 0)$ and $y^2 = (-2, f(2))$ are both feasible (treating commodity 1 as the input) but $y^1 = \frac{1}{2}y^0 + \frac{1}{2}y^2 = (-1, \frac{1}{2}f(2))$ is not feasible since $f(1)$ is the maximum output from one unit of input and $f(1) < \frac{1}{2}f(2)$.

The next example illustrates why an approximate equilibrium exists if the initial range of increasing returns to scale is small relative to the market, even though there may not be a price system that exactly balances demand and supply in every market. There is one household, one firm, and two commodities.

$$X_1 = R_+^2, \quad w_1 = (\tfrac{3}{2}, 0) \qquad u_1(x) = \min\{x_1, x_2\}$$
$$Y_1 = \{y \in R^2 : 0 \geq y_1 \geq -\tfrac{8}{5} \text{ and } (y_1 + 2)(y_2 + \tfrac{1}{2}) \leq 1$$
$$\text{or } y_1 \leq -\tfrac{8}{5} \text{ and } y_2 \leq -y_1 - \tfrac{8}{5} + 2\}$$

The technology set is portrayed in Figure 6.1. The first commodity is an input in production and the second is an output. Note that $(0, 0)$ and $(-\frac{8}{5}, 2)$ belong to Y_1 but $(-\frac{4}{5}, 1) = \frac{1}{2}(0, 0) + \frac{1}{2}(-\frac{8}{5}, 2)$ does not since $(-\frac{4}{5} + 2)(1 + \frac{1}{2}) = \frac{9}{5}$. The maximum that can be produced with four-fifths of a unit of input is determined by solving $\frac{6}{5}(y_2 + \frac{1}{2}) = 1$. The plan that results is $y = (-\frac{4}{5}, \frac{1}{3})$. If we double both input and output, the plan $b = (-\frac{8}{5}, \frac{2}{3})$ is obtained, and this plan is feasible since $(-\frac{8}{5} + 2)(\frac{2}{3} + \frac{1}{2}) < 1$. For low levels of input $(y_1 > -\frac{8}{5})$ there are increasing returns to scale. For example, the most output that can be obtained with four-fifths of a unit of input is $\frac{1}{3}$, but if the input is doubled, the firm can produce six times as much output: $(-\frac{8}{5}, 2)$ is feasible. On the other hand, if $y_1 < -\frac{8}{5}$, there are decreasing returns to scale. If y is efficient (y belongs to Y_1 and there is no b in Y_1 such that $b \geq y$ and $b \neq y$), then λa is not feasible for any $\lambda > 1$ if $y_1 \leq -\frac{8}{5}$.

There is only one Pareto-optimal allocation in this economy. If (x, y) is Pareto optimal, then $x = (\frac{1}{2}, \frac{1}{2})$ and $y = (-1, \frac{1}{2})$. Let us see why. Because $x_1 \geq 0$, we must have $y_1 \geq -\frac{3}{2} > -\frac{8}{5}$. Therefore, (x, y) is feasible only if

$$0 \geq y_1 \geq -\tfrac{3}{2}, \ (y_1 + 2)(y_2 + \tfrac{1}{2}) \leq 1, \quad x \geq 0, \quad \text{and } x \leq y + (\tfrac{3}{2}, 0)$$

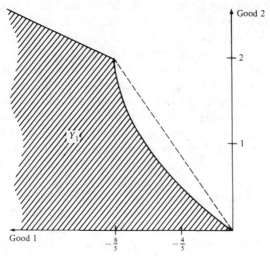

Figure 6.1

Pareto optimality obviously requires $x = y + (\frac{3}{2}, 0)$ and $x_1 = x_2$, which we can set equal to δ. Then $y = (\delta - \frac{3}{2}, \delta)$ and $(\delta - \frac{3}{2} + 2)(\delta + \frac{1}{2}) = 1$ so $\delta = \frac{1}{2}$. Therefore, $(x, y) = ((\frac{1}{2}, \frac{1}{2}), (-1, \frac{1}{2}))$. If this is a competitive equilibrium allocation, then there is a price system p at which the production plan $(-1, \frac{1}{2})$ is at least as profitable as $(0, 0)$ and at least as profitable as $(-\frac{8}{5}, 2)$. Therefore, $py \geq p0 = 0$. Since $(-\frac{8}{5}, 2) = \frac{8}{5}(-1, \frac{1}{2}) + (0, \frac{12}{10})$, we have $p(-\frac{8}{5}, 2) = \frac{8}{5}py + \frac{12}{10}p_2 > py$ since $py \geq 0$ and $p_2 > 0$ at equilibrium, contradicting the assertion that $(-1, \frac{1}{2})$ maximizes profit. Thus, (x, y) is not an equilibrium allocation with respect to any price system.

The best way to isolate the source of difficulty caused by nonconvexities in the production set is to examine the supply behavior of the firm in this example. Fix the price of input at unity $(p_1 = 1)$ and set $p_2 = P$. Now, trace the supply of output as a function of P. If $P < \frac{4}{5}$, then no feasible plan gives a positive profit and only the plan $y = 0$ maximizes profit. Nothing is supplied until P rises to $\frac{4}{5}$, at which point there are exactly two profit-maximizing plans, $(0, 0)$ and $(-\frac{8}{5}, 2)$. If $\frac{4}{5} \leq P < 1$, the firm's profit is $2P - \frac{8}{5}$, which is zero for $P = \frac{4}{5}$ and positive if $P > \frac{4}{5}$. If $P = 1$, then any production plan $(y_1, -y_1 + \frac{2}{5})$, for $y_1 \leq -\frac{8}{5}$, is profit maximizing with profit equaling $\frac{2}{5}$. If $P > 1$, the firm's supply will be arbitrarily large, since profit can be increased without limit by increasing the scale.

The utility function implies $x_1 = x_2$ (for $P > 0$). This and the budget equation implies that $x_1 = x_2 = $ (income)$/(P + 1)$. The household's in-

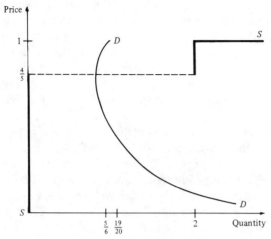

Figure 6.2

come will be $\frac{3}{2}$ plus profit income. Therefore, the household's demand for output, $x_2(P)$, is easily computed:

$$x_2(P) = \begin{cases} \frac{3}{2}(P + 1) & \text{if } 0 < P < \frac{4}{5} \\ (2P - \frac{1}{10})/(P + 1) & \text{if } \frac{4}{5} \le P \le 1 \end{cases}$$

This demand function, illustrated in Figure 6.2, is the general equilibrium demand, which allows for the effect of price on household income.

There is no equilibrium because the firm will not operate if $0 \le P < \frac{4}{5}$, although there will be a positive demand for output. If $P = \frac{4}{5}$, the firm will be indifferent between zero and two units of output: Either decision produces the maximum profit of zero. But demand is $\frac{5}{6}$ in that case, and the supply of output is either too much or too little. If $\frac{4}{5} < P < 1$, then profit is maximized by producing two units of output, but demand cannot be greater than $\frac{3}{2}$. If $P = 1$, then demand is $\frac{19}{20}$, but supply is at least 2.

If we make the supply curve continuous by connecting the dots (Figure 6.2), then an equilibrium would exist since the demand and supply curves would intersect. As it is, there is a discontinuity, or jump, in supply at $P = \frac{4}{5}$ and there can be no market clearing price.

Let us see why the supply discontinuity, caused by the region of increasing returns to scale, becomes relatively less troublesome as the number of consumers and firms increases. Suppose there are n households and m firms. Set $P = \frac{4}{5}$. A firm will produce either zero or two units of output. Let r be the number of firms that produce two units. The demand will be

$\frac{5}{6}n$. If $\frac{5}{6}n = 2r$ for some integer r between 1 and m inclusive, then *both* markets will clear. (Verify that the demand for input equals the supply.) If $\frac{5}{6}n$ is substantially larger than $2m$, then an equilibrium will occur in the decreasing returns-to-scale region. In general, let r be the integer such that $2(r-1) \leq \frac{5}{6}n \leq 2r$. If either r or $r - 1$ firms operate and produce two units each, then there will be excess demand or supply of two units or less, but the per capita difference between demand and supply will be small if n is large.

One important case remains. Suppose that there is one firm but n consumers. As n increases, the demand curve of Figure 6.2 shifts to the right. For n large enough the demand curve will eventually intersect the supply curve, identifying an exact competitive equilibrium. However, if the number of firms is small, they are unlikely to behave competitively. If the range of increasing returns is substantial, there will only be a few firms, since any firm that produces a large quantity of output will have significantly lower average costs than its smaller rivals and the latter will be driven out of the industry.

6.7   The counterexamples reconsidered

Obviously, increasing returns to scale contravenes the convexity requirement of the existence theorem.

If a consumer's endowment is on the boundary of his consumption set, his budget correspondence may not be continuous, violating another hypothesis.

In the case of the rational expectations example, the existence of market clearing prices can easily be established assuming that each agent has full knowledge of the state of nature, but the Shafer–Sonnenschein theorem does not guarantee that the equilibrium price regimes will be different for different states. It is highly unlikely that they will be identical, however, so the nonexistence of a rational expectations equilibrium is logically possible but unlikely. Another way of putting this is that if one of the parameters of one of the utility functions is changed even slightly, a rational expectations equilibrium will then exist.

An equilibrium is not guaranteed in the Rothschild–Stiglitz model of competitive insurance markets because an individual's constraint set is not convex. Two contracts are offered. An individual may choose either one, but not a convex combination of the two. This restriction is imposed by insurance companies so that they can separate the two risk categories.

The average cost taxation mechanism satisfies all of the criteria of the existence theorem, but when one introduces a planner in order to adjust prices *and* to ensure that the household demands for public goods are, in effect, equal, one is stymied. In other words, it is not possible to formulate this mechanism as an abstract economy in which the planner's preferences, which reflect the adjustment rule, are continuous.

The Shafer-Sonnenschein existence theorem does not apply to the majority rule example since the latter permits any *group* of individuals to change their messages, or ballots. The former proves that there is a message configuration from which no one *individual* would want to depart.

6.8 Summary

On the one hand, existence of equilibrium can be established by means of assumptions that are not at all extraordinary. On the other hand, there are important situations in which one or more of these assumptions are not satisfied.

6.9 Background

Walras (1874–7) was the first to describe the market system in a model with enough structure to permit one to ask if there is at least one price regime under which all markets will clear. Walras himself recognized the need for addressing the existence question. The formal proof of existence of an exact competitive equilibrium in a model of the private ownership market economy with a finite number of agents has been accomplished over the last fifty years. Three distinct episodes can be identified.

The first episode concludes with the first existence proof by Wald in 1936. Wald's results were published in German and are summarized in Wald (1951). The second attack on the problem yielded an existence proof under very general assumptions on preferences and technologies. Arrow and Debreu (1954), McKenzie (1968), and Gale (1955) led the way, elucidating the central role played by convexity. (McKenzie's paper first appeared in 1955.) The last episode, beginning with Mas-Colell (1974), provides a proof of existence of equilibrium under extraordinarily weak assumptions on household preference. This approach culminates with Gale and Mas-Colell (1975) and Shafer and Sonnenschein (1975).

Arrow and Hahn (1971) and Debreu (1982) discuss other approaches to the existence question in addition to the one outlined in this chapter.

EXERCISES

6.1 Define a simple two-person, two-commodity exchange economy e: $X_i = \{x_i = (x_{i1}\ x_{i2}):x_i \geq 0\}$, $u_i(x_i) = \min\{2x_{i1}, x_{i2}\}$, $i = 1, 2$, and $w_1 = (0, 1)$, $w_2 = (0, 1)$. (i) Construct an economy e' that is the same as e except that each i's consumption set X_i is replaced by $X_i' = \{x_i \geq 0{:}x_i \leq b\}$. Choose the vector b so that e and e' have the same Walrasian competitive equilibrium. (ii) Prove that e' satisfies each of the conditions in the hypothesis of the Shafer–Sonnenschein theorem. (iii) Characterize the Walrasian competitive equilibria of e.

6.2 Consider a two-commodity exchange economy with n identical consumers. Set $w_i = (1, 1)$ and

$$u_i(x_i) = \begin{cases} (x_{i1})^{1/4}(x_{i2})^{3/4} & \text{if } x_{i1} \leq x_{i2} \\ (x_{i1})^{3/4}(x_{i2})^{1/4} & \text{if } x_{i1} \geq x_{i2} \end{cases}$$

(i) Show that the utility function does not generate convex preferences. (ii) Derive the demand correspondence $x_i(p) = (x_{i1}(p_1, p_2), x_{i2}(p_1, p_2))$. Calculus will help here, but ingenuity and clear thinking are also required. (iii) Prove that there is no Walrasian competitive equilibrium for $n = 1$. (iv) What is the smallest value of n for which an equilibrium exists? If the consumers are identical in every respect, what is the source of the gains from trade at equilibrium? (v) For arbitrary n find the price system that reduces excess demand to its smallest possible value. Show that per capita excess demand approaches zero as n approaches infinity.

6.3 Construct a simple exchange economy for which preferences have all of the properties required by the Shafer–Sonnenschein theorem *and* for some individuals utility increases as consumption *decreases*. Find a price regime under which there is no positive excess demand for any good. Prove that one cannot insist on a zero price for any good that is in excess supply and still have nonnegative excess demand in every market. (You are required to design your example so that it has this property.)

6.4 Consider a simple "division of a cake" problem with three individuals. Each possible division corresponds to a nonnegative triple $x = (x_1, x_2, x_3)$ such that $x_1 + x_2 + x_3 \leq 1$. Now construct an abstract economy with one agent who prefers x to y if and only if $x_i > y_i$ for at least two i (division by majority rule). Prove that the preference scheme of this "agent" does not satisfy the convexity condition (6.8) of the Shafer–Sonnenschein theorem. Show that every division is defeated by some majority.

6.5 Let X be a closed, bounded, and nonempty convex set in R^k. Consider an individual whose preferences satisfy conditions (6.7)–(6.9) for $M_a = X = M$. Prove that there is some x^* in X such that no x in X is strictly preferred to x^* by constructing a one-agent abstract economy and applying the Shafer–Sonnenschein theorem.

6.6 Consider a simple economy with one private good and one public good. There are three consumers and one firm. The firm requires a minimum of $f(z)$ units of the private good to produce z units of the public good. Assume that $f' > 0$ and $f'' > 0$ at all points. Individual i's utility function is $u_i(x_i, z) = x_i + \delta_i z - \frac{1}{2}z^2$, where $\delta_i > 0$ and x_i is i's consumption of the private good. Establish conditions under which there exists a competitive equilibrium of the Groves–Ledyard mechanism.

CHAPTER 7

Welfare properties of the Walrasian mechanism

This chapter briefly summarizes the welfare implications of Walrasian competitive equilibrium. It complements Chapter 3 by highlighting the particular economic assumptions that render the welfare theorems non-vacuous. (A theorem is vacuous if the conditions of its hypothesis cannot be met. For example, if we prove that an equilibrium is Pareto optimal, we have to show that an equilibrium exists for the result to be non-vacuous.) To simplify the exposition, attention will be confined to pure exchange private goods economies. An allocation x specifies a bundle x_i of private goods for each household $i = 1, 2, \ldots, n$. As usual, p denotes a price vector and w_i is i's endowment vector.

We begin by recalling some basic definitions. A utility function u_i for individual i is *self-regarding* if it is independent of the consumption of other individuals. It is implicit throughout this chapter that utility functions are self-regarding and that markets are *complete:* Every good that affects someone's utility is traded in some market. An allocation is *Pareto optimal* if it is feasible and there is no feasible allocation that would make everyone better off. A feasible allocation is *strongly Pareto optimal* if there is no other feasible allocation that would make at least one person better off and leave no one worse off. It will usually be implicit that conditions are such that the two definitions are equivalent. If, for example, there is some commodity that everyone possesses and that is *desirable* in the sense that any increase in its consumption leads to an increase in utility, then the definitions are equivalent if each utility function is continuous. (See Exercise 2.1.)

Our discussion of the welfare implications of the Walrasian model of the private ownership market economy is inspired by the following three statements:

First welfare statement: If (p, x) is a Walrasian competitive equilibrium, then x is Pareto optimal.

Second welfare statement: If x is Pareto optimal, then there exists a redistribution of endowments and a price system p such that (p, x) is a Walrasian competitive equilibrium with respect to the new endowments.

147

Third welfare statement: If allocation y emerges at equilibrium when some, but not all, consumers can purchase some good at a subsidized price, then there is a redistribution of endowments giving rise to a Walrasian competitive equilibrium (p, x) such that each individual prefers x to y.

None of these statements is true and nonvacuous without a panoply of assumptions in addition to those already introduced. We proceed to identify the critical assumptions.

7.1   The first welfare statement

Theorem 3.1 establishes Pareto optimality of the competitive equilibrium allocation. The only restriction is that preferences are self-regarding. For the theorem to be nonvacuous, however, further restrictions must be placed on individual preference to ensure that an equilibrium exists in the first place. From an economic standpoint the most problematic of these restrictions is convexity of the set of commodity vectors that are strictly preferred by individual i to a given vector x_i. Section 6.6 provides an example of an exchange economy for which an equilibrium does not exist even though all of the conditions in the hypothesis of the Shafer–Sonnenschein existence theorem are met except for convexity of individual preference.

Nevertheless, there is no serious economic difficulty as long as the number of households is large and the individual preferences are continuous. Anderson, Khan, and Rashid (1982) prove that an approximate equilibrium will exist in this case. An approximate equilibrium is a price allocation pair (p, x) such that each household i chooses x_i under the budget constraint defined by p and per capita excess demand is exceedingly small, if not zero. In that case x will be *approximately Pareto optimal:* It is approximately feasible and no feasible allocation would make everyone better off. The second claim is proved in the standard way. If each i prefers y_i to x_i, then $py_i > pw_i$. (Because x_i was chosen, y_i must not have been affordable.) Then $p\Sigma_{i=1}^n y_i > p\Sigma_{i=1}^n w_i$, which is inconsistent with $\Sigma_{i=1}^n y_i \leq \Sigma_{i=1}^n w_i$, and y cannot be feasible.

Not only is this proof invalid – for both exact and approximate equilibria – when one person's utility depends directly on the consumption of another, the first welfare statement itself also is invalid at that level of generality. If $w_1 = (1, 0)$, $w_2 = (0, 1)$, $u_1(x) = x_{11} + x_{12} - x_{22}$, and $u_2(x) = x_{21} + x_{22}$, then (p, w) is a Walrasian competitive equilibrium for $p_1 = p_2 = 1$ but $y = ((0, \frac{2}{3}), (1, \frac{1}{3}))$ gives both persons more utility than w.

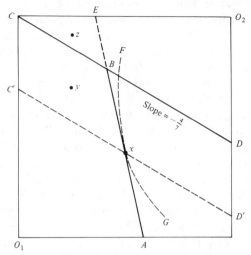

Figure 7.1

7.2   The second welfare statement

If individual preference is representable by a self-regarding utility function, then virtually any hypothesis under which the existence of an equilibrium can be proved will validate the second welfare statement. If x is strongly Pareto optimal, we need only find a Walrasian competitive equilibrium (p, y) for the economy in which preferences are as given and the endowment vector is x. We have $u_i(y_i) \geq u_i(x_i)$ for all i since y_i maximizes u_i subject to $py_i \leq px_i$. If $u_i(y_i) > u_i(x_i)$ for some i, then x is not strongly Pareto optimal since y is feasible (as an equilibrium allocation). Therefore, $u_i(y_i) = u_i(x_i)$ for all i. Therefore, (p, x) is also an equilibrium if x is the endowment vector. In fact, (p, x) is an equilibrium for any endowment vector $\hat{w}$ such that $\Sigma_{i=1}^{n} \hat{w}_i = \Sigma_{i=1}^{n} w_i$ and $p\hat{w}_i = px_i$ for $i = 1, \ldots,$ n. We can even think of redistribution as taking the form of a transfer of purchasing power – money? – so that each i has exactly px_i "dollars" of purchasing power.

Let us examine this argument with a little more care. Consider the two-person, two-commodity exchange economy represented in Figure 7.1. The set of commodity vectors preferred to x_1 by person 1 is the set of points above the straight line CBD. The set of feasible allocations that assign a vector to person 2 that 2 prefers to x_2 is the area $ABCO_1$, not including the boundary section ABC. If (p, x) is a competitive equilibrium, then the budget line will have to coincide with line AB. If it does not, there will be an affordable bundle below or above x that 2 prefers to x_2. However, if the budget line is ABE, then there will be points that 1 can afford and are preferred by 1 to x_1 (z_1, for example). Therefore, there is no redistribution of endowments for which x is an equilibrium allocation. But x is Pareto optimal since $ABCO_1$ and CDO_2 have no points in common except the common boundary BC and points on this line segment are preferred to x by neither individual. We have a Pareto-optimal allocation that is not an equilibrium allocation for any redistribution of endowments.

Consider two alternative specifications of individual 1's preference scheme in Figure 7.1. First, define the utility function u_1: $u_1(a) = 0$ for any a on or between lines CD and $C'D'$. If a is above CD, let $u_1(a)$ be the distance, by the shortest route, from a to CD. If a is below $C'D'$, let $u_1(a)$ be the negative of the distance from a to $C'D'$. In that case x is Pareto optimal but not strongly Pareto optimal and the argument at the beginning of this section does not apply. [Then $u_1(y_1) = 0 = u_1(x_1)$ but person 2 strictly prefers y_2 to x_2.] The problem is that the preferences of 1 do not satisfy *local nonsatiation* (LNS): There is a region around x_1 that does not contain any point strictly preferred by 1 to x_1. Evidently, without LNS the second welfare statement is valid only for the strong form of Pareto optimality.

The second specification of 1's preference scheme cannot be expressed by a utility function. Suppose 1 strictly prefers a to b if and only if $4a_1 + 7a_2 > 4b_1 + 7b_2 + \frac{3}{2}$. Then $(\frac{3}{4}, 0)$ is indifferent to $(\frac{1}{2}, 0)$, which is indifferent to $(\frac{1}{4}, 0)$. Equation $u_1(\frac{3}{4}, 0) = u_1(\frac{1}{2}, 0) = u_1(\frac{1}{4}, 0)$ would contradict the strict preference of $(\frac{3}{4}, 0)$ over $(\frac{1}{4}, 0)$. When indifference is not transitive, the weaker definition of Pareto optimality should be employed; strong Pareto optimality refers to individual indifference, the welfare significance of which is unclear in many cases where someone's preference scheme is not compatible with a utility function. As we have shown, x is Pareto optimal but there is no price system p for which (p, x) is a Walrasian competitive equilibrium regardless of the specification of endowments.

The difficulty illustrated by Figure 7.1 can be eliminated by invoking LNS. In economic terms this means that some change, however small, results in a preferred allocation if the change is in the right direction. Geometrically, LNS means that x_i is on the boundary of the set of commodity bundles strictly preferred by i to x_i. This requires a modification of the example so that the boundary of 1's preferred set goes through x. Suppose that this boundary is $C'D'$. Then x is no longer Pareto optimal; y is strictly preferred to x by both 1 and 2. For x to be Pareto optimal when each preference scheme satisfies local nonsatiation, the preferred sets must have x as a common boundary point and have no allocation in common. Suppose, for example, that the broken curve FG is the boundary of the set of allocations preferred by 1 to x. In that case, the budget line AE confirms the second welfare statement. Any endowment point on AE, including x itself, will result in a Walrasian competitive equilibrium (p, x) as long as $-p_1/p_2$ equals the slope of AE.

In general, if x is Pareto optimal and for each i the set of bundles strictly preferred by i to x_i is convex and contains x_i as a boundary point, then the second welfare statement is true. (Convexity is discussed in relation to Figure A.1 of Appendix 1; see also Figure A.3.) The proof is based on the *separating hyperplane theorem* (Nikaido, 1968: 26). In two dimensions a hyperplane is a straight line, and we see in Figure 7.1 that there is a line (AE) separating the preferred sets of 1 and 2 because the preferred sets do not have any points in common (Pareto optimality) and they are convex. Convexity is a crucial part of the hypothesis of the separating hyperplane theorem. In economic terms this requires that z be strictly preferred to x_i by i if a and b are strictly preferred to x_i and z is a weighted average of a and b. (Specifically, $z = \lambda a + (1 - \lambda)b$ for some number λ between zero and unity.) In even plainer words, there is no premium on extremes in consumption. The economic counterpart of the separating hyperplane is a price regime p. A hyperplane is the set of all points a such that $p_1a_1 + p_2a_2 + \cdots + p_ka_k = \alpha$, given the nonzero k-vector p and the real number α. In two dimensions it is a line with slope $-p_1/p_2$. (Refer to the original interpretation of Figure 7.1 to confirm that two disjoint convex sets cannot necessarily be separated by a hyperplane at a point x unless x is on the boundary of both sets. Translate the geometry back into economics: boundary = LNS, etc.)

Although we did not need to assume LNS in verifying the second welfare statement when each i's preference scheme is representable by a utility function, LNS was implicit. Otherwise, Pareto optimality may not imply strong Pareto optimality. If u_1 does not satisfy LNS at x_1, there is some small reduction in 1's consumption of each good that will not cause u_1 to fall. If u_2 is monotonic, then the goods so released can be transferred to person 2 to increase u_2 without decreasing u_i for any $i \neq 2$; the original allocation x is not strongly Pareto optimal. (LNS is also employed to ensure that demand equals supply at equilibrium, but $\Sigma x_i \neq \Sigma w_i$ is usually incompatible with Pareto optimality of x.)

As an exercise the reader can try to generalize the argument of the beginning of this section to cases where preferences cannot be represented by utility functions. Let e be an exchange economy for which LNS holds at x_i for each i and suppose that x is strongly Pareto optimal. Construct an economy e' with endowments $w' = x$ and contrived utility functions u_i ($\forall i$) defined as follows: Δ_i is the boundary of the set of y_i strictly preferred by i to x_i. If a is strictly preferred to x_i, then $u_i(a)$ is the distance, by the shortest route, from a to Δ_i. If $a \in \Delta_i$, then $u_i(a) = 0$. Otherwise, $u_i(a)$ is the negative of the distance from a to Δ_i. Show, geometrically or rigorously, that $\{a: u_i(a) > u_i(b)\}$ is convex *if* the set $\{a: a$ is strictly preferred by i to x_i in economy $e\}$ is convex. There exists a "quasi-equilibrium" (p, y) for e' such that $(\forall i)\ py_i \le px_i$ and $u_i(a) > u_i(y_i)$ implies $pa > px_i$ $(\forall a)$. $(\Sigma y_i = \Sigma x_i$ may not hold.) Strong Pareto optimality of x in e implies $u_i(y_i) = u_i(x_i)\ \forall i$. Let $\hat{e}$ be the economy with the same individual preferences as e but with endowments $\hat{w} = x$. Then (p, x) is a Walrasian competitive equilibrium for $\hat{e}$: If a is strictly preferred by i to x_i, then $u_i(a) > u_i(x) = u_i(y_i)$ and hence $pa > px_i = p\hat{w}_i$.

(If each preference scheme satisfies convexity and LNS, the second welfare statement may still be false if $x_{ic} = 0$ for some i and c. As demonstrated by the second counterexample of Section 6.1, if i's endowment is on the boundary of the consumption set, an equilibrium may not exist due to a discontinuity in i's demand.)

7.3   The third welfare statement

The third welfare statement is just a vehicle for conveying the significance of the second. If different individuals face different prices, their marginal rates of substitution will not be equal, and the equilibrium will not be Pareto optimal. Whatever equity goals were intended can be met, and surpassed, according to the third welfare statement, by redistribution followed by individual optimization with respect to market-determined prices. In order to prove this claim, it is necessary to assume that the preference scheme of each individual i is representable by a continuous utility function u_i. A smoothness assumption guaranteeing the existence of marginal rates of substitution is also required. The next example, a two-person, two-commodity exchange economy, shows why.

$$w_1 = (\tfrac{1}{4}, \tfrac{3}{4}) \qquad w_2 = (\tfrac{3}{4}, \tfrac{1}{4})$$
$$u_1(a) = \min\{a_1, a_2\} \qquad u_2(b) = b_1(b_2)^{1/2}.$$

Let $p = (1, 1)$ and $q = (2, 1)$ be price vectors. Individual 1 is allowed to consume under regime p and individual 2 consumes under regime q. Both are able to sell goods 1 and 2 at the prices q_1 and q_2, respectively. Individual 1 maximizes u_1 subject to the budget constraint and will therefore demand $y_1 = (\tfrac{1}{2}, \tfrac{1}{2})$: Individual 1 receives two dollars for every unit of good 1 sold and not consumed by himself but cannot sell a unit for two dollars and then buy it back for one dollar. He pays one dollar for every unit of good 1 purchased over and above his endowment of $\tfrac{1}{4}$. The budget line is ABC in Figure 7.2; DEF is the indifference curve through y. If 1 purchases y_1, his net demand for good 1 is $\tfrac{1}{4}$, and since the government is

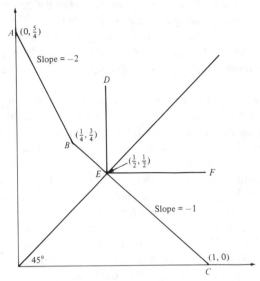

Figure 7.2

providing a one-dollar subsidy per unit of good 1 purchased by household 1, the amount of the subsidy is $\frac{1}{4}$. Therefore, individual 2 will pay a tax of $\frac{1}{4}$ and will maximize u_2 subject to $qy_2 \leq qw_2 - \frac{1}{4}$. Then 2 will demand $y_2 = (\frac{1}{2}, \frac{1}{2})$. We have a competitive equilibrium in this tax-subsidy modification of the Walrasian mechanism. Even though persons 1 and 2 are adjusting to difference prices, the allocation y is Pareto optimal. If $u_2(x_2) > u_2(y_2)$, then either $x_{21} > \frac{1}{2}$ or $x_{22} > \frac{1}{2}$. If x is also feasible, either $x_{11} < \frac{1}{2}$ or $x_{12} < \frac{1}{2}$, so $u_1(x_1) = \min\{x_{11}, x_{12}\} < \frac{1}{2} = u_1(y_1)$.

This example shows that the third welfare statement is false in general, even under the hypothesis that suffices for existence of equilibrium. This counterexample is not a trivial one for which y is a Walrasian equilibrium allocation for several different price vectors. There is no price vector $\hat{p}$ for which $(\hat{p}, y)$ is a Walrasian equilibrium with respect to endowments w_1 and w_2. We would have to have $\hat{p}_1 = 2\hat{p}_2$ if 2 is to demand y_2, so that the marginal rate of substitution at y_2 equals the price ratio. But if $\hat{p}_1 = 2\hat{p}_2$, then individual 1 cannot afford $y_1 = (\frac{1}{2}, \frac{1}{2})$ since $\hat{p}w_1 = \frac{5}{4}\hat{p}_2 < \frac{6}{4}\hat{p}_2 = \hat{p}y_1$.

To avoid this possibility, it will be assumed that marginal rates of substitution are defined at every point for every individual. In addition, each i's preference is assumed to be representable by a continuous utility function u_i, and for each x_i the set $\{x_i' : u_i(x_i') > u_i(x_i)\}$ is convex and has x_i as one of its boundary points (LNS). Marginal rates of substitution are guaranteed by the following *smoothness* assumption for arbitrary commodity vector x_i: If the price vectors p and q both have the property $px_i' > px_i$ and $qx_i' > qx_i$ whenever $u_i(x_i') > u_i(x_i)$, then $p = \lambda q$ for some real number $\lambda > 0$. The maximum amount of good k individual i would be prepared to sacrifice for an additional unit of good c, given initial consumption x_i, is $p_c/p_k = \lambda p_c/\lambda p_k = q_c/q_k$.

Now, suppose that a set I_1 of consumers purchase commodities at prices specified by p and the remaining consumers purchase goods under price regime q. Suppose that the resulting vector y of demands clears every market and that q is not equal to λp for any $\lambda > 0$. Let $(\hat{p}, x)$ be a Walrasian competitive equilibrium for the economy in which each i has an endowment y_i and the utility function u_i. We have $u_i(x_i) \geq u_i(y_i)$ for each i. If $u_i(x_i) = u_i(y_i)$ for each i, then $(\hat{p}, y)$ is an equilibrium also. By smoothness, $\hat{p} = \lambda_i p$ for each i in I_1 and $\hat{p} = \lambda_i q$ for each i not in I_1, contradicting the hypothesis that p is not proportional to q. Therefore, $u_i(x_i) > u_i(y_i)$ for some i. We have a Walrasian equilibrium allocation x that everyone finds at least as desirable as y and some find strictly more desirable. Now construct the feasible allocation x' from x by having some i for whom $u_i(x_i) > u_i(y_i)$ give a tiny amount of some desirable good to every other consumer in such a way that $u_i(x_i') > u_i(y_i)$ for all i. Let (p'', x'') be a Walrasian competitive equilibrium in the economy with endowment vector x'. We have $u_i(x_i'') \geq u_i(x_i') > u_i(y_i)$ for all i.

7.4   Summary

The conditions that ensure the existence of a Walrasian competitive equilibrium are precisely those needed to show that the first and second welfare statements are both true and nonvacuous. For the second welfare theorem to be used to claim that price controls are Pareto inferior to a strictly market-determined equilibrium corresponding to some redistribution of wealth, it is necessary to add a new condition, smoothness of indifference curves, to the hypothesis. Of course, practical and political considerations, beyond the scope of this book, may warrant a modification of the way that markets determine prices.

7.5   Background

The background notes to Chapter 3 are relevant to this chapter as well.

EXERCISES

7.1 Define a two-person, two-commodity exchange economy: $u_i(x_i) = (x_{i1})^{1/2}x_{i2}$ and $w_1 = (0, 1)$, $w_2 = (1, 0)$. (i) Characterize the set of Pareto-optimal allocations being careful with the cases where $x_{ic} = 0$ for some i and c and $x_{1c} + x_{2c} < 1$. (ii) Prove that every Pareto-optimal allocation is a Walrasian competitive equilibrium allocation for some distribution of wealth. (iii) Find the Walrasian competitive equilibrium for the given endowments. (iv) Suppose that the government wishes to assist individual 2 by subsidizing his consumption of commodity 2. If the announced price vector is $p = (p_1, p_2)$, then person 2 will pay $\frac{1}{2}p_2$ per unit of good 2 demanded and the subsidy is financed by a flat tax on 1's wealth. Determine the equilibrium that results from this tax-subsidy program. (v) Find a Pareto-optimal allocation that both individuals prefer to the equilibrium of (iv) and also a direct transfer of purchasing power from 1 to 2 for which this allocation would emerge at the corresponding Walrasian competitive equilibrium.

7.2 There are two countries, A and B, two commodities, and two households in each country. Assume that production has already taken place and has led to the following endowments:

	Country A	Country B
Consumer 1	(0, 12)	(0, 12)
Consumer 2	(12, 0)	(12, 0)

Each consumer in A has the utility function $u_i(x_i) = x_{i1}x_{i2}$ and each consumer in B has the utility function $u_i(x_i) = x_{i1}(x_{i2} + 8)$. Normalize so that the price of commodity 2 is always unity in each country. Let P be the price of commodity 1. (i) Find the Walrasian competitive equilibrium for each country, assuming they are not allowed to trade with each other. (ii) Find a world allocation that leaves every individual better off than under the no-trade equilibrium of (i). [Use the marginal rates of substitution of the allocation of (i) to suggest a welfare improving direction of trade.] (iii) Find the free trade equilibrium by computing each household's demand for good 1 as a function of P. Compute the utility of each consumer at the equilibrium. (iv) Explain the difference in utility levels at the allocations determined in (i), (ii), and (iii). Find a transfer of income *between consumers in A* and a resulting free trade equilibrium that would leave both consumers in A better off than in the no-trade situation (i).

Appendix 1: Elements of consumer choice

This chapter is concerned exclusively with individual choice. Let X be the universal set of alternatives. We wish to represent the individual's preferences in such a way that his choice from a subset B of X can be obtained from that representation. We begin with choice over two-element sets and build from there.

Definition: A *binary relation* Q on X is a subset of $X \times X$. If (x, y) belongs to Q, we write xQy. Relation Q is *complete* if, for all $x, y \in X$, either xQy or yQx holds; Q is *transitive* if, for all $x, y, z \in X$, xQy and yQz imply xQz. A complete and transitive binary relation is called a *weak order* and is represented by the letter R.

Since R is complete, we have xRx (set $y = x$). Since x cannot be strictly preferred to itself, the statement xRy must mean that x is at least as desirable as y: It may be that x is equally desirable as y, as in the case $y = x$, or that x is strictly preferred to y. We can be sure that y is not strictly preferred to x if xRy holds.

If x belongs to B and xRy for all $y \in B$, then x belongs to the set of *best* (or *most-preferred*) elements in B. A weak order allows us to determine choice on *any* finite set from choice on two-element sets. First, note that any complete binary relation Q is precisely a formula for expressing choice on two-element sets. Set $B = \{x, y\}$. If xQy and yQx, then B itself is the set of best elements from B. If xQy but not yQx, then $\{x\}$ is the set of best elements from B. Then a complete and transitive relation R determines a nonempty set of best elements for any finite set $B = \{x^1, x^2, \ldots, x^n\}$: Let C^t be the set of best elements from $\{x^1, x^2, \ldots, x^t\} = B^t$. Clearly, C^1 is not empty. Suppose that C^t is not empty, say $x \in C^t$ and xRy for all $y \in B^t$. If xRx^{t+1}, then x is best in B^{t+1}. If $x^{t+1}Rx$, then for any $y \in B^t$, $x^{t+1}Rx$ and xRy. Therefore, $x^{t+1}Ry$ by transitivity and hence x^{t+1} is best in B^{t+1}. Since R is complete, either xRx^{t+1} or $x^{t+1}Rx$ must hold. Then we have proved that B^1 contains a best element, and for any t, B^{t+1} contains a best element if B^t does. Therefore, B^n contains a best element.

Definition: If *xRy* and *yRx* both hold, we say that *x* and *y* are indifferent and write *xIy*. If *xRy* holds but *yRx* does not, we say that *x* is strictly preferred to *y* and write *xPy*.

From now on we take the universal set *X* to be the nonnegative orthant of *k*-dimensional Euclidean space.

Definition: A subset *A* of *k*-dimensional Euclidean space is *convex* if for all *x*, *y* $\in$ *A* the vector $\lambda x + (1-\lambda)y$ belongs to *A* for any real number λ such that $0 \le \lambda \le 1$.

To interpret convexity geometrically, pick an arbitrary vector *z*. Then $\{\lambda z: \lambda \in L\}$, where *L* is the real line, is the ray through *z* and the origin (set λ equal to 1 and 0, respectively). And for any *y* the set $\{y + \lambda z: \lambda \in L\}$ is the ray through *y* and parallel to the ray $\{\lambda z: \lambda \in L\}$ since we can write

$$\{y + \lambda z: \lambda \in L\} = \{y\} + \{\lambda z: \lambda \in L\}$$

If we confine λ to values in the closed interval $[0, 1] = \{\lambda \in L: 0 \le \lambda \le 1\}$, then we define a line segment $\{y + \lambda z: \lambda \in [0, 1]\}$. If we set $z = x - y$, we have

$$\{y + \lambda z: \lambda \in [0, 1]\} = \{y + \lambda(x - y): \lambda \in [0, 1]\}$$
$$= \{\lambda x + (1-\lambda)y: \lambda \in [0, 1]\}$$

which is the line segment between *x* and *y*, that is, that part of the ray through *y* and parallel to $\{\lambda(x - y): \lambda \in L\}$ and lying between *x* (set $\lambda = 1$) and *y* (set $\lambda = 0$). Therefore, *A* is convex if and only if for every *x*, *y* in *A* the line segment between *x* and *y* lies in *A*. This is illustrated in Figure A.1.

If *k* = 2, we may derive this geometric expression of convexity by computing the slope of the line through *x* and *y* and the slope of the line through *x* and $\lambda x + (1-\lambda)y$ for $0 < \lambda < 1$. The latter is

$$\frac{\lambda x_2 + (1 - \lambda)y_2 - x_2}{\lambda x_1 + (1 - \lambda)y_1 - x_1} = \frac{(1 - \lambda)(y_2 - x_2)}{(1 - \lambda)(y_1 - x_1)} = \frac{y_2 - x_2}{y_1 - x_1}$$

which obviously equals the slope of the line joining *x* and *y*. If two lines have the same slope and a point *x* in common, they coincide. Hence, $\lambda x + (1 - \lambda)y$ is on the line through *x* and *y*, and if $0 < \lambda < 1$, it lies between *x* and *y*.

Many results in economic theory turn on whether the *upper contour set* $Rx = \{y \in X: yRx\}$ is convex at an arbitrary point *x*.

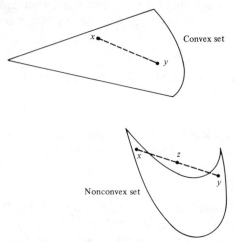

Figure A.1

Definition: R is a convex preference relation if Rx is convex for each x in X.

Definition: R is strictly convex if it is convex and if for all $y \in X$ and $x \in Ry$ such that $x \neq y$ we have zPy if $z = \lambda x + (1 - \lambda)y$ and $0 < \lambda < 1$.

Proposition A.1. *If R is a strictly convex binary relation on X and B is a convex subset of X, then there is at most one $x \in B$ such that xRy for all $y \in B$.*

Proof: Suppose $x \in B$, xRy for all $y \in B$. Suppose $y \in B$ and $y \neq x$. Set $z = \frac{1}{2}x + \frac{1}{2}y$. Then $z \in B$ since B is convex. Now, zPy since R is strictly convex. Therefore, yRz does not hold.   Q.E.D.

The significance of Proposition A.1 stems from the fact that the set of affordable commodity vectors is convex. It will be convenient to have a formal representation of this set.

Definition: A price system p is a nonnegative, nonzero k-vector $p = (p_1, p_2, \ldots, p^k)$ of real numbers. Of course, p_i is the price of commodity i. The income level m is a nonnegative real number. Then $B(p, m) = \{x \in X : px \leq m\}$ is the set of affordable commodity vectors for price system p and income level m.

Lemma A.1. $B(p, m)$ *is a convex set.*

Proof: If $x, y \in B(p, m)$, then $px \le m$ and $py \le m$. If $0 \le \lambda \le 1$, then $1 - \lambda \ge 0$ and thus both $\lambda px \le \lambda m$ and $(1 - \lambda)py \le (1 - \lambda)m$ hold. Then $\lambda px + (1 - \lambda)py \le \lambda m + (1 - \lambda)m = m$. But $\lambda px + (1 - \lambda)py = p(\lambda x) + p(1 - \lambda)y = p[\lambda x + (1 - \lambda)y]$. Therefore, $p[\lambda x + (1 - \lambda)y] \le m$ and $\lambda x + (1 - \lambda)y \in B(p, m)$. Hence, $B(p, m)$ is convex. Q.E.D.

Proposition A.2. *If R is strictly convex, then for any price system p and income level m, $B(p, m)$ contains at most one vector x such that xRy for all $y \in B(p, m)$.*

Proof: Lemma A.1 and Proposition A.1. Q.E.D.

If R is a weak order, then every *finite* nonempty set B contains at least one alternative x such that xRy for all y in B. Alternative x is a most-preferred alternative in B. Are completeness and transitivity sufficient for the existence of a most-preferred commodity vector in the budget set $B(p, m)$ for $p \gg 0$? The following is a counterexample.

Example: $k = 2$ and xRy if and only if $f(x) \ge f(y)$ where the function $f: X \rightarrow L$ is defined as follows:

$$f(x) = \begin{cases} 0 & \text{if } x_2 = 0 \\ x_1 & \text{if } x_2 > 0 \end{cases}$$

The relation $\ge$ is complete and transitive on L and thus R is complete and transitive. However, for any $m > 0$ the budget set $B(p, m)$ does not contain any x such that xRy for all $y \in B(p, m)$. If $x_2 > 0$, then yPx for $y = (x_1 + p_2x_2/2p_1, x_2/2)$. Since $py = px$, we have $y \in B(p, m)$ if $x \in B(p, m)$. If $x_2 = 0$, then $y = (m/2p_1, m/2p_2) \in B(p, m)$ and yPx.

The problem is that the preference relation is not continuous: The sequence $\{(1, n^{-1}): n = 1, 2, \ldots\}$ converges to $(1, 0)$ and $f(1, n^{-1}) = 1$ for all $n = 1, 2, \ldots$. But $f(1, n^{-1})$ converges to 1 although $f(1, 0) = 0$.

We need some new assumptions in order to establish the existence of a demand, or best commodity vector, in a budget set when preferences are represented by means of a weak order R.

Definition: The function u is a *utility representation* of R, or a *utility function* if there is no danger of ambiguity, if u is a real-valued function on X such that xRy if and only if $u(x) \geq u(y)$ for all $x, y \in X$.

Given a real-valued function u on X, we let R^u denote the weak order generated by u in the obvious way: xR^uy if and only if $u(x) \geq u(y)$. It is easy to verify that R^u is a weak order.

It is not the case that every complete and transitive ordering R is representable by a utility function. The following is the standard counterexample:

$k = 2$ and xRy if and only if (1) $x_1 > y_1$ or (2) $x_1 = y_1$ and $x_2 > y_2$.

This is called the lexicographic ordering. The reader can easily verify that R is a weak order. Debreu (1959:72) proves that it is not representable by a utility function.

We now proceed to some assumptions that are sufficient for representability.

Definition: R is monotonic if, for all x and y in X, $x \geq y$ implies xRy and $x \gg y$ implies xPy.

Definition: R is strongly monotonic if, for all x and y in X, $x \geq y$ and $x \neq y$ implies xPy.

In words, R is strongly monotonic if x is strictly preferred to y whenever x offers more of some good and at least as much as every good. And R is monotonic if y is not strictly preferred to x in this case and x is strictly preferred to y if the former offers more of every good.

Definition: R is partly continuous if, for all x and y in X, yPx implies λyIx for some real number $\lambda \geq 0$.

Suppose that R is represented by the *continuous* utility function u. Then if R is strongly monotonic, it is partly continuous: If λyRx for $\lambda = 0$, then $x = 0$ by strong monotonicity and hence $0yIx$. If $x \neq 0$, then $xP\lambda y$ for $\lambda = 0$ and λyPx for $\lambda = 1$ if yPx. That is, $u(1 \cdot y) > u(x) > u(0 \cdot y)$. If u is continuous, then $f(\lambda) = u(\lambda y)$ is a continuous function of λ (with y fixed). By the intermediate value theorem we have $f(\lambda) = u(x)$ for some λ between zero and unity since $f(1) > u(x) > f(0)$. Then λyIx for this value of λ.

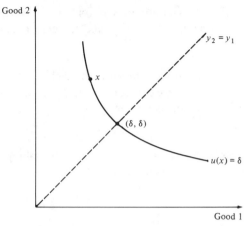

Figure A.2

Theorem A.1. *If R is a monotonic and partly continuous weak order, then it is representable by a utility function.*

Proof: Define $u(x)$: If $x_1 = x_2 \cdots = x_k$, set $u(x) = x_1$. If $x_i \neq x_j$ for some i and j, set $\beta = \max\{x_1, x_2, \ldots, x_k\}$ and $y = (2\beta, 2\beta, \ldots, 2\beta)$. Then yPx by monotonicity. And λyIx for some λ. Suppose we also had $\lambda'yIx$ for $\lambda' \neq \lambda$. If $\lambda' > \lambda$, we have $\lambda'yP\lambda y$ by monotonicity since $y_i > 0$ for all i and hence $\lambda'y_i > \lambda y_i$ for all i. But λyIx and $xI\lambda'y$ so $\lambda yI\lambda'y$ by transitivity of I. (Prove that I is transitive if R is.) But this contradicts $\lambda'yP\lambda y$. Similarly, $\lambda > \lambda'$ leads to a contradiction. Therefore, $\lambda' = \lambda$ and λ is unique. Now set $u(x) = \lambda y_1$.

   (In words, $u(x) = \delta$ for that value of δ for which $(\delta, \delta, \ldots, \delta)$ is indifferent to x. See Figure A.2.)

   Then u, as defined, represents R: Suppose xRy. Now aIx and yIb where $a = (u(x), u(x), \ldots, u(x))$ and $b = (u(y), u(y), \ldots, u(y))$. This follows from the definition of u. Then aRb by transitivity of R (aRy since aRx and xRy, and aRb since aRy and yRb). But if aRb and R is monotonic, we must have $u(x) \geq u(y)$. That is, xRy implies $u(x) \geq u(y)$. Now suppose $u(x) \geq u(y)$. Then xIa and yIb for a and b as defined above. Also aRb by monotonicity. Therefore, xRa, aRb, and bRy so xRy by transitivity of R. Hence $u(x) \geq u(y)$ implies xRy. In short, $u(x) \geq u(y)$ if and only if xRy.   Q.E.D.

From now on we will assume not only that R is representable by a utility function but also that u is continuous and differentiable.

Definition: The function $u: X \to L$ is continuous if for any convergent sequence $\{x^n\}$ in X the sequence $\{u(x^n)\}$ converges to $u(x^*)$, where x^* is the limit of $\{x^n\}$.

Definition: The function $u: X \to L$ is differentiable if for each $x \gg 0$ in X the partial derivatives $u^i(x) \equiv \partial u(x)/\partial x_i$ exist, for $i = 1, 2, \ldots, k$, and for any vector $dx = (dx_1, \ldots, dx_k)$ of increments

$$du = dx_1 u^1(x) + dx_2 u^2(x) + \cdots + dx_k u^k(x)$$

can be made arbitrarily close to $\Delta u = u(x + dx) - u(x)$ by taking dx sufficiently close to zero *and du* converges to the zero vector.

Specifically,

$$\lim_{dx \to 0} \frac{u(x+dx) - u(x) - dx_1 u^1(x) - dx_2 u^2(x) - \cdots - dx_k u^k(x)}{\sqrt{(dx_1)^2 + (dx_2)^2 + \cdots + (dx_k)^2}} = 0 \tag{A.1}$$

Now suppose $dx_j = -\varepsilon\, dx_i$ and $dx_c = 0$ for $i \neq c \neq j$. In words, $x + dx$ is obtained from x by sacrificing good j for good i, or vice versa, at the margin and at the rate of ε units of the former per unit of the latter. Then, if we set $\Delta u = u(x + dx) - u(x)$ and $du = dx_i\, u^i(x) + dx_j\, u^j(x) = dx_i\, u^i(x) - \varepsilon\, dx_i\, u^j(x)$, we have, as a special case of equation (A.1),

$$\lim_{dx_i \to 0} \frac{\Delta u - du}{dx_i \sqrt{1 + \varepsilon^2}} = 0$$

This reduces to

$$\lim_{dx_i \to 0} \frac{\Delta u}{dx_i} - [u^i(x) - \varepsilon u^j(x)] = 0 \tag{A.2}$$

Suppose $\varepsilon < u^i(x)/u^j(x)$ and $u^j(x) > 0$. Then $\alpha = u^i(x) - \varepsilon u^j(x) > 0$. As dx_i varies, α remains constant. Therefore, equation (A.2) can be written

$$\lim_{dx_i \to 0} \frac{\Delta u}{dx_i} = \alpha$$

By definition of a limit, there exists a real number $\delta > 0$ such that $|\Delta u/dx_i - \alpha| < \frac{1}{2}|\alpha|$ if $|dx_i| < \delta$. Then $\alpha > 0$ implies $\Delta u/dx_i > \frac{1}{2}\alpha > 0$ if $\delta > dx_i > -\delta$. Therefore, $\Delta u > 0$ if $0 < dx_i < \delta$, and $\Delta u < 0$ if $0 > dx_i > -\delta$. Similarly, if $\alpha < 0$, then $\Delta u < 0$ if $0 < dx_i < \delta$, and

$\Delta u > 0$ if $0 > dx_i > -\delta$. Therefore, we have proved the following basic result.

Lemma A.2. *Suppose that u is differentiable and $u^i(x) > 0$ for all i and x (positive marginal utility). For any $x \in X$ and any two goods i and j such that $x_i > 0$ and $x_j > 0$, if $\varepsilon > 0$, $dx_j = -\varepsilon\, dx_i$, and $dx_c = 0$ for $i \neq c \neq j$, then there exists a positive real number δ such that the following hold:*

$$\varepsilon < u^i(x)/u^j(x) \quad \text{implies } u(x + dx) > u(x) \quad \text{if } 0 < dx_i < \delta$$
$$\varepsilon < u^i(x)/u^j(x) \quad \text{implies } u(x + dx) < u(x) \quad \text{if } 0 > dx_i > -\delta$$
$$\varepsilon > u^i(x)/u^j(x) \quad \text{implies } u(x + dx) < u(x) \quad \text{if } 0 < dx_i < \delta$$
$$\varepsilon > u^i(x)/u^j(x) \quad \text{implies } u(x + dx) > u(x) \quad \text{if } 0 > dx_i > -\delta$$

In words, if good i can be exchanged for good j at the rate ε, then there is some small trade at that rate that will increase utility provided that the individual increases the consumption of good i if and only if the ratio $u^i(x)/u^j(x)$ exceeds the exchange rate ε.

Lemma A.2 justifies our using the ratio of marginal utilities, called the *marginal rate of substitution* of commodity j for commodity i, as the maximum amount of j the individual would be willing to sacrifice per additional unit of commodity i. Let $\rho_{ij}(x)$ denote the ratio of marginal utilities, $u^i(x)/u^j(x)$. If $\varepsilon < \rho_{ij}(x)$, a small exchange between j and i at the rate ε will leave the individual better off, and thus the maximum acceptable rate of exchange is larger than ε. Similarly, if $\varepsilon' > \rho_{ij}(x)$, a small exchange at the rate ε' will reduce utility so the maximum acceptable exchange rate is less than ε'. We can think of ρ_{ij} as a ratio of subjective prices of the two goods. This is justified by the next theorem.

Theorem A.2. *Suppose that $k = 2$ (there are only two commodities), u is continuous and differentiable, and R^u is monotonic and strictly convex. For any x in X such that $x \gg 0$ if $p_1/p_2 = \rho_{12}(x)$, then for any y in X, $u(y) > u(x)$ implies $py > px$. (In words, if y is strictly preferred to x, then y has a greater value than x at the subjective prices entailed in the marginal rate of substitution at x.)*

Proof: Suppose that p is a price vector for which $p_1/p_2 = \rho_{12}(x)$ and $u(y) > u(x)$ but $py \leq px$. Since u is continuous, we can find a positive number λ less than 1 but close enough to 1 such that $u(\lambda y) > u(x)$. Since

$p \gg 0$, we have $p\lambda y < px$. Hence, there actually exists a commodity bundle z such that $u(z) > u(x)$ and $pz < px$. This means that

$$(p_1/p_2)(z_1 - x_1) < x_2 - z_2$$

Since R^u is monotonic, $u(z) > u(x)$ and $pz < px$ implies either

$$z_1 > x_1 \quad \text{and} \quad z_2 < x_2 \tag{A.3}$$

or

$$z_1 < x_1 \quad \text{and} \quad z_2 > x_2 \tag{A.4}$$

Suppose that (A.3) holds. Then $p_1/p_2 < \varepsilon$ for $\varepsilon = (x_2 - z_2)/(z_1 - x_1)$. Set $dx_1 = z_1 - x_1$ and $dx_2 = -\varepsilon \, dx_1$. We have $z = x + dx$ so $u(x + dx) > u(x)$. Now suppose $0 < \lambda < 1$. Then $u(x + \lambda \, dx) > u(x)$. This follows from strict convexity and the fact that $x + \lambda \, dx = \lambda(x + dx) + (1 - \lambda)x$. Since $u(x + \lambda \, dx) > u(x)$ holds for $\lambda > 0$ arbitrarily small, we have a contradiction. Lemma A.2 establishes that $\rho_{12}(x)$ is the maximum rate of exchange between the two goods for which utility does not decrease for arbitrarily small exchanges. But $\varepsilon > \rho_{12}(x) = p_1/p_2$ and $dx_2 = -\varepsilon \, dx_1$. Similarly (A.4) leads to a contradiction with ε and dx as defined above, and $p_1/p_2 > \varepsilon$ this time.   Q.E.D.

Demand theory is the study of the way in which the best or most-preferred commodity vector in the budget set depends on prices and income. There are two potential difficulties: A most-preferred vector may not exist or it may not be unique. Proposition A.2 establishes uniqueness in case R^u is strictly convex. Existence is implied by continuity of u and $p \gg 0$ since $B(p, m)$ will be closed and bounded: The extreme-value theorem asserts that any continuous function assumes a maximum on an arbitrary closed, bounded, and nonempty subset of k-dimensional Euclidean space. Therefore, under modest assumptions on preference there exists a *Marshallian demand function d* specifying the unique commodity vector $d(p, m)$ in the budget set $B(p, m)$ such that $d(p, m)Ry$ for all y in $B(p, m)$. The last two theorems give some elementary properties of this demand function.

Theorem A.3. *Suppose that R is monotonic and strictly convex and representable by a continuous and differentiable utility function with positive marginal utilities everywhere. Then for any $p \gg 0$, $m > 0$, and any two goods i and j, if $d(p, m) = x$, then*

$$u^i(x)/p_i = u^j(x)/p_j \quad \text{and} \quad \rho_{ij}(x) = p_i/p_j$$

as long as $x_i > 0$ and $x_j > 0$.

Proof: Suppose, without loss of generality, that $u^i(x)/p_i > u^j(x)/p_j$. Then $\rho_{ij}(x) > p_i/p_j$. Setting $\varepsilon = p_i/p_j$ in Lemma A.2 demonstrates the existence of a vector dx of increments such that

$$dx_i > 0 \qquad dx_j = -\varepsilon \, dx_i \qquad dx_c = 0 \quad \text{if } i \neq c \neq j \qquad (A.5)$$

and

$$u(x + dx) > u(x) \quad \text{for } x = d(p, m) \qquad (A.6)$$

But (A.5) implies that $p(x + dx) = px$ ($p \, dx = 0$) if $\varepsilon = p_i/p_j$ so $x + dx$ is affordable since x is. Then (A.6) contradicts the definition of $d(p, m)$. Therefore, $\rho_{ij}(x) = p_i/p_j$ must hold.   Q.E.D.

Theorem A.2 can be employed to obtain a partial converse of the preceding result in case $k = 2$.

Theorem A.4. *Suppose that R is monotonic and strictly convex and representable by a continuous and differentiable utility function with positive marginal utilities everywhere. Suppose also that $k = 2$. Then for any $p \gg 0$ and $m \geq 0$, $d(p, m) = x$ if $px = m$ and $\rho_{12}(x) = p_1/p_2$.*

Proof: If $u(y) > u(x)$, then $py > px = m$ by Theorem A.2. Therefore, x maximizes utility in the budget set.   Q.E.D.

Appendix 2: The Edgeworth exchange economy

The two-person, two-commodity exchange economy provides a remarkable amount of insight into resource allocation in general and the market mechanism in particular. Accordingly, assume that production has already taken place and that all net output is owned by households. Each household wishes to exchange goods that it holds in abundance for the goods it lacks.

There are two commodities and two consumers. An *allocation* $x = (x_1, x_2)$ assigns a nonnegative commodity bundle $x_i = (x_{i1}, x_{i2})$ to each individual $i = 1, 2$. Individual i's preference relation is assumed to be strongly monotonic and strictly convex and representable by a continuous and differentiable utility function $u_i(x_i)$ with positive marginal utilities everywhere ($i = 1, 2$). These assumptions will be implicit in the hypotheses of both of the theorems to follow.

Household i ($i = 1, 2$) has an endowment vector $w_i = (w_{i1}, w_{i2})$, and $w_1 + w_2$ specifies the total stock of each of the two goods available to the community. Allocation x is *feasible* if $x \geq 0$ and $x_1 + x_2 \leq w_1 + w_2$. An allocation $x \geq 0$ is *balanced* if $x_1 + x_2 = w_1 + w_2$. Allocation x is *Pareto optimal* if it is feasible and there is no feasible allocation y such that $u_1(y_1) > u_1(x_1)$ and $u_2(y_2) > u_2(x_2)$. Since strong monotonicity is assumed, every Pareto-optimal allocation is balanced: If $x_{1c} + x_{2c} > w_{1c} + w_{2c}$ for some good c, then x is not feasible, and if $x_{1c} + x_{2c} < w_{1c} + w_{2c}$, then each household will have a higher level of utility if the underdistributed surplus of commodity c is divided between them.

Since there are only two goods and two households, balanced allocations can be represented in the plane: Specification of x_1 determines $x_2 = w_1 + w_2 - x_1$, and 2's utility can be exhibited as a function of x_1, $u_2(w_1 + w_2 - x_1)$. Therefore, the economy can be represented as the Edgeworth box, $\{x_1 = (x_{11}, x_{12}): 0 \leq x_1 \leq w_1 + w_2\}$, depicted in Figure A.3. Let I_1' and I_1'' be typical indifference curves for individual 1, each tracing the set of balanced allocations (x_1 can be viewed as a balanced allocation with $x_2 = w_1 + w_2 - x_1$ implied) that give 1 a constant level of utility. Let I_2', I_2'', and I_2''' be indifference curves for person 2. Each traces

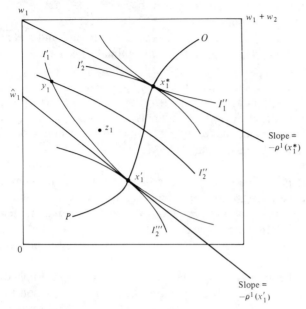

w_1 $w_1 + w_2$

O

Slope = $-\rho^1(x_1^*)$

Slope = $-\rho^1(x_1')$

Figure A.3

the set of balanced allocations x_1 that give 2 a constant level of utility. They look like conventional indifference curves when the diagram is rotated 180° so that the upper right-hand corner becomes the origin.

To simplify the discussion, attention will be restricted to *interior allocations*: x is interior if $x_1 \gg 0$ and $x_2 \gg 0$. Geometrically, an interior balanced allocation is one that is in the box but not on any of the four sides. Let $\rho^i(x_i)$ denote i's marginal rate of substitution at x_i:

$$\rho^i(x_i) = \frac{\partial u_i(x_i)}{\partial x_{i1}} \Big/ \frac{\partial u_i(x_i)}{\partial x_{i2}}$$

Theorem A.5. *An allocation x that is both interior and balanced is Pareto optimal if and only if $\rho^1(x_1) = \rho^2(x_2)$.*

Proof: (i) Suppose that $\rho^1(x_1) \neq \rho^2(x_2)$. Choose ε between the two numbers. Without loss of generality, suppose that $\rho^1(x_1) > \varepsilon > \rho^2(x_2)$. Then by Lemma A.2 of Appendix 1 we can find $dx = (dx_1, dx_2)$ sufficiently small, with $dx_1 > 0$ and $dx_2 = -\varepsilon \, dx_1$ such that $u_1(x_1 + dx) > u_1(x_1)$ and $u_2(x_2 - dx) > u_2(x_2)$. Since $x_1 + dx + x_2 - dx = x_1 + x_2$, the feasible allocation x is not Pareto optimal because $(x_1 + dx, x_2 - dx)$ is also feasible. (Why is it nonnegative?)

(ii) Suppose that $\rho^1(x_1) = \rho^2(x_2)$, $x_1 + x_2 = w_1 + w_2$, and x is an interior allocation. Suppose x is not Pareto optimal. Then there is some feasible allocation y such that $u_1(y_1) > u_1(x_1)$ and $u_2(y_2) > u_2(x_2)$. Using Theorem A.2 and the fact that $\rho^1(x_1) = \rho^2(x_2)$, we have $py_i > px_i$ for $i = 1, 2$ if $p_1/p_2 = \rho^1(x_1)$. Then $py_1 + py_2 > px_1 + px_2 = pw_1 + pw_2$. But $p(y_1 + y_2) > p(w_1 + w_2)$ contradicts $y_1 + y_2 \le w_1 + w_2$ since $p \ge 0$. Therefore, y cannot be feasible if it is preferred by both individuals to x, and x must be Pareto optimal.   Q.E.D.

It is evident from Theorem A.5 that there are an infinite number of Pareto-optimal allocations. These can be generated by fixing u_2, the utility level of person 2, and maximizing u_1 along the corresponding indifference curve to find the point where marginal rates of substitution are equal. In so doing, we trace out the curve PO (Figure A.3) of Pareto-optimal allocations.

Now, bring Theorem A.5 together with Theorem A.3 of Appendix 1. Suppose that x^* is a competitive equilibrium in the two-person market economy. If x^* is an interior allocation, then $\rho^i(x_i^*) = p_1^*/p_2^*$ for the equilibrium price system p^* since x_i^* was chosen by i. Therefore, the marginal rates of substitution are equal. Since x^* is an equilibrium, demand equals supply: $x_1^* + x_2^* = w_1 + w_2$. Then we can apply part (ii) of Theorem A.5 and assert that x^* is Pareto optimal. In fact, the proof in part (ii) suggests a much more general argument. If x^* is a competitive equilibrium for price system p^* and x^* is not Pareto optimal, there is some allocation y such that $u_i(y_i) > u_i(x_i^*)$ for $i = 1, 2$. Then $p^*y_i > p^*w_i$ since p^*w_i is i's income. (Since y_i was not chosen but is preferred to the actual demand x_i^*, the former must have been too expensive.) Then $p^*(y_1 + y_2) > p^*(w_1 + w_2)$, which implies that y is not feasible. Therefore, x^* is Pareto optimal after all. No assumptions on preference are required by this argument. (One could even replace the statement "$u_i(y_i) > u_i(x_i^*)$" by the statement "Consumer i strictly prefers y_i to x_i^*.") There is a point to the assumptions of Appendix 1, however. Something close to these conditions are required to ensure that an equilibrium exists. And we learn more about why the market system is successful under ideal conditions by observing that the subjective price ratios, $\rho^i(x_i^*)$, agree with the market price ratio p_1^*/p_2^*. Each person knows the subjective value that others place on marginal units of the goods, and the exercise of maximizing utility subject to a budget limitation at prices that reflect the value to others, at the margin, of the various goods causes each person's decision to reflect the welfare of others. Consumers do not know that they know the subjective values of others, but the market system entails incentives that lead consumers to act *as if* they perceived the significance of the price ratios and were trying to cooperate with others in producing a Pareto-optimal allocation.

There is one more significant observation that can be extracted from the last theorem. If allocation x is an interior Pareto-optimal allocation, then $\rho^1(x_1) = \rho^2(x_2)$. Choose a price vector p such that $p_1/p_2 = \rho^i(x_i)$ and set $m_i = px_i$. Then $d_i(p, m_i) = x_i$, i's demand at price system p and income m_i. This follows from Theorem A.4 of Appendix 1. Therefore, x is a competitive equilibrium for any redistribution $\hat{w}_1$, $\hat{w}_2$ of endowments such that $\hat{w}_1 + \hat{w}_2 = w_1 + w_2$ and $p\hat{w}_i = m_i$. Since $\hat{w}_2 = w_1 + w_2 - \hat{w}_1$, we merely have to find a solution to

$$\rho^1(x_1)\hat{w}_{11} + \hat{w}_{12} = \rho^1(x_1)x_{11} + x_{12}$$

This is a linear equation in two unknowns, $\hat{w}_{11}$ and $\hat{w}_{12}$, and there are many solutions. We state this as a final theorem.

Theorem A.6. *If x is an interior Pareto-optimal allocation, there is some redistribution of endowments such that x is a competitive equilibrium allocation for the new endowments and the original preferences.*

Refer back to Figure A.3 to make these ideas concrete. Both x^* and x' are Pareto optimal since consumers' marginal rates of substitution are identical at each of these points. Allocation y is not Pareto optimal since marginal rates of substitution are not equal: Allocation z puts both consumers on "higher" indifference curves. Think of z being obtained from y by having individuals trade goods, with person 1 giving up some of commodity 2 and acquiring additional units of the other good from person 2. The exchange rate is $(y_{12} - z_{12})/(z_{11} - y_{11})$. This exchange rate is smaller than the subjective value individual 1 places on good 1, and he is willing to sacrifice some of good 2 to get an additional unit of good 1 at that rate. The exchange rate is larger than the subjective value individual 2 places on good 1 at the margin, so he is willing to sacrifice good 1 at that rate of exchange. Both gain as a result: $u_i(z_i) > u_i(y_i)$ for both i.

Allocation x^* is the competitive equilibrium for the prices implicit in the budget line connecting w_1 and x_1^*. Each i would demand x_i^* since x_i^* is in i's budget set and any bundle strictly preferred to i is not affordable. Demand equals supply since $x_2^* = w_1 + w_2 - x_1^*$ by definition. Allocation x' is not a competitive equilibrium for the endowment w. The budget line connecting x_1' and w_1 contains points preferred by 1 to x_1'. But if individual 1 were required to transfer $w_{12} - \hat{w}_{12}$ units of commodity 2 to individual 2, then x' would be a competitive equilibrium for the resulting endowment vector $\hat{w}$. Refer to the beginning of Section 3.6 for a numerical example illustrating Theorems A.5 and A.6.

Appendix 3: Proof of the
Shafer–Sonnenschein theorem

The existence theorem proved in Shafer and Sonnenschein (1975) relies on a weaker convexity assumption than condition (6.8), namely, *quasiconvexity*: P_a is quasiconvex if for all $m \in M$ the convex hull of $P_a(m)$ does not contain m_a. (A convex combination of members of a set A is any weighted average of a finite number of points in A such that the weights are nonnegative and sum to unity. The convex hull of A, denoted CH(A), is the set of all convex combinations of members of A.) Note that quasiconvexity is implied by conditions (6.8) and (6.9).

Theorem A.7. *Suppose that M is a nonempty, convex, closed, and bounded subset of some finite-dimensional Euclidean space [conditions (6.3) and (6.4)]. If, for each $a = 1, 2, \ldots, N$, P_a is quasiconvex and has an open graph [condition (6.7)] and B_a is a continuous [condition (6.5)] and convex-valued [condition (6.6)] correspondence, then there exists some $m \in M$ such that $m_a \in B_a(m)$ and $B_a(m) \cap P_a(m) = \varnothing$, $a = 1, 2, \ldots, N$.*

Proof: For any agent a and any $(m^1, m_a^2) \in M \times M_a$ let

$$U_a(m^1, m_a^2) = \min\{\|(m^1, m_a^2) - (m^3, m_a^4)\|: m_a^4 \notin P_a(m^3)\}$$

The set $\{(m^3, m_a^4): m_a^4 \notin P_a(m^3)\}$ is closed since P_a has an open graph. Therefore, U_a is well defined. Also, $U_a(m^1, m_a^2)$ is nonnegative and strictly positive if and only if $m_a^2 \in P_a(m^1)$. The function U_a is continuous by condition (6.7).

Now define the correspondence $F_a: M \to M_a$:

$$F_a(m) = \{m_a^1 \in B_a(m): U_a(m, m_a^1) \geq U_a(m, m_a^2) \ \forall \ m_a^2 \in B_a(m)\}$$

Because U_a is continuous and B_a is a continuous and compact-valued correspondence, the correspondence F_a has a closed graph (and $F_a(m) \neq \varnothing \ \forall m \in M$).

Define the correspondence $G: M \to M_a$:

170

$$G(m) = \text{CH}[F_1(m)] \times \text{CH}[F_2(m)] \times \cdots \times \text{CH}[F_N(m)]$$

Then G is a convex-valued correspondence with a closed graph – see Nikaido (1968, Theorems 4.5 and 4.8). By Kakutani (1941) there is some $m^* \in M$ such that $m^* \in G(m^*)$. We will prove that m^* is an equilibrium.

For any a, $F_a(m^*) \subset B_a(m^*)$ by definition and $B_a(m^*)$ is convex so $\text{CH}[F_a(m^*)] \subset B_a(m^*)$. Therefore, $m_a^* \in B_a(m^*)$. It remains to show that $B_a(m^*) \cap P_a(m^*) = \varnothing$. If $m_a \in B_a(m^*) \cap P_a(m^*)$, then $U_a(m^*, m_a) > 0$. Therefore, $U_a(m^*, m'_a) \geq U_a(m^*, m_a) > 0$ for all $m'_a \in F_a(m^*)$. Therefore, $F_a(m^*) \subset P_a(m^*)$, which implies $\text{CH}[F_a(m^*)] \subset \text{CH}[P_a(m^*)]$. Since $m^* \in G(m^*)$, we have $m_a^* \in \text{CH}[F_a(m^*)]$, and therefore $m_a^* \in \text{CH}[P_a(m^*)]$, contradicting quasiconvexity of P_a. Therefore, $B_a(m^*) \cap P_a(m^*) = \varnothing$ for arbitrary a. Q.E.D.

References

Akerlof, G. 1970. The market for "lemons": Quality uncertainty and the market mechanism, *Quarterly Journal of Economics* 84: 488–500.

Allen, B. 1982. Strict rational expectations equilibria with diffuseness, *Journal of Economic Theory* 27: 20–46.

Anderson, R. M., M. A. Khan, and S. Rashid. 1982. Approximate equilibrium with bounds independent of preferences, *Review of Economic Studies* 44: 473–5.

Anderson, R. M., and H. Sonnenschein. 1982. On the existence of rational expectations equilibrium, *Journal of Economic Theory* 26: 261–78.

Arrow, K. J. 1951. "An extension of the basic theorems of classical welfare economics," in J. Neyman (ed.), *Proceedings of the Second Berkeley Symposium on Mathematical Statistics and Probability*. Berkeley: University of California Press, pp. 507–32.

  1959. "Toward a theory of price adjustment," in M. Abramovitz *et al.*, *The Allocation of Economic Resources*. Stanford: Stanford University Press, pp. 41–51.

  1963. *Social Choice and Individual Values*, 2nd ed. New York: Wiley.

  1970. "Political and economic evaluation of social effects and externalities," in J. Margolis (ed.), *The Analysis of Public Output*. New York: Columbia University Press, pp. 1–23.

  1971. *Essays in the Theory of Risk-Bearing*. Chicago: Markham.

Arrow, K. J., and G. Debreu. 1954. Existence of an equilibrium for a competitive economy, *Econometrica* 22: 265–90.

Arrow, K. J., and F. H. Hahn. 1971. *General Competitive Analysis*. San Francisco: Holden-Day.

Arrow, K. J., and R. Radner. 1979. Allocation of resources in large teams, *Econometrica* 47: 361–85.

Aumann, R. J. 1964. Markets with a continuum of traders, *Econometrica* 32: 39–50.

Aumann, R., and B. Peleg. 1974. A note on Gale's example, *Journal of Mathematical Economics* 1: 209–11.

Bergson, A. 1938. A reformulation of certain aspects of welfare economics, *Quarterly Journal of Economics* 52: 310–34.

Brown, D. J., and A. Robinson. 1972. A limit theorem on the cores of large standard exchange economies, *Proceedings of the National Academy of Sciences of the U.S.A.* 69: 1258–60, Correction 69: 3068.

172

Campbell, D. E. 1984. Enforcement of resource allocation mechanisms and second best industrial policy, *Journal of Economic Theory* 34: 319–41.

Clarke, E. H. 1971. Multipart pricing of public goods, *Public Choice* 11: 17–33.

Cournot, A. 1897. *Researches into the Mathematical Principles of the Theory of Wealth.* 1927 translation by N. T. Bacon. New York: Macmillan.

Debreu, G. 1954. Valuation equilibrium and Pareto optimum, *Proceedings of the National Academy of Sciences of the U.S.A.* 40: 588–92.

1959. *Theory of Value.* New York: Wiley.

1982. "Existence of competitive equilibrium," in K. J. Arrow and M. D. Intrilligator (eds.), *Handbook of Mathematical Economics,* Vol. II. New York: North-Holland, pp. 697–743.

Drèze, J., and D. de la Vallée Poussin. 1971. A tâtonnement process for public goods, *Review of Economic Studies* 38: 133–50.

Ekern, S., and R. Wilson. 1974. On the theory of the firm in an economy with incomplete markets, *Bell Journal of Economics and Management Science* 5: 171–80.

Gale, D. 1955. The law of supply and demand, *Mathematica Scandinavica* 3: 155–69.

Gale, D., and A. Mas-Colell. 1975. An equilibrium existence theorem for a general model without ordered preferences, *Journal of Mathematical Economics* 2: 9–15.

Gibbard, A. 1973. Manipulation of voting schemes: A general result, *Econometrica* 41: 587–601.

Green, J. R. 1977. The non-existence of informational equilibria, *Review of Economic Studies* 44: 451–63.

Grossman, S. J. 1981. An introduction to the theory of rational expectations under asymmetric information, *Review of Economic Studies* 48: 541–59.

Groves, T. 1973. Incentives in teams, *Econometrica* 41: 617–31.

Groves, T., and J. Ledyard. 1977. Optimal allocations of public goods: A solution to the "free rider" problem, *Econometrica* 45: 783–809.

Groves, T., and M. Loeb. 1975. Incentives and public inputs, *Journal of Public Economics* 4: 211–26.

Hahn, F. H. 1965. "On some problems of proving the existence of equilibrium in a monetary economy," in F. H. Hahn and F. R. P. Brechling (eds.), *The Theory of Interest Rates.* London: Macmillan, pp. 126–35.

1971. Equilibrium with transactions costs, *Econometrica* 39: 417–39.

1982. "Stability," in K. J. Arrow and M. D. Intrilligator (eds.), *Handbook of Mathematical Economics,* Vol. II. New York: North-Holland, pp. 745–93.

Hammond, P. J. 1979. Straightforward individual incentive compatibility in large economies, *Review of Economic Studies* 46: 263–82.

Harris, R. 1978. Ex-post efficiency and resource allocation under uncertainty, *Review of Economic Studies* 45: 427–36.

Helpman, E., and J.-J. Laffont. 1975. On moral hazard in general equilibrium theory, *Journal of Economic Theory* 10: 8–23.

Herstein, I. N., and J. Milnor. 1953. An axiomatic approach to measurable utility, *Econometrica* 21: 291–7.

174   References

Hotelling, H. 1938. The general welfare in relation to problems of taxation and of railway and utility rates, *Econometrica* 6: 242–69.

Hurwicz, L. 1960. "Optimality and informational efficiency in resource allocation processes," in K. J. Arrow, S. Karlin, and P. Suppes (eds.), *Mathematical Methods in the Social Sciences 1959*. Stanford: Stanford University Press, pp. 27–46.

1972. "On informationally decentralized systems," in C. B. McGuire and R. Radner (eds.), *Decision and Organization*. Amsterdam: North-Holland, pp. 297–336.

1973. The design of mechanisms for resource allocation, *American Economic Review Papers and Proceedings* 63: 1–30.

1977. "On the dimensional requirements of informationally decentralized Pareto-satisfactory processes," in K. J. Arrow and L. Hurwicz (eds.), *Studies in Resource Allocation Processes*. Cambridge: Cambridge University Press, pp. 413–24.

1979a. Outcome functions yielding Walrasian and Lindahl allocations at Nash equilibrium points, *Review of Economic Studies* 46: 217–25.

1979b. On allocations attainable through Nash equilibria, *Journal of Economic Theory* 21: 140–65.

1979c. "On the interaction between information and incentives in organizations," in K. Krippendorff (ed.), *Communication and Control in Society*. New York: Gordon and Breach, pp. 123–47.

Hurwicz, L., and D. Schmeidler. 1978. Construction of outcome functions guaranteeing existence and Pareto optimality of Nash equilibria, *Econometrica* 46: 1447–74.

Jordan, J. S. 1982a. The generic existence of rational expectations equilibrium in the higher dimensional case, *Journal of Economic Theory* 26: 224–43.

1982b. The competitive allocation process is informationally efficient uniquely, *Journal of Economic Theory* 28: 1–18.

Jordan, J. S., and R. Radner. 1982. Rational expectations in microeconomic models: An overview, *Journal of Economic Theory* 26: 201–23.

Kakutani, S. 1941. A generalization of Brouwer's fixed point theorem, *Duke Mathematical Journal* 8: 457–9.

Knight, F. H. 1924. Some fallacies in the interpretation of social cost, *Quarterly Journal of Economics* 38: 582–606.

Kreps, D. 1977. A note on "fulfilled expectations" equilibria, *Journal of Economic Theory* 14: 32–43.

Lange, Oscar. 1942. The foundations of welfare economics, *Econometrica* 10: 215–28.

Ledyard, J., and J. Roberts. 1974. "On the incentive problem with public goods," *Centre for Mathematical Studies in Economics and Management Science*. Discussion Paper No. 116. Northwestern University.

Lerner, A. P. 1933. The concept of monopoly and the measurement of monopoly power, *Review of Economic Studies* 1: 157–75.

1944. *The Economics of Control*. New York: Macmillan.

Lindahl, E. 1919. *Die Gerechtigkeit der Besteuerung*. Translated (in part) as "Just taxation: A positive solution," in R. A. Musgrave and A. T. Peacock (eds.), *Classics in the Theory of Public Finance*. 1967. London: Macmillan, pp. 168–76.

Lippincott, B. (ed.) 1938. *On the Economic Theory of Socialism*. New York: McGraw-Hill.

Lippman, S. A., and J. J. McCall. 1982. "The economics of uncertainty: Selected topics and probabilistic methods," in K. J. Arrow and M. D. Intrilligator (eds.), *Handbook of Mathematical Economics,* Vol. I. Amsterdam: North-Holland, pp. 211–84.

McKenzie, L. W. 1968. "Competitive equilibrium with dependent consumer preferences," in P. Newman (ed.), *Readings in Mathematical Economics,* Vol. I. Baltimore: The Johns Hopkins Press, pp. 129–46.

Makowsky, L. 1980. A characterization of perfectly competitive economies with production, *Journal of Economic Theory* 22: 208–21.

Malinvaud, E. 1971. A planning approach to the public good problem, *Swedish Journal of Economics* 73: 96–112.

Marschak, J. 1955. Elements for a theory of teams, *Management Science* 1: 127–37.

Marschak, J., and R. Radner. 1972. *Economic Theory of Teams*. New Haven: Yale University Press.

Mas-Colell, A. 1974. An equilibrium existence theorem without complete or transitive preferences, *Journal of Mathematical Economics* 1: 237–46.

Maskin, E. 1977. "Nash equilibrium and welfare optimality," mimeo. Department of Economics, Massachusetts Institute of Technology.

Maskin, E. S., and K. W. S. Roberts. 1980. "On the fundamental theorems of general equilibrium," *Economic Theory Discussion Paper* 43. University of Cambridge.

Meade, J. E. 1952. External economies and diseconomies in a competitive situation, *Economic Journal* 62: 54–67.

Meunch, T., and M. Walker. 1981. "Samuelson's conjecture: Decentralized provision and financing of public goods," *Economics Research Bureau,* Discussion Paper No. 235, Stony Brook: State University of New York.

Mount, K., and S. Reiter. 1974. The informational size of message spaces, *Journal of Economic Theory* 8: 161–92.

Nash, J. F. 1950. Equilibrium points in *N*-person games, *Proceedings of the National Academy of Sciences of the U.S.A.* 36: 48–9.

Nikaido, H. 1968. *Convex Structures and Economic Theory*. New York: Academic Press.

Novshek, W. 1980. Cournot equilibrium with free entry, *Review of Economic Studies* 47: 473–86.

  1985. Perfectly competitive markets as the limits of Cournot markets, *Journal of Economic Theory* 35: 72–82.

Novshek, W., and H. Sonnenschein. 1978. Cournot and Walras equilibrium, *Journal of Economic Theory* 19: 223–66.

Osana, H. 1978. On the informational size of message spaces for resource allocation processes, *Journal of Economic Theory* 17: 66–78.

176   References

Ostroy, J. M. 1973. The informational efficiency of monetary exchange, *American Economic Review* 63: 597–610.

1980. The no-surplus condition as a characterization of perfectly competitive equilibrium, *Journal of Economic Theory* 22: 183–207.

Otani, Y., and J. Sicilian. 1982. Equilibrium allocations of Walrasian preference games, *Journal of Economic Theory* 27: 47–68.

Pareto, Vilfredo. 1927. *Manuel d'Economie Politique,* 2nd ed. Paris: Giard.

Pigou, A. C. 1932. *The Economics of Welfare,* 4th ed. London: Macmillan.

Pratt, J. W. 1964. Risk aversion in the small and in the large, *Econometrica* 32: 122–35.

Radner, R. 1968. Competitive equilibrium under uncertainty, *Econometrica* 36: 31–58.

1974. A note on unanimity of stockholders' preferences among alternative production plans: A reformulation of the Ekern-Wilson model, *Bell Journal of Economics and Management Science* 5: 181–4.

1979. Rational expectations equilibrium: Generic existence and information revealed by prices, *Econometrica* 47: 655–78.

1982. "Equilibrium under uncertainty," in K. J. Arrow and M. D. Intrilligator (eds.), *Handbook of Mathematical Economics,* Vol. II. Amsterdam: North-Holland, pp. 923–1006.

Roberts, J. 1976. The incentives for correct revelation of preferences and the number of consumers, *Journal of Public Economics* 6: 359–74.

1979. Incentives in planning procedures for the provision of public goods, *Review of Economic Studies* 46: 283–92.

Roberts, J., and A. Postlewaite. 1976. The incentive for price-taking behavior in large exchange economies, *Econometrica* 44: 115–27.

Rothschild, M., and J. E. Stiglitz. 1976. Equilibrium in competitive insurance markets: An essay on the economics of imperfect information, *Quarterly Journal of Economics* 90: 629–49.

Samuelson, P. A. 1954. The pure theory of public expenditure, *Review of Economics and Statistics* 36: 387–9.

1955. Diagrammatic exposition of a theory of public expenditure, *Review of Economics and Statistics* 37: 350–6.

Satterthwaite, M. 1975. Strategy-proofness and Arrow's conditions: Existence and correspondence theorems for voting procedures and social welfare functions, *Journal of Economic Theory* 10: 187–217.

Scitovsky, T. 1954. Two concepts of external economies, *Journal of Political Economy* 62: 143–51.

Selten, R. 1975. Reexamination of the perfectness concept for equilibrium points in extensive games, *International Journal of Game Theory* 4: 25–55.

Shafer, W., and H. Sonnenschein. 1975. Equilibrium in abstract economies without ordered preferences, *Journal of Mathematical Economics* 2: 345–8.

Smith, Adam. 1776. *An Inquiry into the Nature and Causes of the Wealth of Nations,* E. Cannan (ed.). 1937. New York: Modern Library.

Sonnenschein, H. 1974. An axiomatic characterization of the price mechanism, *Econometrica* 42: 425–33.

Starr, R. 1973. Optimal production and allocation under uncertainty, *Quarterly Journal of Economics* 87: 81–95.

Starrett, D. 1972. Fundamental nonconvexities in the theory of externalities, *Journal of Economic Theory* 4: 180–99.

Vickrey, W. 1961. Counterspeculation, auctions, and competitive sealed tenders, *Journal of Finance* 16: 1–17.

von Hayek, F. A. 1935. "The present state of the debate," in F. A. von Hayek (ed.), *Collective Economic Planning*. London: Routledge, pp. 201–43.

von Neumann, J., and O. Morgenstern. 1944. *Theory of Games and Economic Behavior*. Princeton: Princeton University Press.

Wald, A. 1951. On some systems of equations of mathematical economics, *Econometrica* 19: 368–403.

Walker, M. 1977. On the informational size of message spaces, *Journal of Economic Theory* 15: 366–75.

　1978. A note on the characterization of mechanisms for the revelation of preferences, *Econometrica* 46: 147–52.

　1981. A simple incentive-compatible scheme for obtaining Lindahl allocations, *Econometrica* 49: 65–71.

　1984. A simple auctioneerless mechanism with Walrasian properties, *Journal of Economic Theory* 32: 111–27.

Walras, Léon. 1874–7. *Eléments d'Economie Politique Pure*. Translated by W. Jaffé. 1954. *Elements of Pure Economics*. Homewood, Ill.: Irwin.

Wicksell, K. 1896. "Ein neues prinzip der gerechten besteuerung." Translated as "A new principle of just taxation," in R. A. Musgrave and A. T. Peacock (eds.), *Classics in the Theory of Public Finance*. 1967. London: Macmillan, pp. 72–118.

Williams, S. R. 1984. "Realization with Nash implementation: Two aspects of mechanism design," Institute for Mathematics and Its Applications, preprint no. 69, University of Minnesota.

Wilson, C. 1977. A model of insurance markets with incomplete information, *Journal of Economic Theory* 16: 167–207.

Young, A. 1913. Pigou's Wealth and Welfare, *Quarterly Journal of Economics* 27: 672–86.

Author index

Subject index